Developing Intermediate-Level Piano Performance with Romantic Style Repertoire

Developing Intermediate-Level Piano Performance with Romantic Style Repertoire

Foundational Concepts and Skills

Lori Ellen Rhoden

BLOOMSBURY ACADEMIC
NEW YORK • LONDON • OXFORD • NEW DELHI • SYDNEY

Online resources to accompany this book are available at https://Bloomsbury.pub/Intermediate-Piano-Performance. If you experience any problems, please contact Bloomsbury at: onlineresources@bloomsbury.com

BLOOMSBURY ACADEMIC
Bloomsbury Publishing Inc, 1359 Broadway, New York, NY 10018, USA
Bloomsbury Publishing Plc, 50 Bedford Square, London, WC1B 3DP, UK
Bloomsbury Publishing Ireland, 29 Earlsfort Terrace, Dublin 2, D02 AY28, Ireland

BLOOMSBURY, BLOOMSBURY ACADEMIC and the Diana logo are trademarks of Bloomsbury Publishing Plc

First published in the United States of America 2026

Copyright © Bloomsbury Academic, 2026

For legal purposes the Acknowledgments on p. vii constitute an extension of this copyright page.

Cover image © iStock.com/djvstock

All rights reserved. No part of this publication may be: i) reproduced or transmitted in any form, electronic or mechanical, including photocopying, recording or by means of any information storage or retrieval system without prior permission in writing from the publishers; or ii) used or reproduced in any way for the training, development or operation of artificial intelligence (AI) technologies, including generative AI technologies. The rights holders expressly reserve this publication from the text and data mining exception as per Article 4(3) of the Digital Single Market Directive (EU) 2019/790.

Bloomsbury Publishing Inc does not have any control over, or responsibility for, any third-party websites referred to or in this book. All internet addresses given in this book were correct at the time of going to press. The author and publisher regret any inconvenience caused if addresses have changed or sites have ceased to exist, but can accept no responsibility for any such changes.

A catalog record for this book is available from the Library of Congress.

ISBN: HB: 979-8-8818-0523-4
PB: 979-8-8818-0524-1
ePub: 979-8-8818-0525-8
ePDF: 979-8-7651-4914-0

Typeset by Deanta Global Publishing Services, Chennai, India
Printed and bound in the United States of America

For product safety related questions contact productsafety@bloomsbury.com.

To find out more about our authors and books visit www.bloomsbury.com and sign up for our newsletters.

Contents

Acknowledgments vii

1 Introduction 1

Part I Musical Elements

2 Melody 9
3 Harmony 23
4 Texture 31
5 Rhythm 57
6 Technique 69
7 Articulation 95
8 Fingering 105
9 Pedaling 111
10 Musical Expression 127

Part II Repertoire Annotations

11 Amy Beach—*Children's Album*, Op. 36 155
12 Johann Burgmüller—*25 Progressive Pieces*, Op. 100 159
13 Johann Burgmüller—*18 Characteristic Studies*, Op. 109 177
14 Cécile Chaminade—*Album for the Young*, Book 1, Op. 123 191
15 Cécile Chaminade—*Album for the Young*, Book 2, Op. 126 199
16 William Gillock—*Lyric Preludes in Romantic Style* 209
17 Edvard Grieg—*Lyric Pieces*, Opp. 12, 38, 43, 47, 54, 57, 62, 65, 68, 71 (Selections) 225
18 Cornelius Gurlitt—*Album for the Young*, Op. 140 253

19	Robert Schumann—*Album for the Young*, Op. 68	267
20	Peter Ilyich Tchaikovsky—*Album for the Young*, Op. 39	299
21	Miscellaneous	315

References	317
Index of Terms	320
Index of Compositions	323

Acknowledgments

When I was a child, I apparently told my mother that I wanted to become a music teacher when I grew up. While I do not remember that specific encounter, I cannot ever remember wanting to pursue any profession other than music teaching. My dear parents always supported my hopes and dreams, and encouraged me to pursue whatever I wanted to do. Music has always permeated every part of my life, from home and church to school and community. Through the influence of my enjoyable school musical experiences in choir and band, I pursued the goal of being a university band director. During my first full-time music teaching position as a middle-school band director, I realized that I missed playing and teaching the piano, and therefore needed to shift my focus. The path from that point on was clear, and I have been blessed with many wonderful opportunities to pursue my craft.

Throughout my entire musical career, I have had a host of amazing music teachers. Every one of them has contributed immeasurably to the musician and teacher that I am today. Their kind, patient, and encouraging teaching and guidance helped me to thrive and achieve my goals. Each day as I try to be the best teacher that I can be, I carry on their legacy and will be forever grateful for their excellent teaching. This book is therefore dedicated to all of the wonderful music teachers who have enriched my life in so many ways. While most of them are now gone, I continue to hear their voices and am forever changed by my interaction with them. To my mentors who are still providing wisdom and insight but prefer to stay out of the spotlight, I continue to be extremely grateful for your exemplary assistance.

In addition, I am grateful for the support of this project from Ball State University, especially Dr. Seth Beckman, dean of the College of Fine Arts, and Dr. Franklin Larey, director of the School of Music. Their ongoing support has made it possible for me to be able to bring this project to completion. I am so thankful for the generous assistance of my School of Music colleague, Dr. Eleanor Trawick, associate professor of music, who provided all of the Finale graphics for this book. I am also thankful for my many musical colleagues, both at Ball State and around the country, who have celebrated this opportunity with me and continue to support my professional growth and development.

I deeply appreciate the assistance of Michael Tan, acquisitions editor for music. His knowledge, patience, and encouragement have been essential in helping me successfully navigate the publishing process. I am thankful for all of the reviewers who determined that this project would be a beneficial contribution to the piano teaching profession.

I was delighted to become acquainted with Ms. Elise Fast, who provided excellent and timely editing for the Introduction and Part I of this book.

To all of my former, current, and future students, thank you for the joy that you bring to my life and for continuing to help me learn more every day.

Finally, I am immensely grateful to my family and friends, whose patience, encouragement, and love continue to sustain me in all that I do. I cannot thank you enough for your steadfast faith in me, and for your enthusiastic and sincere celebration of my accomplishments.

1

Introduction

Numerous piano teaching method books exist for the elementary level, providing teachers and students with many resources for developing musical, technical, and notational foundations in a progressive order. These elementary method books generally cover a relatively consistent set of skills and concepts in preparation for the intermediate and advanced levels of performance. Unfortunately, there are not many similar resources available for teaching the intermediate-level student. Existing pedagogical resources for teachers of intermediate-level students include the following:

1) multi-style period collections, period-specific collections, and composer collections of representative repertoire in either standalone volumes or leveled series
2) graded lists of recommended repertoire in alignment with various rating systems, some including brief annotations for each piece
3) certificate and achievement programs associated with international, national, or state-level music teacher associations that provide graded levels in areas such as technique, aural skills, written music theory, and repertoire
4) online catalogs of repertoire pieces that include selected information about each piece
5) a variety of general piano teaching books.

Many of these resources generally attempt to define levels of instruction through the development of various technical exercises and keyboard skills, written music theory, aural skills, and repertoire. However, few resources at the intermediate level approach these technical and aural skills within the context of how they contribute to the musical elements and expression of a piece.

The current music notation system does not allow for more than basic information in the musical score, so once students reach the intermediate level, they usually learn in-depth musical details from their teachers, passed down from one generation to the next through the heritage of piano teaching. This book aims to further assist students and teachers by providing a detailed exploration of the foundational musical elements of melody, harmony, texture, rhythm, technique, articulation, fingering, pedaling, and musical expression found in intermediate-level Romantic style repertoire. For each element, the author identifies various concepts and skills related to the important technical, musical, and interpretive aspects of a piece. By focusing on mastery of the concepts and skills of the various musical elements, teachers can more confidently determine what their students need to learn. They can be better prepared to understand what makes each piece more or less challenging, and what repertoire can be covered and in what order.

Since the Romantic era covers an extended historical period and a wide range of styles, an exploration of standard teaching collections of this period provides an opportunity to identify common musical elements and challenges. The following chapters encourage teachers and students to explore common musical elements and challenges through the standard teaching collections of this period. The intermediate-level collections referenced in this book include the following:

1) Amy Beach—*Children's Album*, Op. 36
2) Johann Burgmüller—*25 Progressive Pieces*, Op. 100
3) Johann Burgmüller—*18 Characteristic Studies*, Op. 109
4) Cécile Chaminade—*Album for the Young, Book 1*, Op. 123
5) Cécile Chaminade—*Album for the Young, Book 2*, Op. 126
6) William Gillock—*Lyric Preludes in Romantic Style*
7) Edvard Grieg—*Lyric Pieces*, Opp. 12, 38, 43, 47, 54, 57, 62, 65, 68, 71 (selections)
8) Cornelius Gurlitt—*Album for the Young*, Op. 140
9) Robert Schumann—*Album for the Young*, Op. 68 (selections)
10) Peter Ilyich Tchaikovsky—*Album for the Young*, Op. 39

These collections span the entire range of the intermediate level, providing an excellent developmental compendium of Romantic style period repertoire. Mostly composed during the nineteenth and early twentieth centuries, they are readily available within the public domain. The only exception is the twentieth-century *Lyric Preludes in Romantic Style* by William Gillock, which is included because it is widely regarded as an essential early to middle intermediate-level introduction to Romantic-period repertoire. Musical examples have not been included within the chapters due to space limitations. Readers are encouraged to download or purchase the scores for reference while exploring this book. Copies of the musical scores for all of the collections except the Gillock *Lyric Preludes in Romantic Style* are available as PDF documents at https://Bloomsbury.pub/Intermediate-Piano-Performance. Previously published by Summy-Birchard, the *Lyric Preludes in Romantic Style* is now available through Alfred Music.

Readers may be surprised to note that repertoire by well-known composers such as Felix and Fanny Mendelssohn, Frédéric Chopin, and Clara Schumann, among others, is not included. This is because the vast majority of their pieces are at the late intermediate or advanced levels, and the collections by Robert Schumann and Edvard Grieg already cover the late-intermediate level well. The collections by Amy Beach and Cécile Chaminade are included to celebrate lesser-known composers of the period whose music deserves greater promotion. An additional repertoire piece by Franz Liszt is included to illustrate specific concepts and skills. Rather than being a comprehensive survey of the available literature, this book focuses instead on the musical elements and their associated concepts and skills.

Beginning with Chapter 2, this book provides foundational knowledge about each musical element, a listing of some of the specific features of each element, and a maximum of ten selected repertoire pieces that illustrate the concepts and skills. Discussion also includes some of the technical and musical challenges that influence repertoire difficulty levels as well as selected practice suggestions and techniques.

The repertoire leveling is limited to the broader categories of early, middle, and late intermediate, as well as some more advanced pieces. Difficulty levels established by Jane Magrath in her book *Piano Literature for Teaching and*

Performance: A Graded Guide and Annotated Bibliography are provided for pieces that have been rated in this system.[1]

Part II (beginning with Chapter 11) provides an annotated listing of the repertoire collections and pieces, using criteria focusing specifically on the various musical elements. Chapters are organized alphabetically by the composers' last names and individual collection titles.

Important philosophical principles of piano teaching and learning support the pedagogy in this book:

1) Student learning should involve "sound before sight" and "experience before explanation." Students should hear music before they see it in notation, and they should experience music before hearing theoretical explanations about the music. The introduction of new concepts and skills should be approached aurally whenever possible.
2) Students should learn concepts and skills in their easiest settings first. Easier settings include those that have consistent, patterned musical elements in areas such as articulation, dynamics, rhythmic patterns, and pedaling. The textural complexity within one hand and between the two hands should be limited. New musical elements and challenges may be introduced in one hand only, while the other hand has less-complicated musical material. Learning should follow a spiral approach, in which the same concepts and skills continually recur in more difficult musical settings.
3) Students should play a lot of different repertoire to experience concepts and skills in many different settings at the same level before moving on to more difficult repertoire.
4) While practicing, students can alter the score in some way to change their perception of it. Often this involves the principle of opposites, such as playing loud passages soft/soft passages loud, *legato* passages detached/detached passages *legato*, dotted rhythms even/even rhythms dotted, slow passages fast/fast passages slow, or reversing normal balances, rhythmic groupings, and so forth. Practicing in this way provides a different perception so that when the students return to playing the passage as notated, their performance improves through their greater musical understanding.

This book is appropriate for students in college and university piano pedagogy courses, as well as for independent piano teachers. Teachers are encouraged to focus on teaching the concepts and skills within the repertoire and to guide students to discover the same concepts and skills in subsequent pieces. A curriculum that focuses on concepts and skills to master prepares students to become independent musicians who can approach new repertoire with confidence.

The concepts and skills explored in these collections also apply to much of the intermediate-level repertoire of other historical style periods. Teachers can transfer this knowledge of musical elements to all styles and genres, including contemporary and popular music.

This book is an accumulation of knowledge that I have acquired through my professional degrees and over thirty-two years of full-time teaching as a college and university piano professor. The content applies to students of all ages who are playing repertoire at the intermediate level or higher. My goal is to provide teachers with an examination of the fundamental musical elements related to piano performance that will serve as a guide for teaching intermediate-level piano students.

Note

1 Jane Magrath, *Piano Literature for Teaching and Performance: A Graded Guide and Annotated Bibliography*, ed. E. L. Lancaster and Albert Mendoza (Kingston, NJ: The Frances Clark Center Piano Education Press, 2021).

Part I

Musical Elements

2

Melody

Melody is perhaps the most dominant musical element in the Romantic period and is often the most memorable and recognizable element of any piece. Melodies found in Romantic-period repertoire may be vocal or instrumental in character, and each type requires different musical and technical skills.

Vocal Melodies

Vocal melodies are expressive, warm, and lyrical. They may portray a range of emotions, from intense and dramatic to introspective, gentle, hopeful, happy, dreamy, sad, and so on. Although vocal melodies can present a variety of tonal colors and characters, their common element is a prominent, sustained melodic line that clearly predominates the rest of the musical texture.

<u>Repertoire: Vocal Melodies</u>
Beach: *Children's Album*, Op. 36, No. 3—Waltz
Burgmüller: *25 Progressive Pieces*, Op. 100, No. 3—Pastorale
Burgmüller: *18 Characteristic Studies*, Op. 109, No. 14—Song of the Gondolier
Chaminade: *Album for the Young*, Book 1, Op. 123, No. 11—Air de Ballet
Chaminade: *Album for the Young*, Book 2, Op. 126, No.1—Idylle
Gillock: *Lyric Preludes in Romantic Style*—An Old Valentine
Grieg: *Lyric Pieces*, Op. 43, No. 6—To the Spring
Grieg: *Lyric Pieces*, Op. 62, No. 5—Phantom
Tchaikovsky: *Album for the Young*, Op. 39, No. 16—Old French Song

Instrumental Melodies

Melodies that do not fall into the lyrical, vocal Romantic category can be described as instrumental in nature. Usually wider in range, these instrumental melodies have more detailed figuration and often include a greater variety of articulation. Instrumental melodies may not be as clearly identifiable as vocal melodies, since there is not a singable "tune" that makes them easily recognizable. Performers may have difficulty identifying a melody in these pieces, because the thematic material may consist of repeated musical motives or brilliant passagework. Instrumental melodies often have a lively, exciting, or dramatic character.

<u>Repertoire: Instrumental Melodies</u>
Burgmüller: *18 Characteristic Studies*, Op. 109, No. 3—The Shepherd's Return
Burgmüller: *18 Characteristic Studies*, Op. 109, No. 10—Velocity
Burgmüller: *18 Characteristic Studies*, Op. 109, No. 17—March
Burgmüller: *18 Characteristic Studies*, Op. 109, No. 18—Spinning Song
Chaminade: *Album for the Young*, Op. 123, No. 4—Rondeau
Chaminade: *Album for the Young*, Op. 123, No. 5—Gavotte
Grieg: *Lyric Pieces*, Op. 71, No. 3—Puck
Schumann: *Album for the Young*, Op. 68, No. 10—The Happy Farmer
Schumann: *Album for the Young*, Op. 68, No. 12—Knight Rupert
Schumann: *Album for the Young*, Op. 68, No. 13—May, Sweet May

Melodic Analysis

The performance of a compelling melody encompasses many different perspectives discovered through both analysis and aural awareness. The analysis begins with a detailed examination of the composer's notational content, combined with an understanding of how various musical elements foster expressive possibilities. Often teachers neglect to introduce analytical tools, leaving students limited in their ability to discover important features of the melody and other elements.

Following the philosophical principle of sound and musical experience before explanation and theoretical understanding, the pianist should first identify and play all melodic lines individually. It is not enough to look at the musical score and be able to identify where the melody is located. The pianist must first hear the melody separate from any of the other parts to grasp it aurally without any distracting accompaniment. This crucial step of isolating the melody is an important foundation for understanding the melodic content as well as its accompanying musical texture. The pianist should next play the melodic line with each of the other individual lines of the texture separately, starting with the bass line. Playing the melodic line with each of the other parts individually, then combining them together, helps the student to hear all of the parts within the entire sound.

Pitch Content

Is the melodic pitch content scalar or triadic, and what scales or modes do the notes imply? Scalar, conjunct melodies in limited ranges will be the easiest to perform well. Triadic or more disjunct melodies require an aural ability to connect the melody through the leaps. Less-experienced students will be more comfortable with melodies that are diatonic and scalar rather than melodies that are more chromatic with unpredictable pitch patterns.

In addition, certain pitches of the scale have a tendency to resolve in a particular direction. Scale degree numbers two and four tend to continue downward, while scale degree number seven, the leading tone, usually resolves upward. Chromatic pitches in the melody also tend to go in particular directions, with notes altered by sharps tending to resolve up and those with flats tending to go down. Becoming aware of these tendencies in the pitch content can provide students with opportunities for more musical expressiveness.

Range

What is the range of the melody? While a well-regulated modern piano demonstrates relative consistency of tone throughout the keyboard, different ranges of the piano can cause challenges in tonal control, dynamic breadth, and balance with the accompaniment. Melodies that include wide leaps require pianists to carry their arm weight through the leaps to achieve consistent tone quality and dynamic control. It is much harder to play with consistency of technique and sound when traveling across leaps through various ranges.

Structure

What is the structure of the melody, including its important motives or themes? Melodic material helps to define the formal structure of the piece. Long melodic lines may exhibit a seamless, continuous line, or they may be constructed from motives or sub-phrases. Many melodies follow a typical phrase shape that intensifies to a climax near the end of the phrase, and then relaxes through its conclusion. Inconclusive phrase chains or phrase groupings can undermine or postpone climaxes and/or cadences. Phrase groupings may include shorter phrases followed by a longer concluding phrase, with the final phrase often possessing the climactic arrival point for the entire section. The delay of significant arrival points often heightens the sense of melodic climax and strengthens the eventual return to the tonic.

Intuitive students may have a natural sense of where the climax of the phrase occurs, especially in music with clearly defined phrase shapes. Other students will need more guidance in determining the point of greatest intensity within the phrase. Phrase climaxes often occur on the highest note, on a strong beat, and/or on a longer note value compared to those around it. The simultaneous joining of two or all three of these criteria strengthens the possibility that the phrase shape may reach its climax at that point.

Repetitions of the melody within the same piece provide the performer with opportunities to vary its shape, so that each one has a distinct or different climax. Since it may be difficult to determine a clear climax point within a phrase, performers should experiment with different arrival points until an intuitive sense of the best choice emerges.

During the Romantic period in music history, individual countries and cultures began to take an interest in developing their own nationalistic musical styles. This music typically includes the use of simple folk melodies that consist of irregular phrase lengths. Formal structures that include phrases of different lengths feel different and may need more musical exploration than phrases that follow regular and symmetrical numbers of measures. Counting the number of measures in each phrase is one easy method to help students become aware of these phrasing irregularities.

Gestures

Playing beautiful melodies and phrases requires playing musical gestures rather than individual notes. The performance of individual notes in an isolated manner promotes "vertical" or "notey" playing. Unfortunately, early music reading approaches that emphasize individual note letter names negatively influence musical perception long beyond the elementary level. The introduction to music reading should focus on melodic patterns and intervals between notes within tonal contexts rather than individual note names. Students should learn rhythms in patterned chunks within a beat-function approach rather than as individual note values. Combining pitch and rhythmic patterns into larger pulse groupings appropriate to the tempo automatically improves the musical perception and is the foundation for developing the ability to perform musical phrases.

Common melodic gestures include:

1) Diatonic scalar passages, moving upward or downward in shorter groups or a longer series of pitches. These may move in one direction only or be joined together in more "circular" gestures that depart from and return to a starting point.
2) Chromatic scalar passages.
3) Melodic patterns that lead away from and then return to the tonic.
4) Arpeggios, sweeping in one or both directions.
5) Ornaments that decorate main notes.

Common rhythmic gestures include:

1) Patterns that begin on weak beats or in-between beats and lead to strong beats.
2) Shorter note values that lead to longer note values.

Dynamic Shape of the Melody

The dynamic shape of a melody may be determined through a variety of approaches. One method is to follow the pitch contour by performing a *crescendo* when the pitches ascend and performing a *diminuendo* when the pitches descend. This is an important and solid approach for developing musical playing at an early level, but is not appropriate for every phrase, since melodies can have many different shapes.

Other musical factors that influence the dynamic shape of the melody include the different note values and their metrical placement, textural setting, and harmonic context. Teachers should introduce students to a variety of melodic shapes to gain experience with different musical contours.

Character and Emotional Effect

Once the basic shape of the melodic phrase has been determined, the performer should explore its character or emotional content. Intuitive performers may immediately suggest descriptive words or thoughts, but many students will need a lot of teacher guidance in probing emotional character. Extrinsic mental imagery can help students connect the music to something tangible that they may have already experienced. Expressive aural modeling by a teacher can inspire intangible subtleties that contribute greatly to intuitive musical understanding. It is not possible for a composer to notate every subtle expressive nuance, nor is it desirable to do so; the musical score would become unreadable or perhaps confusing, and individual artistic personality would diminish.

Melody Curriculum

In the elementary level of piano study, teachers should assign pieces that have clearly defined contours and musical direction through notated dynamic markings so that the shape of the melody is well-defined. Teachers can model beautiful phrase shapes and give students appropriate technical tools to reproduce these. Students who have progressed to intermediate-level repertoire but who have not yet had these preparatory experiences can play late-elementary repertoire to practice performing beautiful melodies within simpler notational and technical contexts.

Consistency and Variety of Sound

The foundation for performing an expressive melody consists of the ability to produce a consistent, solid sound on a series of consecutive, scalar pitches with consistent note values. It is difficult for students to control dynamic changes and variety in tonal colors if they have not first mastered producing a consistent tonal color and dynamic level on successive notes. Consistency of sound is achieved through consistency in arm weight/release (or the absence of tension/physical holding), position of the finger on the key supported by a good hand position, speed of attack into the key, and connections between notes. Mastering these skills on basic scales is an important prerequisite for achieving good melodic playing.

Once students can produce a consistent sound on consecutive notes, they can advance to achieve a broad spectrum of dynamics through variation in the speed of attack on each note. Often students think that they should push or press harder or more forcefully into the keys to play louder, but this can result in physical tension and a harsh, constricted sound that does not sustain well. Focusing on the speed of attack and the approach into the key while maintaining a free and fluid technique can facilitate the performance of beautiful melodies at all dynamic levels.

Patterned Melodies with Continuous Note Values

When moving from technical exercises to repertoire, students should practice performing a smooth melodic line by playing pieces that have melodies with continuous, patterned, short note values, since there is no perceived loss of sound between these notes. They can then work on performing a melodic line with patterned and consistent longer note values. An important concept when playing longer note values is to hear the sound continuing through each long note. Teaching strategies and practice techniques for this may include:

1) Physically moving the hand or arm to sense continuity for the duration of the sound.
2) Singing the tone of any sustained note through to the next note, especially with a *crescendo* through the longer notes.
3) Counting or singing a rhythmic subdivision of the sustained note.
4) Performing repeated notes on the same pitch for the duration of the sustained note to simulate continuity of sound.

Melodies with a Mixture of Note Values—Fading Sound Challenges

Once a student has mastered playing melodies with continuous shorter notes, the next step involves playing melodies with a mixture of shorter and longer note values. A slight *crescendo* through shorter notes leading to longer notes can create a sense of continuity and direction. A significant challenge involves the fading sound decay on longer notes due to the nature of the piano as a percussive instrument. After an initial rise or "bloom" in the tone, the sound will gradually fade until there is no perceptible volume left. The slower the tempo and/or the longer the note value, the more difficult it is for a pianist to sustain the long note and connect it to the next one. This skill must begin with an aural connection. A performer must listen carefully and mentally "sing" through long notes to match them to successive notes in order to create a smooth melodic line. In all cases, the first note following a sustained note should seamlessly "come out of" the previous long note to avoid undesirable accents that disrupt melodies. The aural perception must inspire the appropriate physical movement of a fluid arm and wrist combined with a careful finger approach into the key.

In addition, flowing note values in the accompaniment under longer melody notes can help to give the illusion of a more sustained melody. A slight *crescendo* through these accompaniments can significantly help to propel the melody forward. Students need many opportunities to work on the careful listening and dynamic control necessary for melodies that include a mixture of note values.

Repertoire: Melodies with a Mixture of Note Values—Fading Sound Challenges
Burgmüller: *25 Progressive Pieces*, Op. 100, No. 16—Sorrow
Burgmüller: *18 Characteristic Studies*, Op. 109, No. 9—Morning Bell
Gillock: *Lyric Preludes in Romantic Style*—A Faded Letter
Gillock: *Lyric Preludes in Romantic Style*—Serenade
Grieg: *Lyric Pieces*, Op. 38, No. 6—Elegie
Grieg: *Lyric Pieces*, Op. 43, No. 6—To the Spring
Grieg: *Lyric Pieces*, Op. 54, No. 4—Notturno
Grieg: *Lyric Pieces*, Op. 65, No. 5—Ballad
Gurlitt: *Album for the Young*, Op. 140, No. 18—Serenade
Tchaikovsky: *Album for the Young*, Op. 39, No. 1—Morning Prayer

Right-hand, Single-line Melodies

From the early levels of piano study, students most often perform repertoire with the melody in the right hand and accompaniment in the left hand, so they are more comfortable playing this texture. There are likely many reasons for this, including the acoustical reality that listeners can hear a melody presented in a higher voice more clearly than one residing in the left hand. The fact that the vast majority of individuals are right-handed may be another reason why there are more pieces with right-hand melodies. Whatever the reasons, repertoire pieces with melodies in the right hand are clearly more readily available. Students should master playing right-hand melodies well before moving on to repertoire with the melody in the left hand.

Repertoire: Right-hand, Single-line Melodies
Beach: *Children's Album*, Op. 36, No. 3—Waltz
Burgmüller: *25 Progressive Pieces*, Op. 100, No. 3—Pastorale
Burgmüller: *25 Progressive Pieces*, Op. 100, No. 22—Barcarolle
Gillock: *Lyric Preludes in Romantic Style*—Autumn Sketch
Grieg: *Lyric Pieces*, Op. 68, No. 4—Evening in the Mountains
Gurlitt: *Album for the Young*, Op. 140, No. 3—The Sky is Bright
Gurlitt: *Album for the Young*, Op. 140, No. 18—Serenade

Schumann: *Album for the Young*, Op. 68, No. 5—Little Piece (with left-hand duet)
Tchaikovsky: *Album for the Young*, Op. 39, No. 15—Italian Song
Tchaikovsky: *Album for the Young*, Op. 39, No. 16—Old French Song (with some left-hand duets)

Left-hand, Single-line Melodies

Teachers should assign plenty of repertoire with left-hand melodies. The most obvious challenge in playing left-hand melodies is balancing them against the more dominant right-hand accompaniment, which will likely be in a more prominent range of the keyboard. The lower range can make it more difficult for students to hear the melody clearly underneath the higher accompaniment. Melodic movement in the left hand may also feel less natural physically, since the pianist is moving more across the body rather than away from it. Pianists may need to sit a little further back or lean back slightly when a left-hand melody moves higher in the range.

Repertoire: Left-hand, Single-line Melodies
Burgmüller: *25 Progressive Pieces*, Op. 100, No. 7—The Clear Stream (B section)
Chaminade: *Album for the Young*, Op. 126, No. 2—Aubade
Gillock: *Lyric Preludes in Romantic Style*—Deserted Ball Room
Grieg: *Lyric Pieces*, Op. 12, No. 2—Waltz (B section)
Grieg: *Lyric Pieces*, Op. 43, No. 6—To the Spring (A section)
Gurlitt: *Album for the Young*, Op. 140, No. 4—In the Garden
Schumann: *Album for the Young*, Op. 68, No. 10—The Happy Farmer (A section)

Repertoire: Both Right-hand and Left-hand Single-line Melodies
Burgmüller: *25 Progressive Pieces*, Op. 100, No. 15—Ballade
Burgmüller: *25 Progressive Pieces*, Op. 100, No. 16—Sorrow
Grieg: *Lyric Pieces*, Op. 54, No. 5—Scherzo
Tchaikovsky: *Album for the Young*, Op. 39, No. 21—Sweet Dreams

Melodies with Large Vocal Leaps

Performances by singers and other instrumentalists provide important models for pianists, as they demonstrate techniques and sounds that pianists may not be able to replicate as easily. Observing the physical singing of lyrical melodies provides a greater understanding of their expressive nature. Vocal melodies often possess expressive leaps that require some effort by singers but may seem to be easier to perform on the piano. Pianists should physically sing melodies with expressive vocal leaps and use this experience to help them transfer this sound to the piano. Exaggerating the dynamic shape of a vocal leap can make its expression even more convincing.

Pianists should seek to create the same gesture of a vocal leap by involving the entire arm and hand in the tone production, using the natural arm weight that comes from a freely released arm. The pianist's arm, hand, and fingers should consistently transfer weight from one note to the next, combined with skillful pedaling and an overlapped finger *legato* to achieve a beautifully connected vocal line.

<u>Repertoire: Melodies with Large Vocal Leaps</u>
Beach: *Children's Album*, Op. 36, No. 3—Waltz
Burgmüller: *25 Progressive Pieces*, Op. 100, No. 3—Pastorale
Burgmüller: *25 Progressive Pieces*, Op. 100, No. 15—Ballade (B section)
Burgmüller: *25 Progressive Pieces*, Op. 100, No. 22—Barcarolle
Burgmüller: *18 Characteristic Studies*, Op. 109, No. 9—Morning Bell
Chaminade: *Album for the Young*, Book 2, Op. 126, No.1—Idylle
Grieg: *Lyric Pieces*, Op. 62, No. 5—Phantom
Gurlitt: *Album for the Young*, Op. 140, No. 7—The Festive Dance (A section)
Gurlitt: *Album for the Young*, Op. 140, No. 18—Serenade
Tchaikovsky: *Album for the Young*, Op. 39, No. 23—The Handorgan Man

Melodies with Rapid Changes of Direction, Requiring Rotation or Rolling Weight

Instrumental melodies, in particular, often possess frequent changes of direction, challenging the pianist to move arm weight consistently through each shift. While the keys on a piano clearly move vertically up and down, a more horizontal approach perceiving movement directionally from left to right combined with a continuous fluid motion yields smoother and consistent melodies. The technique of rotation from the elbow is particularly helpful, especially when these changes of direction consist of broken intervals.

Repertoire: Melodies with Rapid Changes of Direction, Requiring Rotation or Rolling Weight
Burgmüller: *25 Progressive Pieces*, Op. 100, No. 3—Pastorale
Burgmüller: *25 Progressive Pieces*, Op. 100, No. 7—The Clear Stream
Burgmüller: *25 Progressive Pieces*, Op. 100, No. 12—The Farewell
Burgmüller: *18 Characteristic Studies*, Op. 109, No. 3—The Shepherd's Return
Gillock: *Lyric Preludes in Romantic Style*—Dragon Fly
Gillock: *Lyric Preludes in Romantic Style*—Soaring
Grieg: *Lyric Pieces*, Op. 47, No. 6—Norwegian March
Grieg: *Lyric Pieces*, Op. 57, No. 6—Homesickness
Gurlitt: *Album for the Young*, Op. 140, No. 10—The Little Norwegian
Schumann: *Album for the Young*, Op. 68, No. 12—Knight Rupert

Fragmented or Interrupted Melodies

The easiest melodies for students to perform will be single-line melodies that remain within one hand and have a *legato* consistency of sound between notes. Vocal melodies can also include rests that can serve as expressive tools for enhancing the intensity of the melodic line. Melodies more instrumental in character may also have various interruptions, such as being suspended across rests or traveling between hands. An important principle is to remember that the melodic notes have to continue a sense of musical connection even if the notes do not actually have a physical *legato* connection. Rests can be a visual barrier, with students often seeing the rests as a stopping point. The melody still continues, however, and needs to be shaped and defined as if there were no rests.

A useful practice technique to change the perception of these melodies is to eliminate the rests or interruptions and play the melody as if it is a lyrical, *legato* line. This provides an excellent aural model, so that when the pianist reverts to playing it as notated with the rests or interruptions, the connected aural image is still in their memory.

<u>Repertoire: Fragmented or Interrupted Melodies</u>
Beach: *Children's Album*, Op. 36, No. 2—Gavotte
Burgmüller: *18 Characteristic Studies*, Op. 109, No. 2—The Pearls
Burgmüller: *18 Characteristic Studies*, Op. 109, No. 5—The Spring
Burgmüller: *18 Characteristic Studies*, Op. 109, No. 7—Lullaby
Burgmüller: *18 Characteristic Studies*, Op. 109, No. 8—Agitato
Burgmüller: *18 Characteristic Studies*, Op. 109, No. 11—Serenade
Burgmüller: *18 Characteristic Studies*, Op. 109, No. 15—Sylphs
Burgmüller: *18 Characteristic Studies*, Op. 109, No. 17—March
Chaminade: *Album for the Young*, Book 1, Op. 123, No. 10—Tarentelle
Schumann: *Album for the Young*, Op. 68, No. 33—Vintage Times

Finally, melodies are dependent upon their accompaniments and various textures, so pianists must always let the musical context guide their performance. The same practice and perception principles already discussed apply to melodies within complex textures as well.

Harmony

Jean Phillipe Rameau's 1722 *Treatise on Harmony* outlines the major and minor tonal system that is the basis of much of Western art music. Unfortunately, students sometimes view this important theoretical knowledge as an intellectual pursuit, with little connection to the interpretive understanding of a piece. An integration of theoretical knowledge with its emotional and/or dramatic impact on the various elements of music can significantly improve a student's expressive playing and prepare them for more difficult repertoire.

Individual Chords

Individual chords can be consonant or dissonant. A consonant chord is one that seems pleasant, peaceful, and stable, while a dissonant chord may feel tense, dramatic, or perhaps even "wrong" to some Western ears. A consonant chord is usually major or minor, while a dissonant chord might be a diminished chord or a cluster chord with non-consonant intervals. Dissonant chords suggest tension or intensity and a stronger dynamic level, followed by a *diminuendo* into their resolution.

Functional Harmony

Individual chords are defined by their letter name and chord quality: for example, a C-major triad or a G-diminished triad. Chords need a tonal context to become "functional," and this functionality then defines the role of each chord. In Western classical music within the common practice period, the tonic is the name of the key, the first note of the major scale, and the center of tonal stability. Compositions revolve around the tonic both melodically and harmonically to create a sense of completion and conclusion.

Chords are built upon scale degrees identified by Roman numerals. Major chords use uppercase numerals (I, V) and minor chords use lowercase numerals (i, iv). Both primary triads (I/i, IV/iv, V) and secondary triads (ii/ii°, iii/III, vi/VI, vii°/VII) are considered to be diatonic or native to the key, and each scale degree has a designation:

I/i—tonic, ii/ii°—supertonic, iii/III—mediant, IV/iv—subdominant, V—dominant, vi/VI—submediant, vii° leading tone, VII—subtonic.

Harmonic Progressions and Cadences

The sequence of functional harmonies within a piece is referred to as a harmonic progression. Throughout the history of Western music, various chord progressions have been significant in defining the style and aesthetic of each period. Harmonic progressions help define musical phrasing, form, and character.

Cadential patterns are common chord progressions with clear paths to the tonic through various chord function categories. The cadence with the strongest route to the tonic is the authentic cadence (V-I). Composers sometimes extend the dominant (V) harmony as a way of making a stronger and more dramatic arrival to the tonic. The plagal cadence (IV-I) is another route to the tonic, frequently used as the "amen" ending of a hymn. An inconclusive chord progression that ends on the dominant is a half cadence (I-V). Some chords do not progress to where they are expected to go, such as the deceptive cadence that prolongs the arrival to the tonic (V-vi). Regular cadential patterns confirm tonality and provide harmonic stability. Figure 3.1 shows common chord progressions and their substitute chords.

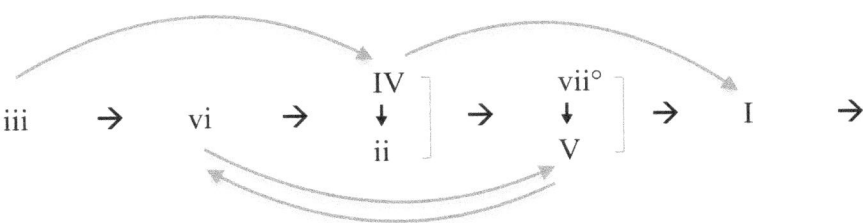

Figure 3.1 Common harmonic progressions (author owned).

Harmonic Analysis

Once students understand the concept of functional harmony, they can study harmonic analysis through chord progression exercises. Most elementary-level students learn their I-IV-I-V7-I cadential patterns, but they may not play them with any understanding of the musical significance of the progression. One possible teaching strategy is to think of the I chord as "home," the IV chord as going somewhere exciting "away from home," and the V7 chord as nearing the end of the journey "on my way back to home." Playing chord progressions with this type of analytical understanding brings new meaning to these important harmonic excursions.

Following experience with basic cadential chord progressions, students are ready to explore harmonic progressions within their repertoire. While they may not be able to identify every harmony or chord progression, exploring this process will begin to open up their understanding of the significance of various chords and progressions. One analytical challenge for inexperienced students is to identify non-chord tones, such as passing tones, neighbor tones, appoggiaturas, escape tones, anticipations, pedal points, suspensions, and retardations. Students must be able to identify these within their repertoire in order to analyze chords properly. Teachers may need to improve their own analytical skills to be prepared to assist students with harmonic analysis and demonstrate the application of analysis to musical interpretation.

Non-typical Chord Progressions

Composers often use a departure from common chord progressions to convey surprise, interest, and heightened emotional content. Chords that do not follow typical chord progressions usually do not have a conventional movement to the tonic. The lack of a strong cadence into the tonic results in more ambiguity and a different character in the music. Sometimes composers may not establish a clear tonality at the beginning of a piece, which can create a sense of uncertainty or even unease. Teachers and students must be alert to the expressive possibilities of unconventional chord progressions.

Harmonic Rhythm

Harmonic rhythm, the rate at which chords change, also influences interpretation and musical character. A slow harmonic rhythm often projects a sense of peace and stability. A faster harmonic rhythm usually conveys more energy, excitement, or urgency. Changes in the harmonic rhythm affect the expressive content. Analysis of the harmonic rhythm in combination with other musical elements helps students explore what the composer may be communicating.

Non-diatonic Harmonies and Modulations

Through the inclusion of chords outside of the established key, composers generate more interest and a sense of "going somewhere" musically. This may be simply a harmonic excursion through the temporary tonicization of another key, or it may result in a modulation to a new key. The establishment of a new key often has a very clear authentic cadence, while a temporary excursion to another key is usually very short. Modulations often happen through a chord that is common to both the previous key and the new key, and thus can be analyzed as being functional in both keys. Modulations can also be abrupt, with no common chord between the old and new keys.

Harmony Curriculum

A thorough foundational knowledge of harmony is essential for understanding the structure of a composition and thus its interpretive possibilities. Essential foundational concepts and skills for the intermediate-level student include the following competencies:

1) Construct and identify major key signatures.
2) Understand key relationships between major and minor, both parallel and relative minor.
3) Construct and identify major scales and all forms of the minor scales.
4) Construct and identify major, minor, augmented, and diminished triads and seventh chords in both root positions and inversions.
5) Construct and identify primary and secondary triads on all scale degrees in major and minor keys. Identify the appropriate scale degree term and chord quality for each chord.
6) Perform elementary- through intermediate-level repertoire in all major and minor keys.

Keys with More Than Four Sharps or Flats

Ideally, students should have previously performed five-note scales and elementary-level repertoire selections in all keys. Unfortunately, much of the elementary-level repertoire stays in easier keys, so intermediate-level students may not have had much experience playing pieces with multiple sharps and flats. It is important for intermediate-level students, therefore, to perform pieces in as many keys as possible to confirm their knowledge of key signatures and gain experience reading pitch patterns in all of these keys. In addition, the keyboard topography feels very different in each tonality and influences technical decisions such as fingering and hand/wrist position on the keys, especially when playing in tonalities that involve a large number of black notes. Teachers have to search carefully for supplementary repertoire that will utilize more difficult keys.

Repertoire: Keys with More Than Four Sharps or Flats
Gillock: *Lyric Preludes in Romantic Style*—Moonlight Mood (B)
Gillock: *Lyric Preludes in Romantic Style*—Procession of the Mandarin (G-flat)
Gillock: *Lyric Preludes in Romantic Style*—Phantom Rider (G-sharp minor)
Gillock: *Lyric Preludes in Romantic Style*—The Silent Snow (E-flat minor)
Gillock: *Lyric Preludes in Romantic Style*—Night Journey (B-flat minor)
Grieg: *Lyric Pieces*, Op. 43, No. 3—In My Native Country (F-sharp)
Grieg: *Lyric Pieces*, Op. 43, No. 6—To the Spring (F-sharp)
Grieg: *Lyric Pieces*, Op. 68, No. 3—At Your Feet (middle section D-flat)
Grieg: *Lyric Pieces*, Op. 71, No. 3—Puck (E-flat minor)

"Color Chords" for Expressive Effects

Consistent, predictable diatonic chords and harmonic progressions convey stability and security. More interest and expressiveness occur when a composer does something unexpected, such as using a chord that is not common to the key. These "color" chords call for special treatment. One of my former teachers used to say that they need a little extra "tender loving care." A progression that arrives at one of these chords, for example, might not arrive in a typically increasing dynamic climax, but might be more compelling and dramatic through a slight delay and sudden drop in the dynamic level on the color chord. Teachers need to help students identify common chords and harmonic progressions so that they can recognize unconventional progressions and chords that provide opportunities for greater expressiveness.

Repertoire: "Color Chords" for Expressive Effects
Chaminade: *Album for the Young*, Book 2, Op. 126, No. 7—Élégie
Grieg: *Lyric Pieces*, Op. 12, No. 1—Arietta
Grieg: *Lyric Pieces*, Op. 43, No. 2—Solitary Traveler
Grieg: *Lyric Pieces*, Op. 54, No. 4—Notturno
Grieg: *Lyric Pieces*, Op. 57, No. 2—Gade
Grieg: *Lyric Pieces*, Op. 62, No. 5—Phantom
Grieg: *Lyric Pieces*, Op. 68, No. 3—At Your Feet
Schumann: *Album for the Young*, Op. 68, No. 21—***

Schumann: *Album for the Young*, Op. 68, No. 32—Sheherazade
Schumann: *Album for the Young*, Op. 68, No. 34—Theme

Obscure Tonalities and Harmonic Progressions

Just as unexpected chords can provide unique opportunities for dramatic expressiveness, obscure tonalities and unconventional harmonic progressions also create more interest and intensity. When a composer does not establish clear and regular departures from and returns to the tonic, the music can feel uncertain, restless, or anxious. Phrase chains that end with inconclusive cadences might project an increasing sense of urgency, with more relief created once the tonic has finally arrived.

<u>Repertoire: Obscure Tonalities and Harmonic Progressions</u>
Grieg: *Lyric Pieces*, Op. 43, No. 1—Butterfly
Grieg: *Lyric Pieces*, Op. 43, No. 3—In My Native Country
Grieg: *Lyric Pieces*, Op. 54, No. 4—Notturno
Grieg: *Lyric Pieces*, Op. 62, No. 5—Phantom
Grieg: *Lyric Pieces*, Op. 68, No. 3—At Your Feet
Schumann: *Album for the Young*, Op. 68, No. 21—***
Schumann: *Album for the Young*, Op. 68, No. 26—***

Harmony is an important foundation of the formal structure of a piece and guides musical interpretation and artistry. While an intermediate-level student may not possess enough analytical tools to identify exactly how every chord functions within a particular key, they can begin to find chords and harmonic progressions that don't fit the normal expectations. Combining this awareness with other musical elements will likely yield more interesting possibilities for expression.

4

Texture

Musical texture refers to the number and variety of different musical lines or layers within a piece and the ways in which those lines relate to each other. In broad terms, textures may be (1) monophonic, consisting of a single line of music, (2) homophonic, a melody-dominated texture with supporting parts, or (3) polyphonic, a texture with at least two independent lines of music. Textures may be thick or thin and vary in complexity and relationships between voices.

The musical texture of a piano work has a great deal to do with the difficulty level of the piece, since each hand may have to manage multiple parts at one time. The more different elements that a pianist has to control at the same time, the more difficult the piece becomes.

Because the dominant element in much of the Romantic-period music is melody, the element of texture in this chapter will be considered as it relates to how melody is presented within the musical texture. Five broad categories of textures are discussed: (1) monophonic textures, (2) homophonic textures with single-line melodies and various accompaniments, (3) homophonic textures with complex settings, (4) polyphonic textures with multiple distinct voices, and (5) mixed textures.

Monophonic Textures

A monophonic texture consists of a single musical line without any accompaniment. For the purpose of discussion in this book, monophonic textures include single musical lines in either hand or lines that move back and forth between each hand, creating one single musical line. Lines doubled at the unison octave between hands, within one hand, or within both hands are examined in the homophonic texture sections.

Single Musical Lines in the Right Hand

Single musical lines played by the right hand are the easiest to perform. Since many individuals are right-hand dominant and much elementary-level music consists of pieces with the melody in the right hand, the pianist has likely developed more technical skills in the right hand than in the left hand. Right-hand melodies are usually located in a higher range that is easier to hear clearly and are thus more common than left-hand melodies. Pieces with single musical lines provide wonderful preparation for students to learn how to shape and pace similar cadenza-like passages that appear in Romantic-period repertoire.

Repertoire: Single Musical Lines in the Right Hand
Grieg: *Lyric Pieces*, Op. 68, No. 4—Evening in the Mountains
Liszt: *Forgotten Romance* (Romance Oubliée), S. 527

Single Musical Lines in the Left Hand

Single musical lines in the left hand are by nature more difficult for students because they are more infrequent in the elementary-level repertoire, and they usually appear in a lower range. It is much easier for performers to hear a right-hand melody that appears in the uppermost voice than to listen to a melody that is lower in range. Since the left hand more often plays accompaniments than melodies, a performer's left hand may not be as developed in performing lyrical, singing melodies. As the repertoire advances, the prevalence of left-hand melodies increases. Students need as much experience as possible performing left-hand single musical lines in easier settings.

Repertoire: Single Musical Lines in the Left Hand
Liszt: *Forgotten Romance* (Romance Oubliée), S. 527

Single Musical Lines that Move between Hands

A single musical line divided between the hands requires careful listening for tonal consistency. Students should begin playing this type of texture by studying single musical lines that have less-frequent changes between the two hands. Easier pieces will be those that are very patterned in how the line moves from one hand to the other. Most of these pieces have lines that are instrumental in character, consisting primarily of figuration rather than lyrical melodies.

Repertoire: Single Musical Lines that Move between Hands
Burgmüller: *25 Progressive Pieces*, Op. 100, No. 21—Angels' Voices
Burgmüller: *18 Characteristic Studies*, Op. 109, No. 8—Agitato
Liszt: *Forgotten Romance (Romance Oubliée)*, S. 527
Schumann: *Album for the Young*, Op. 68, No. 14—Little Study

Single Musical Lines that Move between the Hands with Hand Crossings (One or Both Hands Crossing)

Single musical lines that move between the two hands with hand crossings have an additional technical challenge. Both the *rate of speed* at which one or both hands must cross and the *distance* that the crossing hand must travel will influence the difficulty level of the piece. It is crucial for the performer to maintain technical freedom and fluidity of movement when crossing hands in order to produce a smooth tonal and dynamic musical line. Because the speed of attack affects both dynamics and tone color, the performer will need to control the speed of attack carefully on the notes played immediately following the hand crossing. Performers should move quickly but fluidly to get to the next note sooner than they actually have to play it so that they can control the speed of attack into the key carefully.

Repertoire: Single Musical Lines that Move between the Hands with Hand Crossings (One or Both Hands Crossing)
Burgmüller: *25 Progressive Pieces*, Op. 100, No. 24—The Swallow

Single Musical Lines that Alternate Rapidly between Hands on Every Pitch

The most difficult single musical line is one that alternates every pitch between the two hands. This type presents a number of challenges for the performer: rhythmic precision, metrical continuity in larger pulse groupings, technical freedom and consistency, tonal consistency, and often the voicing of a melodic line within a line. Rhythmic precision improves when pianists group pitches into the largest possible pulse groupings as determined by the tempo. Pianists can place a subtle emphasis on the strong beat of each pulse group to maintain metrical continuity. The perception of larger pulse groupings promotes physical gestures that gather multiple notes in one physical motion rather than separate motions for each note. Grouping of the pitches into larger pulse units also promotes technical freedom, since the recurring strong beats can provide a regular point of release within a perpetual-motion line.

In addition to the use of metrical grouping as a means of gaining technical freedom, performers must retain fluidity and flexibility within arms and wrists to negotiate the keyboard topography changes. Once students are able to play with consistency of sound, rhythmic precision, and metrical continuity, they can then begin to shape the melodic line-within-a-line. Since most repertoire pieces with this texture have many challenges, they are usually advanced-level works.

Homophonic Textures

Perhaps the most prevalent texture in Romantic-period piano music is homophonic. This texture is also perhaps the most varied of any texture type, as there are many accompaniment types and ways in which a melody is paired with its supporting parts. Within this section, "melodies" refers to only single-line melodies, while "accompaniments" refers to all other supporting parts. Students should experience a lot of single-line melodies in each hand combined with different types of accompaniments. They should become very comfortable playing single-line melodies with accompaniments prior to performing more complicated textures in which the melody is supported by chords or other lines within the same hand, requiring finger independence within one or both hands.

The easiest homophonic textures will be those that are the most consistent and patterned in one or more musical elements. Some examples of this would be consistency of articulation, such as *legato* melodies with *legato* accompaniment or detached melodies with detached accompaniment, or a consistent, patterned rhythm in each hand, such as a melody in continuous eighth notes over a smooth chordal accompaniment with consistent harmonic rhythm.

Homophonic Textures—Melodies Doubled at the Octave

Melodies can be doubled in unison between the two hands, with an additional octave within one of the hands or with octaves in both hands.

Melodies with Unison Doubling between the Hands

Melodies doubled in unison octaves split between the two hands present several considerations. The first challenge is fingering, since fingering for parallel motion lines is not symmetrical between the two hands. Many students find it challenging to play the same pitches in each hand using different fingerings. The second is voicing, since the performer will likely need to differentiate the parts dynamically. The choice of which voice to highlight requires careful consideration and has a great impact upon the musical character. The default voicing option is usually to highlight the top voice, but performers should not accept this as the only option. The process of experimenting with different voicing and different tonal colors between the two hands can yield some imaginative results. Highlighting the top voice results in a brighter color and character. Bringing out the lower voice yields a darker tone that may feel more somber or subdued. Sometimes the voices should be relatively equal, which would also result in a different sound and character.

<u>Repertoire: Melodies with Unison Doubling between the Hands</u>
Burgmüller: *18 Characteristic Studies*, Op. 109, No. 15—Sylphs (B section)
Grieg: *Lyric Pieces*, Op. 68, No. 2—Grandmother's Minuet (B section)

Schumann: *Album for the Young*, Op. 68, No. 12—Knight Rupert (A section)

Melodies with Unison Doubling in Octaves within the Same Hand

Melodies doubled in octaves within one hand present an additional challenge. The performer must have a well-developed octave technique to be able to play a smooth and expressive melody. It is physically impossible to play a melody in octaves completely *legato* with fingers only. Performers with large enough hands can include the use of the fourth finger on some of the top notes to create more of a *legato* line. If it is possible to play the top notes of the octaves with *legato* fingering, the whole texture will sound more *legato*, since the listener will be following the top voice. Careful dynamic shaping, tonal control, and subtle use of the damper pedal help the performer create an illusion of *legato* when it is not physically possible.

Pianists should perform octaves using good wrist technique rather than trying to play them with a forearm motion, because the forearm cannot move fast and relying on it can quickly lead to fatigue. Intermediate-level students will not encounter too many octave passages, especially rapid ones, which are generally characteristic of higher difficulty levels. Repertoire pieces with many octaves in one hand are most likely at the late-intermediate level or higher. Playing octaves within one hand while playing an accompaniment in the other hand increases the difficulty level of the piece.

Repertoire: Melodies with Unison Doubling in Octaves within the Same Hand
Burgmüller: *18 Characteristic Studies*, Op. 109, No. 16—Parting
Grieg: *Lyric Pieces*, Op. 62, No. 5—Phantom
Schumann: *Album for the Young*, Op. 68, No. 31—Song of War
Schumann: *Album for the Young*, Op. 68, No. 37—Sailor's Song (with alternating redistribution)

Melodies with Unison Doubling in Octaves within Both Hands

All of the previously discussed criteria for melodies doubled at the octave in one hand also apply to melodies doubled in octaves in both hands, with the added challenge that balance and voicing must be determined between the two hands as well as within one hand. Frequently, a desirable voicing is to emphasize the highest note in the right hand and the lowest note in the left hand, with the inner voices softer. This choice of voicing creates a clearer texture for the listener.

Homophonic Textures with Single-line Melodies and Various Accompaniments

Romantic-period repertoire is full of soaring melodies with various types of accompaniments. The most basic role of these accompaniments is to provide a harmonic foundation for the melody, but accompaniments contribute to the musical fabric in many other ways. Pianists must be able to delineate the role of each of the different lines of these textures clearly.

Maintaining good balance between the two hands in homophonic repertoire is challenging. The "ghosting" practice technique is one of the most successful ways to improve good balance between the two hands. While playing a simple melody with accompaniment, the student plays the melody normally with full sound, while only slightly depressing the keys of the accompaniment so that they produce no sound. Next, the student plays the melody again, while allowing a few of the accompaniment notes to sound. Finally, the student plays the piece normally, allowing all notes to sound but with the accompaniment softer than the melody. This approach virtually always yields better balance in any textural setting.

Accompaniments can be distracting, and pianists must be able to control the shape and phrasing of the melody while maintaining good balance with the accompaniment. An appropriate curriculum begins with single-line melodies with simple accompaniments, progresses to more complex accompaniments, then to more complex melodies, and finally to mixed textures that may change frequently.

Single-line Melodies with Continuous Blocked-chord Accompaniment

An important principle to remember when selecting repertoire for students is to consider the number of musical elements that the performer must manage at one time. The introduction of concepts and skills in their easiest settings is another important guiding principle. Students should begin playing homophonic textures with single-line melodies and continuous blocked-chord accompaniments. Slow-moving chords provide the opportunity for the pianist to focus more on the melody.

Repertoire: Single-line Melodies with Continuous Blocked-chord Accompaniment
Burgmüller: *25 Progressive Pieces*, Op. 100, No. 1—Sincerity
Burgmüller: *25 Progressive Pieces*, Op. 100, No. 20—Tarantelle
Gurlitt: *Album for the Young*, Op. 140, No. 8—The Music Box
Gurlitt: *Album for the Young*, Op. 140, No. 9—Thoughtful Moments

Single-line Melodies with Intermittent Blocked-chord Accompaniment

Sometimes composers will create an accompaniment consisting of intermittent blocked chords. Often students will have a tendency to accent these accompanying chords each time they enter after a rest, which may cause the student to also accent the melody notes at the same time. The accompaniment chords therefore may affect the consistency and flow of the melody. Students must listen carefully and continuously sing through long melody notes, which will help to maintain the balance between the two hands.

Repertoire: Single-line Melodies with Intermittent Blocked-chord Accompaniment
Burgmüller: *25 Progressive Pieces*, Op. 100, No. 17—The Chatterbox
Gillock: *Lyric Preludes in Romantic Style*—Deserted Ball Room
Schumann: *Album for the Young*, Op. 68, No. 8—Wild Rider
Tchaikovsky: *Album for the Young*, Op. 39, No. 21—Sweet Dreams (B section)

Single-line Melodies with Continuous or Detached Repeated-chord Accompaniment

Accompaniments with repeated chords present additional challenges. In the Burgmüller *Pastorale*, the repeated chords provide a gentle pulsating accompaniment that continues the energy and flow. When playing a series of repeated chords, students will often "land" on the last one, creating an unwanted accent. A slight *diminuendo* through each chord repetition can help to avoid these accents. The pianist will need to use the pedal to play the chords smoothly, which will increase the amount of volume built up with each repeated chord. Careful listening, shallow pedaling, and more frequent pedal changes can help the pianist keep the accompaniment dynamically beneath the melody. Since the speed of attack is a large determinant of dynamics, pianists should keep their fingers in contact with the keys while playing the chords to avoid louder attacks through the repetitions. The student must keep the melody notes "alive" aurally by singing through long notes and listening for fading sound. If the repeated chordal accompaniment is detached rather than continuous, the pianist will have even more of a challenge to keep the volume of the chords controlled.

Repertoire: Single-line Melodies with Continuous Repeated-chord Accompaniment
Burgmüller: *25 Progressive Pieces*, Op. 100, No. 3—Pastorale
Burgmüller: *25 Progressive Pieces*, Op. 100, No. 8—Gracefulness
Grieg: *Lyric Pieces*, Op. 12, No. 2—Waltz (B section)
Schumann: *Album for the Young*, Op. 68, No. 11—Sicilienne

Repertoire: Single-line Melodies with Detached Repeated-chord Accompaniment
Burgmüller: *25 Progressive Pieces*, Op. 100, No. 22—Barcarolle
Burgmüller: *25 Progressive Pieces*, Op. 100, No. 23—The Return (B section)
Schumann: *Album for the Young*, Op. 68, No. 10—The Happy Farmer
Tchaikovsky: *Album for the Young*, Op. 39, No. 18—Neapolitan Dance Song

Single-line Melodies with Alberti-bass, Broken-chord, or Broken-interval Accompaniment

Accompaniments consisting of Alberti-bass lines and other broken-interval patterns increase the difficulty level, as there is more potential interference with the melody. These accompaniment patterns are likely to be more rhythmically active than the melody and their constant directional changes can present challenges. The pianist should approach most broken-chord patterns with forearm rotation to make them easier to play and to achieve a smoother, more consistent sound than is possible from relying solely on finger motion. Depending upon the keyboard topography of the passage, students should adapt their wrists to whatever position will allow them to play fluidly and comfortably. Playing broken-chord patterns that include black keys likely means that the wrist needs to be higher or that the hand position needs to be tilted at a different angle. Students should practice these broken-chord patterns first as blocked chords to find comfortable hand positions and fingerings, then practice the blocked chords with the melody, and finally practice the broken chords with the melody as written.

Repertoire: Single-line Melodies with Alberti-bass, Broken-chord, or Broken-interval Accompaniment
Burgmüller: *25 Progressive Pieces*, Op. 100, No. 7—The Clear Stream (B section)
Burgmüller: *18 Characteristic Studies*, Op. 109, No. 13—The Storm
Chaminade: *Album for the Young*, Book 2, Op. 126, No. 1—Idylle
Chaminade: *Album for the Young*, Book 2, Op. 126, No. 7—Élégie
Gillock: *Lyric Preludes in Romantic Style*—Autumn Sketch
Grieg: *Lyric Pieces*, Op. 43, No. 1—Butterfly
Gurlitt: *Album for the Young*, Op. 140, No. 3—The Sky is Bright
Gurlitt: *Album for the Young*, Op. 140, No. 18—Serenade
Schumann: *Album for the Young*, Op. 68, No. 5—Little Piece
Tchaikovsky: *Album for the Young*, Op. 39, No. 14—Polka

Single-line Melodies with Waltz-bass Accompaniment

A typical waltz pairs melodies with waltz-bass accompaniments. A student's first waltz experience should not be the more advanced waltzes of Schubert, Chopin, and other Romantic-period composers. Students need to have experience performing simpler waltzes prior to these mature works. The easiest waltzes will have a single-line melody in the right hand accompanied by a waltz-bass pattern in the left hand that is limited in distance and consists of simple chords in regular inversions.

One of the challenges with the waltz-bass accompaniment is that the melody and the bass line are frequently moving in opposite directions. The practice technique of "air playing" is extremely helpful for practicing the waltz-bass accompaniment as well as any other traveling movements throughout the range of the keyboard. "Air playing" involves the pianist moving their hands and arms above the keyboard to the appropriate positions as if they are playing the piece. The purpose of "air playing" is to help the pianist to focus on the larger physical movements rather than individual fingers as a way of creating smooth, coordinated movement patterns. When pianists do not have to focus on playing the individual notes, they can develop a greater awareness of their larger physical gestures.

Repertoire: Single-line Melodies with Waltz-bass Accompaniment
Beach: *Children's Album*, Op. 36, No. 3—Waltz
Burgmüller: *25 Progressive Pieces*, Op. 100, No. 14—Austrian Dance
Grieg: *Lyric Pieces*, Op. 12, No. 5—Popular Melody
Gurlitt: *Album for the Young*, Op. 140, No. 7—The Festive Dance
Tchaikovsky: *Album for the Young*, Op. 39, No. 8—Waltz
Tchaikovsky: *Album for the Young*, Op. 39, No. 15—Italian Song

Single-line Melodies with Waltz-bass Accompaniment, with Accompaniment Split between Hands

Pieces become much more complicated when the accompaniment involves both hands. This requires careful dynamic control of the different voices. The hand playing both the melody and also some of the accompaniment notes needs much finger independence to differentiate between them. Mastering this technique can be helpful for preparing to play more difficult repertoire where each hand may have to play multiple voices of the texture.

Repertoire: Single-line Melodies with Waltz-bass Accompaniment, with Accompaniment Split between Hands
Grieg: *Lyric Pieces*, Op. 38, No. 7—Waltz

Single-line Melodies with Multi-voice Accompaniment

More challenging homophonic pieces present accompaniments with multiple voices, requiring control of the melody while also demonstrating finger independence in the opposite hand. Tchaikovsky's *Old French Song* requires the left hand to play two different voices, all while paying attention to the beautiful melody in the right hand. *Sweet Dreams* requires greater finger independence by requiring the accompaniment hand to hold down longer note values while also playing off beats. The challenge of the accompaniment threatens to disrupt the singing melody in the other hand.

Repertoire: Single-line Melodies with Multi-voice Accompaniment
Tchaikovsky: *Album for the Young*, Op. 39, No. 16—Old French Song
Tchaikovsky: *Album for the Young*, Op. 39, No. 21—Sweet Dreams

Single-line Melodies that Move Below or Within the Accompaniment

A single-line melody in the right hand over an accompaniment in the left hand is the most basic homophonic texture and the easiest to balance. When the melody is within or beneath the accompaniment, the student has many more challenges. Students should follow the previously recommended practice techniques of playing the melody alone first to aurally follow it across the range changes. Following this, the "ghosting" practice technique works very well to help students master the extra balance challenges. As with all challenging textures, extremely slow practice enables the student to hear everything, which in turn helps textural control.

Repertoire: Single-line Melodies that Move Below or Within the Accompaniment
Burgmüller: *18 Characteristic Studies*, Op. 109, No. 10—Velocity
Gillock: *Lyric Preludes in Romantic Style*—Serenade
Grieg: *Lyric Pieces*, Op. 57, No. 2—Gade
Schumann: *Album for the Young*, Op. 68, No. 40—Little Fugue (Fugue section)

Single-line Melodies with Line-within-a-line Texture

Composers frequently create and notate an additional melody within a single line of music, commonly referred to as a line-within-a-line melody. In this type of writing, the composer has succeeded in giving the illusion of creating

Figure 4.1 Burgmüller: *18 Characteristic Studies*, Op. 109, No. 1—Confidence, m. 1 (author owned).

an additional melodic line within the texture, even though an additional line has not actually been added (See Figure 4.1).

These line-within-a-line notes function therefore both as melodic notes and as part of a continuous accompaniment. The composer notates this by putting double stems in opposite directions on the melody notes, so that the notes visually belong to both the melody and accompaniment. Another practice is to notate the melody pitches with full-size note heads and make the accompaniment pitches a smaller size.

Line-within-a-line melodies often appear in the top voice but may also appear on the bottom or anywhere in the middle. The location of the line-within-a-line melody contributes to the difficulty level of the work; melodies on the top will be the easiest to perform, melodies on the bottom will be the next easiest, and melodies that fall in the middle will be the most challenging. Melodies in which the line-within-a-line moves between different voices are even more challenging to control, since the texture is constantly shifting.

Typically, a line-within-a-line texture involves a melody of longer note values held through and connected to the next longer melody note, while the moving part continues underneath. The composer notates this by giving the double-stemmed melody pitches longer note values than the accompaniment. For example, the melody pitches may be notated as quarter notes while the accompaniment pitches are notated as triplets. The pianist should voice the melody pitches louder than the accompaniment notes so that the melodic outline is clear, while the accompaniment stays in the background. The pianist must clearly delineate the vertical balance between the melody and accompaniment, but also connect the melody notes together dynamically and tonally, carefully shaping their linear contour.

One helpful practice technique is to block these notes as a chord, voicing the designated melody notes more strongly. Another balance technique is to play the voiced melodic note immediately preceding the rest of the chord. This practice technique is easier when the melody notes are on the top and the bottom but much more difficult when the melody notes are in the middle of the chord.

A line-within-a-line melody does not have to be a sustained melody of longer notes over the accompaniment; it can also simply consist of melodic pitches that the composer wants to bring out of the continuous line to highlight their significance. Composers notate these non-sustained melodic pitches with the same rhythmic values as the rest of the accompaniment notes, but with the addition of double stems.

An additional complication occurs when the same notes can be either a part of the melody or a part of the accompaniment at different times. These challenging lines require very slow practice, since the same note must have a different volume and different tonal color depending upon its function.

Performing a line-within-a-line melody requires significant independence and control, and is a more difficult challenge than normal single-line melodies. Students need extensive experience with defining the melody in these combined lines, since this type of writing appears extensively in Romantic-period piano repertoire. As with many other skills, performing these types of melodies in the right hand is generally easier than playing them with the left hand.

1) *Right-hand, single-line melodies—line-within-a-line texture with melody on top*

Figure 4.2 Burgmüller: *18 Characteristic Studies*, Op. 109, No. 1—Confidence, m. 1 (author owned).

When the melody notes in the combined line are on the "top" of the line, the pianist plays these notes with the fifth finger, which usually sounds prominently. Melody notes on the top of the line are the easiest to hear (See Figure 4.2).

Repertoire: Right-hand, single-line melodies—line-within-a-line texture with melody on top
Burgmüller: *18 Characteristic Studies*, Op. 109, No. 1—Confidence
Burgmüller: *18 Characteristic Studies*, Op. 109, No. 7—Lullaby
Burgmüller: *18 Characteristic Studies*, Op. 109, No. 11—Serenade
Gillock: *Lyric Preludes in Romantic Style*—Forest Murmurs
Gurlitt: *Album for the Young*, Op. 140, No. 11—Longing

2) *Right-hand, single-line melodies—line-within-a-line texture with melody on bottom*

Melody notes on the bottom of the musical line are usually played with the thumbs. This makes the melodic contour harder to control dynamically but is still easier because these melodies use a dominant finger on the inside of the hand. Pianists must create a consistent *legato* melody through careful pedaling because it is impossible to connect the melody notes played by the thumb only (See Figure 4.3).

Figure 4.3 Burgmüller: *25 Progressive Pieces*, Op. 100, No. 7—The Clear Stream, m. 1 (author owned).

Repertoire: Right-hand, single-line melodies—line-within-a-line texture with melody on bottom
Burgmüller: *25 Progressive Pieces*, Op. 100, No. 7—The Clear Stream
Gillock: *Lyric Preludes in Romantic Style*—Soaring
Schumann: *Album for the Young*, Op. 68, No. 5—Little Piece (left hand plays a line-within-a- line duet with the melody)

3) *Right-hand, single-line melodies—line-within-a-line texture with melody in the middle*

Melody notes that fall in the middle of the texture are much harder to define and control, since the pattern is less consistent with the melody notes played by different fingers (See Figure 4.4).

Figure 4.4 Burgmüller: *18 Characteristic Studies*, Op. 109, No. 5—The Spring, m. 1 (author owned).

Repertoire: Right-hand, single-line melodies—line-within-a-line texture with melody in the middle
Burgmüller: *18 Characteristic Studies*, Op. 109, No. 5—The Spring

4) *Right-hand, single-line melodies—line within-a-line texture with melody in various places within the same piece*

Finally, when the melody notes move around in the texture within the same piece, the pianist has to make quick adjustments in voicing. This is the most difficult texture.

Repertoire: Right-hand, single-line melodies—line within-a-line texture with melody in various places within the same piece
Burgmüller: *25 Progressive Pieces*, Op. 100, No. 13—Consolation
Gillock: *Lyric Preludes in Romantic Style*—Night Song
Gurlitt: *Album for the Young*, Op. 140, No. 5—Murmuring Brook

Homophonic Textures with Melodies in Complex Settings

Textures become much more complicated when the hand playing the melody also has to play parallel intervals or chords within the same hand, or when the melody is on the top of chords that alternate hands.

Melodies with Parallel Intervals with Single-line Accompaniment

Composers can create a variety of textures by adding parallel intervals to melodies. Standard fingerings for parallel thirds (1-3, 2-4, 3-5) facilitate a chain of smooth thirds with a limited number of changes in hand position. Parallel sixths are more awkward and provide more challenges, especially because the thumb often has to play adjacent pitches, requiring the hand to move frequently. Students should practice these parallel intervals beginning with pieces in which the other hand is less-complicated and/or slower moving. Pieces with parallel intervals and single-note accompaniments provide a good starting level, since the technical demands for the hand playing the single-note accompaniment are less than for the hand playing the parallel intervals.

Repertoire: Melodies with Parallel Intervals with Single-line Accompaniment
Burgmüller: *25 Progressive Pieces*, Op. 100, No. 4—The Little Party (parallel thirds, sixths)
Schumann: *Album for the Young*, Op. 68, No. 36—Italian Sailor's Song (parallel thirds)

Melodies with Parallel Intervals with Chordal Accompaniment

Melodies with parallel intervals that have a chordal accompaniment will be easier if the chords have longer note values, if they do not change frequently, or if changes are very patterned and consistent.

Repertoire: Melodies with Parallel Intervals with Chordal Accompaniment
Burgmüller: *25 Progressive Pieces*, Op. 100, No. 23—The Return (A section, various intervals)
Grieg: *Lyric Pieces*, Op. 38, No. 2—Popular Melody (various)
Grieg: *Lyric Pieces*, Op. 47, No. 6—Norwegian Dance (parallel sixths)
Tchaikovsky: *Album for the Young*, Op. 39, No. 17—German Song (limited parallel thirds and horn fifths)

Melodies with Parallel Intervals with Mixed-texture Accompaniment

As with most piano repertoire, the more complicated the accompaniment becomes, the more difficult these parallel intervals will be for the student.

Repertoire: Melodies with Parallel Intervals with Mixed-texture Accompaniment
Chaminade: *Album for the Young*, Book 1, Op. 123, No. 1—(untitled)
Grieg: *Lyric Pieces*, Op. 47, No. 6—Norwegian March (parallel sixths)
Grieg: *Lyric Pieces*, Op. 54, No. 4—Notturno (horn fifths, *più mosso* section)

Homophonic Textures—Chords

Legato Chordal Textures with Melody on Top of Chords within the Same Hand

Chordal textures exist in solo and collaborative piano repertoire as well as vocal-style works such as hymns and chorales. Chordal playing has multiple challenges for pianists, including fingering choices with frequent hand-position changes and consistency of sound transfer from one chord to the next. In chordal repertoire, the melody usually appears in the top notes of the chords, requiring clear voicing. If these chords are *legato*, it is easier for the pianist to connect, voice, and shape the melody notes on top of the chords, especially if the chords have the same rhythmic patterns.

As with all homophonic textures, students need to begin by playing the melody separate from the chords using an altered fingering (as necessary) to produce a *legato*, since this will provide an aural model for the linear shape of the melody. Next, they should play the melody alone using the fingering that will be required when playing all of the notes of the chords, focusing on maintaining the tonal and rhythmic control previously achieved. When students can control the melodic line using the normal fingering, they can add pedaling to assist with the *legato*. Finally, students can play the entire chordal texture, focusing on voicing the melody above the rest of the notes.

Repertoire: *Legato* Chordal Textures with Melody on Top of Chords within the Same Hand
Burgmüller: *25 Progressive Pieces*, Op. 100, No. 19—Ave Maria
Chaminade: *Album for the Young*, Book 2, Op. 126, No. 9—Patrouille
Grieg: *Lyric Pieces*, Op. 43, No. 2—Solitary Traveler
Gurlitt: *Album for the Young*, Op. 140, No. 2—Morning Song
Gurlitt: *Album for the Young*, Op. 140, No. 12—In the Church (Chorale)
Schumann: *Album for the Young*, Op. 68, No. 15—Spring Song
Tchaikovsky: *Album for the Young*, Op. 39, No. 1—Morning Prayer
Tchaikovsky: *Album for the Young*, Op. 39, No. 7—The Doll's Burial

Tchaikovsky: *Album for the Young*, Op. 39, No. 12—The Peasant Plays the Accordion
Tchaikovsky: *Album for the Young*, Op. 39, No. 24—In Church

Melody on Top of Detached Chords within the Same Hand

In pieces where the chords are detached, it may be more difficult for pianists to maintain control over the voicing of the melody. Students can first play these pieces more *legato*, following the same approach discussed above for *legato* chords. When they can perform the melody well using a *legato* touch, then they can attempt to maintain the same voicing and control of the texture while detaching the chords as written.

Repertoire: Melody on Top of Detached Chords within the Same Hand
Burgmüller: *25 Progressive Pieces*, Op. 100, No. 23—The Return
Burgmüller: *18 Characteristic Studies*, Op. 109, No. 4—The Gypsies
Burgmüller: *18 Characteristic Studies*, Op. 109, No. 17—March
Chaminade: *Album for the Young*, Book 1, Op. 123, No. 12—Marche Russe
Grieg: *Lyric Pieces*, Op. 12, No. 8—National Song (Song of the Fatherland)
Grieg: *Lyric Pieces*, Op. 68, No. 1—Sailor's Song
Schumann: *Album for the Young*, Op. 68, No. 29—Strange Man
Schumann: *Album for the Young*, Op. 68, No. 41—Norse Song
Tchaikovsky: *Album for the Young*, Op. 39, No. 3—Hobby-Horse
Tchaikovsky: *Album for the Young*, Op. 39, No. 19—The Nurse's Tale (A section)

Chordal Textures with Melody in Alternating Hands

Chords or melodies with parallel intervals with the melody notes on top that alternate between the two hands require an important perception of melodic continuity. This is a different *legato* concept, since students are more used to connecting melody notes from one finger to the next within the same hand. The most difficult challenge with these melodies is the careful matching of tone, speed of attack, and arm weight from one melodic note to the next, combined with skillful pedaling. Chords or melodies with parallel intervals with the melodies on top have the additional requirement of voicing the melody notes in each hand.

Students should follow the same practice steps outlined previously: (1) play the melody notes *legato* with one or two hands using altered fingerings to hear the continuity of the melody, then (2) play the melody notes using the normal fingering when all of the notes will be played, and finally (3) play the piece as written.

<u>Repertoire: Chordal Textures with Melody in Alternating Hands</u>
Gillock: *Lyric Preludes in Romantic Style*—Moonlight Mood—melody with parallel thirds
Gillock: *Lyric Preludes in Romantic Style*—Procession of the Mandarin—melody with parallel fifths

Polyphonic Textures with Multiple Distinct Voices

Two Distinct Voices

Polyphonic Romantic-period piano music can share the same textures with similar Baroque and Classical repertoire. An important difference is that the Romantic-period pieces may require a more dramatic and/or rhythmically free approach and more independence of the parts. As with music from the earlier periods, the easiest polyphonic textures are going to be the ones limited to one independent part in each hand. Pianists should master independent voices between the two hands before attempting to master independent voices within one hand, or voices traveling between the hands.

<u>Repertoire: Two Distinct Voices</u>
Burgmüller: *25 Progressive Pieces*, Op. 100, No. 6—Progress
Chaminade: *Album for the Young*, Book 1, Op. 123, No. 5—Gavotte
Chaminade: *Album for the Young*, Book 1, Op. 123, No. 6—Gigue
Gillock: *Lyric Preludes in Romantic Style*—Interlude
Gurlitt: *Album for the Young*, Op. 140, No. 12—In the Church (Präludium)

Three Distinct Voices—Melody, Inner Voice, and Bass Line

Romantic-period repertoire with multiple independent lines presents different textural control challenges. Pianists may face independent lines within one or both hands or one or more voices that move between the two hands. A common texture is one with a melody on the top, an inner voice that crosses back and forth between hands, and a supportive bass line. This texture is more difficult, since the hand that plays the inner voice is constantly shifting, requiring a great amount of expressive and textural control.

Repertoire: Three Distinct Voices—Melody, Inner Voice, and Bass Line
Gillock: *Lyric Preludes in Romantic Style*—A Faded Letter (left hand acts as one voice)
Grieg: *Lyric Pieces*, Op. 12, No. 1—Arietta
Grieg: *Lyric Pieces*, Op. 57, No. 6—Homesickness (m. 9–16)
Schumann: *Album for the Young*, Op. 68, No. 35—Mignon
Tchaikovsky: *Album for the Young*, Op. 39, No. 21—Sweet Dreams

Four Distinct Voices

Repertoire with four distinct parts often has two independent parts within each hand. Pieces that have at least one or two lines that are not very active, such as a pedal point bass line and/or slow-moving inner voice, will generally be easier to play. If all four parts are very active with different rhythmic patterns, different articulation, and so on, the texture will be much more challenging, requiring a lot of finger independence and control.

Repertoire: Four Distinct Voices
   Tchaikovsky: *Album for the Young*, Op. 39, No. 23—The Handorgan Man

Mixed Textures

Pieces that maintain consistency of musical elements within the texture are usually easier to play, and pieces in which the texture changes frequently require many technical and musical adjustments. The speed and frequency of these changes have a significant impact on the difficulty level.

Chords or Intervals Alternating with Single Notes in One or Both Hands

Playing chords and playing single-note passagework each have different musical and technical requirements. Most performers find single-note passagework easier to play, as it typically follows normal scale fingerings and fingering principles. Technique for fingers, hands, and arms is usually fluid and consistent in passagework, and presents limited challenges even when navigating through changes in the keyboard topography. In contrast, chordal playing requires constant fingering and hand-position shifts, and different technical requirements to transfer weight between the chords consistently and smoothly. Chordal playing can be quite awkward, depending upon the shapes of the chords related to the keyboard topography, putting the entire arm and hand in many different positions. Shifting between chords and single notes is extremely awkward, requiring careful listening combined with physical awareness of the choreography required to play these passages smoothly and musically.

Repertoire: Chords or Intervals Alternating with Single Notes in One or Both Hands
Burgmüller: *25 Progressive Pieces*, Op. 100, No. 25—Knight Errant
Grieg: *Lyric Pieces*, Op. 12, No. 3—Watchman's Song
Grieg: *Lyric Pieces*, Op. 12, No. 4—Dance of the Elves (Elfin Dance)
Grieg: *Lyric Pieces*, Op. 12, No. 7—Album-leaf (B section)
Grieg: *Lyric Pieces*, Op. 71, No. 3—Puck
Schumann: *Album for the Young*, Op. 68, No. 6—Poor Orphan
Schumann: *Album for the Young*, Op. 68, No. 7—Hunting Song
Schumann: *Album for the Young*, Op. 68, No. 28—Remembrance
Tchaikovsky: *Album for the Young*, Op. 39, No. 5—March of the Tin Soldiers
Tchaikovsky: *Album for the Young*, Op. 39, No. 20—The Witch

More Than One Independent Voice in One or Both Hands

Maintaining independence of voices when there is more than one part in each hand is challenging for all pianists, especially when the parts each have different note values. For example, if there is a longer note in the melody, but a more active rhythm in an inner voice, the student's melodic line may seem to wander back and forth between the melody notes and accompaniment so that the texture is not clear. A useful analogy to improve this is to think of a highway that does not allow any lane changes, so all parts must stay in their own aural "lane." Students must maintain their aural attention on the melody and keep the secondary lines dynamically underneath it. A useful practice technique is to play each part alone first, followed by playing all of the various combinations of parts. Students should master balance within each hand before tackling balance with all of the parts in both hands.

Repertoire: More Than One Independent Voice in One or Both Hands
Gillock: *Lyric Preludes in Romantic Style*—An Old Valentine
Grieg: *Lyric Pieces*, Op. 43, No. 6—To the Spring
Grieg: *Lyric Pieces*, Op. 54, No. 2—Norwegian March
Grieg: *Lyric Pieces*, Op. 62, No. 2—Gratitude
Grieg: *Lyric Pieces*, Op. 65, No. 2—Peasant's Song
Schumann: *Album for the Young*, Op. 68, No. 26—***
Tchaikovsky: *Album for the Young*, Op. 39, No. 1—Morning Prayer

Single-line Melodies with Chords in the Same Hand, with Accompaniment

A texture that includes chords within the same hand as the melody is even more challenging than one that has more than one independent line in the same hand. Significant finger independence is required to be able to hold the chordal notes down while other fingers are playing a moving line. Pianists should not develop tension in their fingers, hands, or arms when holding chord tones down, since there is no need to apply any pressure into the key; releasing arm weight will keep the keys from coming back up.

Repertoire: Single-line Melodies with Chords in the Same Hand, with Accompaniment
Schumann: *Album for the Young*, Op. 68, No. 32—Sheherazade

Melody in Parallel Octaves between Hands, with Accompaniment

This texture is extremely challenging because it requires so much finger independence and control of multiple elements at the same time, including very sophisticated pedaling. An earlier section of this chapter explored challenges of playing the melody in octaves between hands, within one hand, and within both hands. Those challenges still exist in these pieces, but the pianist also has to navigate the accompaniment patterns while playing the octaves. Gurlitt's *In the Garden* is one of the easier pieces within this category, because the left hand only has to play the single melodic line while the right hand has to play both the melody and offbeat accompaniment. It is still challenging, though, because the right hand has to use awkward fingering for the *legato* melody. Chromaticism in the melody prevents the pianist from using patterned pedaling to help in playing the melody *legato*, so the pianist has to change the pedal frequently. In addition, the pianist has to smoothly connect and shape the melody notes, while balancing the melody consistently between the two hands. The "ghosting" practice technique would be very helpful for working on the balance of the melody with the accompaniment repeated chords in the right hand.

The well-known Schumann pieces listed below are even more difficult due to the nature of the accompaniment patterns often changing on every eighth note. All of the Grieg works listed below are technically difficult and require great control of dynamics and tonal colors. Practicing these pieces involves a great deal of separation of the different tasks combined with a lot of repetition to make sure that the fingers "remember" the details of control.

Repertoire: Melody in Parallel Octaves between Hands, with Accompaniment
Burgmüller: *18 Characteristic Studies*, Op. 109, No. 15—Sylphs (B section)
Grieg: *Lyric Pieces*, Op. 43, No. 2—Solitary Traveler

Grieg: *Lyric Pieces*, Op. 43, No. 6—To the Spring
Grieg: *Lyric Pieces*, Op. 65, No. 5—Ballad
Gurlitt: *Album for the Young*, Op. 140, No. 4—In the Garden
Schumann: *Album for the Young*, Op. 68, No. 10—The Happy Farmer
Schumann: *Album for the Young*, Op. 68, No. 19—Little Romance

5

Rhythm

Although attention to all musical elements is essential for excellent musicianship, control of tempo and rhythmic precision certainly rank among the most important skills. Rhythmic challenges are also among the most difficult to correct or improve, especially if the student cannot maintain a stable tempo through changes in note values. Rhythm is movement, and young students first learn rhythm through the movement of their bodies. Comprehension of rhythmic patterns begins with experiencing both macro- and micro-beats through listening, moving, drumming, and singing. Beat stability must become internalized. In addition, great musicians do not play like rhythmic robots; they have a keen awareness of the ebb and flow of rhythm and tempo in all of its micro-fluctuations. Understanding how music moves forward in rhythmic chunks and shapes rather than individual beats and notes is an important task in preparing the intermediate-level student for greater musical artistry.

Students should comprehend and coordinate rhythmic patterns prior to playing them on the piano. They should learn new rhythmic patterns using a process of sound before sight: *sound, syllable, and symbol*. Students hear and imitate rhythmic *sounds* on a neutral syllable such as "ba" in a steady beat, speak these rhythmic patterns using rhythmic *syllables*, and finally connect these rhythmic syllables to the rhythmic *symbols* found in music notation. Following this process helps students recognize and perform known rhythmic patterns when they appear in different repertoire.[1]

Prior to learning each new piece, students should speak the rhythmic patterns of each hand using rhythmic syllables. If there is more than one rhythmic pattern within the same hand, they should speak each pattern separately. Since pianists have the challenge of performing different rhythmic patterns in coordination between the hands, the students should also tap all of the rhythmic patterns of both hands simultaneously prior to playing anything on the piano. If there are multiple rhythmic patterns within each hand, the student may need to tap all of the parts using individual fingers rather than tapping with the entire hand. If a student cannot tap the rhythmic patterns accurately and comfortably hands together, they certainly will have trouble playing them with the addition of pitches and other musical details. Mastering the rhythmic patterns first provides a solid foundation for all other musical elements.

Intermediate-level students who need rhythmic remediation should sight-read and practice repertoire pieces at the elementary level that include multiple rhythmic patterns within easier settings. For example, practicing complex rhythmic patterns between the two hands within a five-finger pattern simplifies the pitch requirements and eliminates the challenges of moving around on the keyboard so that students can focus on the rhythm.

Time Signatures and Pulse Groupings

Instructional methodology for teaching time signatures can vary from teacher to teacher. Elementary-level students may learn that time signatures indicate the beat or pulse, so a $\frac{4}{4}$ time signature means that the quarter note is the beat and there are four quarter-note beats in each measure. Depending upon the tempo, however, this is not always the best approach. If the tempo is moving somewhat fast, the most likely pulse grouping is larger than four beats per measure. A piece in $\frac{4}{4}$ often moves in two large beats, while $\frac{3}{4}$ moves in one large beat, and compound meters almost always move in larger beats unless the tempo is extremely slow ($\frac{6}{8}$ is two beats, $\frac{9}{8}$ is three beats, $\frac{12}{8}$ is four beats, etc.).

When learning a new piece, students should speak rhythmic syllables with vocal inflection to articulate the largest pulse grouping possible. Once they reach performance tempo, students should select an appropriate pulse grouping that feels both technically and musically comfortable. An ideal pulse grouping facilitates natural rhythmic flow and ease of movement.

Perceiving tempo and rhythmic patterns in larger pulse groupings provides an important foundation for musical playing. Students who play notes as individual pitches and individual rhythmic note values end up with "vertical," fragmented playing that interferes with a sense of musical progression and shape. Pulse groupings define strong and weak beats (which imply different approaches into the key), as well as the playing of gestures and shapes.

Tempo Stability and Use of the Metronome

Intermediate-level students should be able to play consistently with an external beat source such as a metronome. Teachers need to remember, however, that students who do not already have the ability to maintain a steady beat without a metronome may not be able to stay in time with a metronome. For many years, I asked students who were having rhythmic stability problems if they practiced with their metronome. The response was often a convincing "yes," even though their performance did not seem to correlate with that answer. This left me quite puzzled, as their answers were sincere. Only after many years of teaching did I realize that I needed to follow that first question with a second question: "Are you able to stay in tempo with your metronome?" Once I started asking this question, I realized that many of them were not able to align with the metronome, even though they dutifully tried to practice with it.

Following the philosophy of experiencing concepts and skills in their easiest settings first, intermediate-level students who have never used the metronome or who have not been able to stay in time with the metronome should do a lot of rhythmic stability work away from the keyboard. Once students can track with a steady beat through movement, they can play simple five-note scales or one-octave scales along with the metronome, playing one note to each click of the metronome. A student has to be able to track one note per click before they can play beat divisions, subdivisions, or rhythmic patterns. Another practice technique would be to turn on the metronome, ask the student to play a few measures with the metronome, stop playing briefly while listening to the metronome clicks, play again, stop and listen, and so on.

In general, students should practice repertoire pieces with the metronome beat at the largest pulse grouping possible for the tempo they can currently perform. If they cannot hold the beat steady in the larger pulse grouping, they can temporarily move the metronome to a smaller pulse grouping but should return to the larger pulse as soon as possible. Ultimately, students should be able to follow the metronome consistently while playing their repertoire pieces.

Practicing with the metronome has many purposes. One goal is to help pianists become aware of places where they are not maintaining tempo stability. Especially useful in Romantic-period repertoire, the metronome can be a plumb line to help pianists hear how far their expressiveness deviates from the normal beat. The use of the metronome can help performers gain speed on technique exercises and repertoire by increasing the metronome marker incrementally to gradually increase the tempo. Students can use the metronome to make themselves practice at much slower tempos and to keep themselves from speeding up. The metronome establishes objective tempos, which can be very helpful in collaborative playing if all performers practice consistently at the designated tempo. Establishing a designated performance tempo and practicing it consistently gives the performer a more reliable sense of the chosen tempo, even in the absence of the metronome. Students should also practice performance-ready pieces at different tempos slower than the performance tempo, such as at approximately 50 percent, 75 percent, and 90 percent of performance tempo, in order to maintain rhythmic precision.

Rhythmic Precision within Passagework

Students whose technique is not yet well developed may have trouble playing passagework with rhythmic precision. One of the best practice techniques to achieve rhythmic precision is to practice in rhythmic groupings. In passagework consisting of continuous sixteenth notes in simple meters, students can practice six different rhythmic grouping patterns.

The first two patterns involve changing the equal sixteenth notes to unequal dotted rhythms, often referred to as "long-short" ♪♩ and "short-long" ♩♪ patterns. For the remaining four rhythmic groupings, the performer plays the passage, pausing successively on the first, second, third, and fourth notes of each beat, while playing the notes in between each pause very fast.

Pianists can also construct rhythmic grouping patterns in passages that include other note values by simply adapting the pattern to pause through longer note values as needed. It is also possible to use this concept for time signatures or groupings that are different from the standard sixteenth-note passages in simple meters. The important points to remember are that the pauses must happen consistently within each grouping, repetitions have to include one for each of the note positions within each grouping, and the notes in between pauses must be performed very fast with a solid technique.

Patterns Beginning on Upbeats or Weak Beats

Awareness of rhythmic patterns involves more than merely feeling the basic metrical strong and weak beats. Language spoken with thoughtful vocal inflection offers an intuitive, easily transferrable aural model for both rhythmic patterns and musical inflection. In addition to using basic rhythmic syllable systems such as Takadimi to articulate rhythmic patterns, teachers can pair words with rhythm patterns using words, phrases, and short sentences. A simple two-word upbeat to downbeat pattern could be "a house" or "a dog," while a pattern of several upbeats to downbeat in triple meter might be "it's a house" or "it's a dog." Teachers can ask students to speak the phrases as they normally would say them, model the phrases for them, and even say them incorrectly to demonstrate the differences in inflection. Understanding rhythms within their upbeat and downbeat contexts fosters the development of musical gestures. Because rhythmic patterns beginning on weak beats usually start from either silence or after a long note sustained through a strong beat, students must be careful not to accent notes that begin on a weak beat.

Rhythmic Curriculum

Mastery of foundational rhythmic skills and concepts at the intermediate level should include:
1) Comprehension of note values and their proportionate relationships through at least the level of the subdivision of the beat.

2) Ability to verbally articulate rhythmic patterns using rhythmic syllables in a beat-function system for both simple and compound meters. (My preference is the Takadimi rhythmic syllable system.)
3) Ability to maintain a steady, consistent pulse grouping through changes in note values, rhythmic patterns, and articulations.
4) Ability to keep tempo with an external beat source such as a metronome.
5) Ability to change tempo within a piece.
6) Ability to maintain rhythmic stability while performing with the teacher or other students in intermediate-level duet or duo repertoire.

Syncopation or Other Rhythmic Patterns Emphasizing Weak Beats

Syncopation is a rhythmic pattern that emphasizes weak beats, usually by accenting the weaker beat and suspending it through the following strong beat. It is most effective when the performer emphasizes the strong beat then bounces the syncopated note out of the strong beat. The strong beat becomes a "down" sound, and the syncopated note becomes an "up" or weaker sound. Students often do the exact opposite of this, playing the weak syncopated note as a strong beat, possibly because it is usually longer than the previous note. This completely stops the rhythmic motion, disrupts the larger pulse grouping, and fragments the musical line. The problem is exacerbated with successive syncopated notes, as each strong beat must be heard internally. Even students who have already grasped the concept of pulse groupings and can perform them consistently often struggle with playing syncopated patterns. They will need many experiences with syncopation to play the rhythms accurately, master the appropriate inflection, and maintain the larger pulse.

Repertoire: Syncopation or Other Rhythmic Patterns Emphasizing Weak Beats
Beach: *Children's Album*, Op. 36, No. 3—Waltz
Gillock: *Lyric Preludes in Romantic Style*—Moonlight Mood
Grieg: *Lyric Pieces*, Op. 12, No. 5—Popular Melody
Grieg: *Lyric Pieces*, Op. 54, No. 2—Norwegian March
Grieg: *Lyric Pieces*, Op. 54, No. 4—Notturno

Gurlitt: *Album for the Young*, Op. 140, No. 7—The Festive Dance
Gurlitt: *Album for the Young*, Op. 140, No. 9—Thoughtful Moments
Schumann: *Album for the Young*, Op. 68, No. 15—Spring Song
Tchaikovsky: *Album for the Young*, Op. 39, No. 8—Waltz

Frequent Changes from Duple to Triple Division of the Beat within One Hand or between Hands

Younger pianists may have challenges when the rhythm switches from a duple division of the beat to a triple division of the beat. One reason for this is that they may not maintain the larger beat pulse grouping. Another possible reason is the lack of rhythmic syllables for triple division of the beat in many counting systems. Teachers may try to make words fit the triple division by speaking them differently, such as saying "*tri-pl-et*" as three syllables rather than "*triplet.*" Also confusing is when teachers use the same syllables for two different rhythmic patterns, such as speaking "*1 and a*" for ♫ and also for ♫. The teacher speaks the same syllables but in a different rhythmic context, which can completely confuse students. The Takadimi rhythmic syllable system provides a different set of rhythmic syllables for the duple and triple division of the beat so there is no confusion. The duple division of the beat in the Takadimi system is Ta-di and the triple division of the beat is Ta-ki-da. The triple division of the beat, Ta-ki-da, is an eighth-note triplet in simple meters ♫ and is three eighth notes beamed together in compound meters ♫. Within the Takadimi system, the triple division of the beat always has the same syllables, regardless of the meter, easily facilitating smooth transitions between duple and triple division of the beat.[2]

Repertoire: Frequent Changes from Duple to Triple Division of the Beat within One Hand or between Hands
Burgmüller: *25 Progressive Pieces*, Op. 100, No. 25—The Knight Errant
Grieg: *Lyric Pieces*, Op. 12, No. 6—Norwegian Melody
Grieg: *Lyric Pieces*, Op. 38, No. 6—Elegie
Grieg: *Lyric Pieces*, Op. 43, No. 6—To the Spring
Grieg: *Lyric Pieces*, Op. 47, No. 6—Norwegian Dance

Grieg: *Lyric Pieces*, Op. 54, No. 4—Notturno
Grieg: *Lyric Pieces*, Op. 68, No. 4—Evening in the Mountains
Schumann: *Album for the Young*, Op. 68, No. 33—Vintage Times

Polyrhythms between Hands

A common rhythmic challenge in Romantic-period repertoire is playing asymmetrical rhythmic patterns between the hands and sometimes within one hand. The first example that students usually encounter is the duple against triple pattern, either as an eighth-note triplet against two eighth notes or a quarter-note triplet against two quarter notes. Following the *sound, syllable, symbol* learning process previously discussed, students should echo each pattern back to the teacher using a neutral *sound* such as "ba," then echo patterns using the Takadimi *syllables*, before finally connecting the syllables to the notational *symbols*.

In the Takadimi system, the duple division of the beat in simple meter is Ta-di, and the triple division of the beat in compound meter is Ta-ki-da (Figure 5.1).

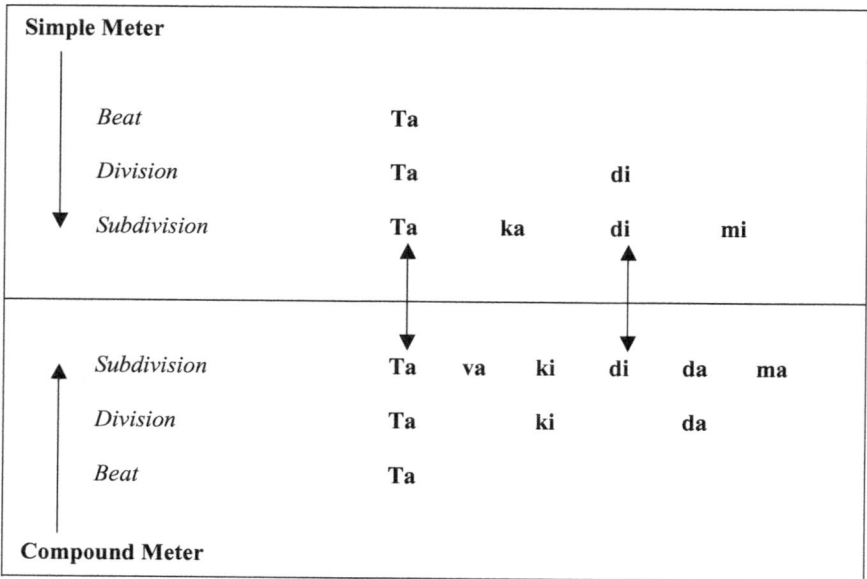

Figure 5.1 From *Sound Connections: A Comprehensive Approach to Teaching Music Literacy* (p. 60), by D. P. Ester, 2021, Self-published. Reprinted with permission.

The subdivision of the compound meter is Ta-va-ki-di-da-ma, demonstrating that the syllables for both the duple and triple division of the beat line up perfectly when performed simultaneously. As long as the students already know these syllables well, they should be able to tap these two patterns with hands together accurately. By speaking the subdivision of the beat using Ta-va-ki-di-da-ma syllables and tapping the duple in one hand and the triple in the other hand, students discover that two against three involves tapping on the syllables Ta, ki, di, and da. Speaking these syllables Ta, ki-di, da while tapping the correct patterns for each hand should feel completely clear, as seen in Figure 5.2.

Figure 5.2 Takadimi syllables: simple meter division of the beat and compound meter subdivision of the beat (author owned).

As previously noted, students should practice tapping the rhythms with both hands simultaneously on the fallboard until they are comfortable with them before adding pitches at the piano. When first learning complex rhythmic patterns such as these (by rote prior to studying them in repertoire), students should practice switching which hand has the triple and which hand has the duple, so that they can become comfortable playing these patterns either way. The easiest patterns will be those in which each hand plays the complete pattern normally without any rests, ties, or dotted rhythms. Students can modify patterns that have rests or ties by substituting notes for rests and replaying tied notes to perceive the rhythmic patterns more clearly, before playing the patterns as written.

Other asymmetrical patterns between the two hands become more complicated, such as four against three or other complicated patterns with many notes in each hand, as is often found in the music of Chopin. In complex patterns larger than two against three, it is important to make sure that both hands arrive together on the main beats. While it is usually mathematically possible to find the lowest common denominator and figure out exactly how the two rhythms fit together, this may result in nonmusical, stilted rhythmic playing that often loses its larger pulse grouping. One purpose of asymmetrical rhythmic patterns is to add a certain ambiguous expressiveness to the piece. With complicated patterns, it may not be as important to play them mathematically correct, but instead let each hand keep its own expressive pace and arrive together at main beats. The important point is to perform these polyrhythms as an expressive, fluid unit rather than as individual rhythmic patterns.

In complicated patterns between the hands, a good practice strategy is for the student to tap the pulsation beats with one hand while the other hand taps the given rhythmic pattern to feel the general speed of the rhythmic pattern. Next, the student should use the same process but switch hands. Finally, the student should tap the rhythmic patterns in both hands simultaneously in successively slower tempos, maintaining the pulse grouping while hearing rhythmically even notes in each voice.

Repertoire: Polyrhythms between Hands
Grieg: *Lyric Pieces*, Op. 38, No. 6—Elegie
Grieg: *Lyric Pieces*, Op. 43, No. 6—To the Spring
Grieg: *Lyric Pieces*, Op. 54, No. 4—Notturno
Grieg: *Lyric Pieces*, Op. 54, No. 5—Scherzo
Grieg: *Lyric Pieces*, Op. 62, No. 5—Phantom

Unmeasured, Improvisatory Lines

Romantic-period repertoire often includes unmeasured, improvisatory single lines, usually without a time signature. The pitches may or may not have actual note values, but the absence of note values or time signatures does not imply that the student should play the notes continuously. Composers who provide rhythmic note values provide information about the proportion of the notes in relation to each other. For example, a composer might indicate a ritardando by gradually increasing the note value lengths. Teachers should guide students to find the rhythmic and melodic gestures within these lines, followed by combining the gestures into a musical entity that makes sense.

Repertoire: Unmeasured, Improvisatory Lines
Liszt: *Forgotten Romance (Romance Oubliée)*, S. 527

Notes

1. Don Ester, *Sound Connections—A Comprehensive Approach to Teaching Music Literacy* (Muncie, IN: self-published, 2021), 35.
2. Richard Hoffman, William Pelto, and John W. White, "Takadimi: A Beat-Oriented System of Rhythm Pedagogy," *Journal of Music Theory Pedagogy* 10 (1996): 7–30.

6

Technique

Foundational Technique Principles

The word "technique" evokes visions of pianists playing endless scales, arpeggios, and etudes to develop their performance skills. While these exercises are important tools for developing facility, they only represent one facet of technique. "Technique" more broadly refers to any aspect of performance that serves the desired musical results. This chapter aims to present foundational technique principles for the intermediate-level student rather than discussion of any particular technique "school" or method. Many excellent books, videos, and online resources are available that provide detailed discussions of all facets of piano technique.

Intermediate-level students often have similar technical challenges. They may have developed a physically tense approach to technique produced by the fingers only, with little connection to the rest of their body. Much of their playing has a persistently loud tone quality with limited variety in dynamics or tone color. Other students may not have had much technical development, playing with collapsed hand and finger joints and producing little volume of sound or tone quality definition. These students also have a one-dimensional approach to playing the piano, since much of their playing sounds weak and unfocused. Neither of these approaches provides pianists with the best opportunity to develop a high level of performance.

Pianists should strive to play with the most natural, physically comfortable, free, and efficient technique in which all parts of the body are working together as a balanced, coordinated unit. All pianistic approaches should use the various parts of the body in the way that they normally function, since forcing the body to move unnaturally has the potential for injury and does not promote good performance. Technique is limited, however, if it is not inspired by an internal sound image and an external aural awareness of the sound actually produced.

Sitting Posture

Most elementary-level method books provide instructions and visual references for developing a good sitting posture at the piano. Students should position the bench so that they have adequate room to move their arms freely, sitting on their sitz bones (also called sitting bones) on the front half of the bench while balancing with their feet. Good sitting posture at the piano is not the same as sitting back in a chair, since the latter throws off the physical center of gravity and balance needed for performance. Furthermore, many students sit too close to the keyboard, resulting in cramped positions that restrict their arm movements. Pianists should adjust the distance between the bench and piano to maintain enough room for their arms to be comfortable based upon particular repertoire needs and personal preferences.

In addition to sitting at a good distance from the piano, students need to sit at an appropriate bench height. The student's arms should be slightly above the keyboard to facilitate the proper alignment of arms and hands with the keys. Although not all piano manufacturers supply adjustable benches, they are necessary for optimal performance. If these are not available, students might need to sit on a firm cushion or other solid surface to reach the desirable height. Younger students whose feet do not reach the floor also need a stable footrest.

Good posture allows students to sit comfortably with a stable but flexible body core. The need for a stable core does not imply a fixed sitting position. For example, students will need to rock on their sitz bones to either side to reach the extreme ranges of the keyboard so that their hands and arms are aligned with the keyboard. A flexible core, however, does not mean that students should move around unnecessarily. The principle of "economy of motion" dictates that pianists should move only as much as is necessary to place their hands and arms in proper positions. While some listeners may mistake excessive physical motions for the appearance of greater musical sensitivity, excessive movement can actually prevent the performer's musical intentions from being accomplished.

Fluid Physical Movements

A good sitting posture helps maintain freedom and fluidity in the arms and hands, which can help prevent the accumulation of physical tension. Experience with progressive relaxation exercises can help the pianist become more aware of unnecessary body tension. The goal is not to achieve complete physical relaxation but instead use only the minimal firmness necessary to play. A better strategy is to think of avoiding physical "holding" patterns that create tension and restrict movement. Pianists should avoid any fixed or extreme positions such as overly raised or unnaturally curved fingers, wrists excessively high or low, or tightness in the shoulders, arms, or other parts of the body. Pianists sometimes unconsciously associate musical intensity with physical tension, but this is counterproductive.

Shoulders and Arms

All hand and finger activities are related to the proper use of the pianist's shoulders and arms. Many pianists have a high amount of physical tension in their shoulders, back, and neck. Pianists' arms should hang freely from their shoulders so that they can move their hands wherever needed, including up to the higher plane of the black keys. The arm "weight" or release that comes from free shoulders and arms combined with gravity can be applied into the keys to produce good tone quality and significant volume. Heinrich Neuhaus, in *The Art of Piano Playing*, described the ideal function of the arms and hands as being similar to a suspension bridge, in which the shoulder joint is fixed at one end and the fingers are firm at the other end, but the arms are free and flexible in between.[1]

Wrists and Hands

Wrists and hands should be aligned with the arms, but they must remain flexible to move as needed. The metacarpophalangeal (MCP) joint, also referred to by pianists as the "bridge," is the place where the fingers meet the hands and should be the highest point of the hand most of the time. As pianists extend their hands, the bridge is slightly lower, but it should not collapse completely. A solid bridge allows the fingers to move freely with great speed and facility, while a collapsed bridge puts a strain on the fingers, forcing them into poor positions. The ideal natural hand position occurs when arms hang freely from the shoulders and should be maintained when the hand is raised to the keyboard. Both the distal interphalangeal (DIP) joint (the one closest to the fingertip) and the proximal interphalangeal (PIP) joint (the middle joint) must remain solid but not tightly held.

Types of Hand Motions

In addition to the basic finger motion from the hand bridge, there are several other essential types of hand motions. Lateral motion involves moving the wrist from side to side to keep the hand, arm, and body in alignment with the keys they are playing. An example of the use of lateral motion occurs in major scales when the thumb comes under the third finger. While some teachers advocate for an extreme turning under of the thumb, a more efficient and fluid approach involves the hand gradually shifting laterally to reposition the thumb.

Rotation involves the vertical turning of the forearm from the elbow. Pronation turns the hand toward the thumb, while supination turns the hand toward the fifth finger. Rotation is extremely helpful for playing broken intervals smoothly and easily with a more consistent sound.

Hand extension and contraction help to maintain the natural hand position, but not every finger has to remain over every note after it has been played. Pianists should avoid maintaining extended positions of the hand to avoid straining, especially those with small hands. They should also avoid keeping their hands in excessively flat positions, since our hands are designed with curved, not flat fingers. Pianists should return to the natural position of the hand as often as possible.

Finger Positions on the Keys

The position of the pianist's finger on a key can make a difference in the tone quality and initial articulation of the note. A more vertical finger position with a fast attack creates a brighter sound, while flatter fingers produce a warmer tone quality with a more subtle initiation of the sound.

Proper Use of the Body Parts

While pianists should coordinate and integrate all parts of the body for playing the piano, different physical levers work better for different needs. Fingers are the fastest-moving parts, responsible for articulating the notes to produce a variety of timbres. All too often, however, pianists force their fingers to bear the complete burden of tone production and volume, which usually creates physical tension and a constricted sound. The use of wrist motion is ideal for playing fast intervals, chords, and octaves, and for applying arm weight into the keys for beautiful *cantabile* playing. The forearms, in combination with a very fast speed of attack into the keys, provide strong, powerful playing. Arms and shoulders are responsible for free and efficient movements as well as tone production. Teachers should observe students very carefully to deduce how their body movements relate to the sounds they are producing, guiding students to use the most appropriate parts of the body for each pianistic task.

Injury Prevention

A crucial foundational technique principle is that playing the piano or any musical instrument should not cause any pain or discomfort. The phrase "no pain, no gain" should never apply to piano performance. Students who experience pain while playing should be encouraged to disclose this information to their teachers, and teachers must become knowledgeable in evaluating potential pianistic causes of pain (although only a physician can make a medical diagnosis). The student's first response when experiencing pain should be to stop playing temporarily and do some gentle stretching of hands, arms, neck, and shoulders. A regular practice of physical stretching is an excellent strategy for preventing injuries and promoting healthy technique.

Changes in technical approaches or practice methodology may resolve pain problems, especially if these are due to tension created by an improper use of the body. Continuing to practice while experiencing pain can potentially lead to long-term physical problems. Sometimes simply taking a break from regular practice allows the body time to heal. Students should seek medical advice from physicians and physical therapists if pain persists.

Pianists can experience physical problems and poor performance results from playing repertoire that is too hard for them. A student's technique should develop naturally and steadily through a gradually increasing level of repertoire difficulty. In addition, students need time for technical facility to develop within each individual repertoire piece or exercise. Playing pieces or exercises too fast before their bodies have adapted to playing them can also cause injuries. Furthermore, pianists can risk injury if they are away from the piano for a long time, then suddenly resume hours of intense practicing without letting their body gradually readjust to the physical demands of playing the piano.

Tone Production

Pianists must understand how the piano action operates to produce a good sound. Depressing a key causes its damper to rise as the hammer strikes the string. The string vibrates, and the soundboard amplifies these vibrations. The sound continues until the pianist releases the key and its damper returns to the strings. Activating the damper pedal keeps all of the dampers raised and the sound sustained, even after the pianist has released the key.

While piano technicians can adjust various internal parts of the keyboard action to change variables such as the friction, the pianist can only control how the hammer hits the string, the release of the keys, and any manipulation of the pedals. Pressing into the keys after the sound begins results in a labored, tight sonority and creates more difficulty in playing. Efficient movements, proper positioning, release of arm weight into the keys, and articulation of the notes through the speed of attack and proper approach into the key are foundational tools for excellent pianistic technique.

Technique Curriculum

Students at the intermediate level should master the following technique skills:

1) Perform all major and minor (natural, harmonic, and melodic) scales in both parallel and contrary motion in two or more octaves.
2) Perform all major, minor, diminished, and dominant-seventh arpeggios in parallel and contrary motion in two or more octaves.
3) Perform all major and minor chord inversions in blocked and broken patterns using correct fingering.
4) Perform technical exercises and studies such as Hanon's *The Virtuoso Pianist*, Czerny's *School of Velocity*, Op. 299, and Schmitt's *Preparatory Exercises for the Piano*, Op. 16, to develop speed and facility.
5) Master basic hand motions such as rotation, lateral movement, and hand extension and contraction.
6) Perform repertoire that expands into wider ranges with more challenging hand and fingering positions and has a need for greater control of musical elements.

Scales and Arpeggios

Scales

Students must learn all major and minor scales with correct fingering so that fingering patterns become automatic. Scales should be learned in groups based upon the same fingering patterns, because associating individual pitches with individual finger numbers is not usually effective or reliable. Students must perceive fingering in patterns and groupings such as 1-2-3 and 1-2-3-4. Practicing scales in thirds, sixths, and tenths can help solidify fingering, since beginning the scale with each hand on a different note requires different thought patterns. Students can also practice scales in different rhythmic proportions between hands, for example, playing quarter notes in one hand while the other hand plays eighth notes, triplets, or sixteenth notes. Each pattern should be repeated, alternating the hand that plays the quarter notes. Additional scale challenges involve maintaining consistency in various elements such as tone color, speed of attack, dynamic level, and degree of connection between notes.

Once students can play scales without having to think about notes or fingerings, practicing scales in different ways between the hands can help students develop facility, speed, independence, and control of other musical elements. Each of these examples should be repeated to alternate hands.

1) One hand *staccato*, one hand *legato*.
2) One hand loud, one hand soft.
3) One hand playing a *crescendo*, one hand playing a *diminuendo*.
4) Playing with crossed hands, with either hand on top.
5) One hand playing even rhythms, one hand playing dotted notes or uneven rhythms.

Arpeggios

Arpeggios cover the same keyboard distance more quickly than scales do. Leading arpeggios with arm movement promotes more fluid, comfortable playing and puts fingers in the correct positions relative to the keyboard topography. The arms should move continuously to avoid fingers lingering too long on individual notes. Wrists should remain stable without dropping each time that the thumb is played to avoid accents. Other challenges with arpeggios can include frequent finger crossings, accuracy of notes, and consistency of sound.

Repertoire: Arpeggios
Burgmüller: *25 Progressive Pieces*, Op. 100, No. 11—The Young Shepherdess
Burgmüller: *18 Characteristic Studies*, Op. 109, No. 17—March
Grieg: *Lyric Pieces*, Op. 43, No. 6—To the Spring

Keyboard Mobility

The wide range of the piano poses potential challenges when the pianist begins to move, or travel, across the keyboard range. Traveling can be accomplished using finger crossings, finger substitutions on repeated or sustained notes, hand extension and contraction, and leaping to new locations.

Elementary-level method books differ in their introduction to traveling, with some implementing range changes initially through octave transposition by rote. While students are still performing repertoire within five-finger positions, it is important for them to keep their eyes on the score. Students who are constantly looking at their hands, even when there are no traveling requirements, will have difficulty moving out of the five-finger patterns. Security within the five-finger patterns is necessary before students begin to gradually and systematically venture outside of them. As students progress through intermediate-level repertoire, movement by larger distances through different ranges becomes the norm. Students should look at their hands only as necessary by dropping their eyes to use their peripheral vision without making large head movements.

Left-hand Waltz Bass

A frequent example of traveling in the left hand is the waltz-bass pattern. Some of the important considerations for this pattern include the following:

1) What is the range that the pattern covers?
2) How rapidly does the pattern change, either through rhythmic patterns or tempo?
3) How rapidly does the pattern change direction?
4) Do the upper chords repeat or change notes, and if they change notes, what are the challenges of inversions, fingerings, and so on?
5) What are the textural challenges happening in the opposite hand at the same time as the waltz-bass pattern?

The easiest waltz-bass patterns are those with a limited range and consistency of repeated chords. Waltz-bass patterns usually involve regular, frequent changes of direction that should be perceived as horizontal rather than vertical movements. Pianists can group movements from left to right, moving from bass notes to the upper chords, or group movements from right to left, moving from chords back to the bass notes. Rather than perceiving these movements as separate events, pianists should practice them as one continuous gesture, since continuous movement facilitates consistency and control of sound. The pianist must also be careful to practice the principle of economy of motion, since unnecessary large movements of the arms or hands may slow the tempo or result in an inconsistent tone quality. Pianists should move linearly and not make large circular shapes when traveling. Bass notes are important both harmonically and melodically, so pianists must be aware of their linear importance. Pianists often focus on the one-measure pulse of waltz-bass patterns, placing an accent on each downbeat rather than playing longer phrases. Teachers will need to demonstrate how to retain the one-measure pulse grouping subtly within the longer phrases characteristic of pieces with waltz-bass accompaniments.

Waltz-bass Patterns with Rests

Waltz-bass patterns with rests may cause pianists to pause during the rests instead of maintaining a continuous motion. Rests on beat two can cause the pianist to stay on the bass notes too long, resulting in sudden, uncontrolled movements to the upper chords. The pianist should instead spring off the bass notes in one horizontal motion toward the next position, timing the transition to arrive smoothly at the third beat. Playing the bass notes with an upward motion of the wrist and arm can also create a nice bell-tone effect. When rests appear on beat three, pianists should immediately release the chord played on beat two back in the direction of the bass notes rather than remaining in the chord position during the rest.

Repertoire: Waltz-bass Patterns with Rests
Grieg: *Lyric Pieces*, Op. 62, No. 1—Sylph (mm.1–9)
Tchaikovsky: *Album for the Young*, Op. 39, No. 10—Mazurka (mm. 1–12)

Waltz-bass Patterns Combined with Fast Repeated Chords

In their most basic form, waltz-bass patterns involve the same chords on beats two and three, but composers may repeat chords more rapidly through faster rhythmic patterns. The addition of rapid repeated chords requires a smooth horizontal gesture on the leap, followed immediately by a vertical one using a hand/wrist *staccato* for the repeated chords.

Repertoire: Waltz-bass Patterns Combined with Fast Repeated Chords
Burgmüller: *18 Characteristic Studies*, Op. 109, No. 9—Morning Bell (mm. 10–15)
Tchaikovsky: *Album for the Young*, Op. 39, No. 18—Neapolitan Song (mm. 1–8)

Waltz-bass Patterns with Different Articulations

In some pieces, composers indicate specific articulations for waltz-bass patterns. Pianists must ensure that their approach to these patterns is consistent with both the articulation and the meter. In the Grieg *Waltz*, beats one and two are slurred, implying a strong-weak approach. In Burgmüller's *The Shepherd's Return*, the slur is on beats two and three, putting the strong beat in the middle of the measure and threatening to fragment the pulse grouping into quarter notes. Perceiving the entire measure metrically as one pulse will help prevent the pianist from making an unwanted accent on the second quarter-note beat.

Repertoire: Waltz-bass Patterns with Different Articulations
Burgmüller: *18 Characteristic Studies*, Op. 109, No. 3—The Shepherd's Return (mm. 5–10)
Grieg: *Lyric Pieces*, Op. 12, No. 2—Waltz (mm. 1–7)

Waltz-bass Patterns with at Least One Sustained Voice

Waltz-bass patterns become more difficult if more independence of the voices is required. In Grieg's *Remembrances*, the left hand has to play sustained melodic bass notes while also playing the repeated chords. Depending upon the size of their hands, pianists may consider using finger substitutions to connect the bass line notes and will probably need to add some pedaling. The pianist must also dynamically shape this melodic bass line.

Repertoire: Waltz-bass Patterns with at Least One Sustained Voice
Grieg: *Lyric Pieces*, Op. 71, No. 7—Remembrances (mm. 9–16)

Waltz-bass Patterns with Difficult Chord Changes

An increase in the difficulty of the chord patterns within waltz basses influences the difficulty level of the piece. Chord inversions require position shifts plus changes of fingering, chords covering wider ranges require more rapid position shifts, and chords with a great deal of hand contraction and extension require precision and control—all of which increase the difficulty level.

Repertoire: Waltz-bass Patterns with Difficult Chord Changes
Grieg: *Lyric Pieces*, Op. 38, No. 6—Elegie (mm. 13–19)
Tchaikovsky: *Album for the Young*, Op. 39, No. 17—German Song

Chord Position Shifts

Pieces with rapidly shifting chords are prevalent in Romantic-period repertoire. Some important considerations for these include the following:

1) How quickly do the chord position shifts occur?
2) Are the shifts continuous or are there pauses in between?
3) Do both hands move in the same or different directions?
4) Do both hands move at the same time, or does one hand move before the other?
5) How far do the hands move?
6) Do the position shifts have patterned, predictable movements?
7) Is the fingering difficult due to the chord configurations?
8) Do either or both hands have to cross while changing positions?
9) Is the texture complicated? What additional elements do pianists have to navigate while shifting?

As with other musical elements, position changes that are consistent in one or both hands, within a limited range, with less chromaticism, moving at moderate speeds, and in less-complicated textures, will be easier to accomplish.

Chord Position Shifts, Both Hands at the Same Time

Three pieces from Tchaikovsky's *Album for the Young*, Op. 39, provide examples of hands shifting at the same time. In *A Winter Morning*, the speed of shifting is slower, there is a pause between position changes, the articulation and texture are patterned and consistent, and the grouping of physical movements is clear to the pianist, making this piece an easier one. *The Nurse's Tale* has a moderate tempo, but the chords change rapidly and include frequent use of chromaticism, making this piece moderately difficult. The *Hobby-Horse* is also patterned and consistent, and while there are small shifts within each measure, the more difficult position changes happen regularly between the third beat and the following downbeat. In waltz-bass patterns, pianists may tend to group their physical movements in alignment with the one-measure pulse. Because the position shifts in this piece occur between beats three and one, a better approach is to link the third beat with the next downbeat as one motion. Any change in groupings, however, can potentially cause unwanted accents, so pianists must listen carefully for continuity of tone and dynamics. *The Hobby-Horse* is the most difficult of the three pieces because of its very fast tempo. In Burgmüller's *The Knight Errant*, Op. 100, No. 25, the chords shift at the same time in each hand, but position changes are slower, making it an easier piece.

Repertoire: Chord Position Shifts, Both Hands at the Same Time
Burgmüller: *25 Progressive Pieces*, Op. 100, No. 25—The Knight Errant (mm. 1–8)
Chaminade: *Album for the Young*, Book 2, Op. 126, No. 9—Patrouille
Grieg: *Lyric Pieces*, Op. 12, No. 3—Watchman's Song (various places)
Tchaikovsky: *Album for the Young*, Op. 39, No. 2—A Winter Morning (mm. 1–12)
Tchaikovsky: *Album for the Young*, Op. 39, No. 3—The Hobby-Horse
Tchaikovsky: *Album for the Young*, Op. 39, No. 19—The Nurse's Tale (mm. 1–11)

Chord Position Shifts, Both Hands at Different Times

Hands changing positions at different times can often add to the difficulty of a piece, depending upon the rest of the texture. The pianist should attempt to synchronize movements between the two hands as much as possible and keep both hands flowing continuously in larger gestures.

Repertoire: Chord Position Shifts, Both Hands at Different Times

Gillock: *Lyric Preludes in Romantic Style*—Autumn Sketches
Gurlitt: *Album for the Young,* Op. 140, No. 15—Will-o-the-Wisp

Position Shifts within Passagework

Pianists can accomplish position shifts within passagework through rests, hand contraction and extension, repeated notes, lateral motion, and awkward fingering (when necessary).

Position Shifts within Passagework during Rests

Traveling through passagework is one of the important ways that a pianist moves throughout the different ranges of the keyboard. These pieces are easier when the composer provides rests for transition points.

Repertoire: Position Shifts within Passagework during Rests
Burgmüller: *25 Progressive Pieces,* Op. 100, No. 2—Arabesque
Burgmüller: *25 Progressive Pieces,* Op. 100, No. 18—Inquiétude

Position Shifts within Passagework through Hand Contraction and Extension

Hand contraction and extension are necessary in playing most piano compositions. The pianist must develop great flexibility in the hand and arm to be able to move to different locations with ease. The pianist should attempt to keep fingers in line with the arm rather than turning the hand or reaching for a position without moving the arm. Turning the hands outward laterally rather than changing their position on the keyboard can create ulnar deviation, a position that puts a lot of strain on the hands. Pianists with larger hands might be able to reach notes without moving frequently, but most pianists will need to employ a slight undulating movement of contraction and extension combined with lateral motion to reach the appropriate positions.

Repertoire: Position Shifts within Passagework through Hand Contraction and Extension
Grieg: *Lyric Pieces,* Op. 54, No. 5—Scherzo (mm. 1–16)

Schumann: *Album for the Young*, Op. 68, No. 8—Wild Rider
Schumann: *Album for the Young*, Op. 68, No. 12—Knight Rupert (mm. 25–32)

Position Shifts within Passagework with Repeated Notes

Pianists should consider changing fingerings on repeated notes within passagework to facilitate position shifts. Sometimes this is not possible due to tempo or other considerations, but changing fingerings usually makes the position shifts easier. When changing fingers, pianists should release the first note quickly and shift the fingers with as little extraneous movement as possible.

Repertoire: Position Shifts within Passagework with Repeated Notes
Burgmüller: *25 Progressive Pieces*, Op. 100, No. 20—Tarantelle (mm. 1–4, 9–16)
Tchaikovsky: *Album for the Young*, Op. 39, No. 14—Polka (mm. 11–12, 15–18)

Position Shifts in Passagework through Lateral Motion

Some pieces require the need for much shifting through lateral motion, sometimes combined with contraction and extension. In Tchaikovsky's *Folk-Song*, pianists should primarily use finger *staccato* with lateral motion rather than hand/wrist *staccato*, since the desired movement pattern should be more horizontal than vertical.

Repertoire: Position Shifts in Passagework through Lateral Motion
Tchaikovsky: *Album for the Young*, Op. 39, No. 13—Folk-Song (mm. 13–24)

Position Shifts in Passagework through Awkward Fingering

The music of Schumann and Brahms often involves awkward fingering and hand-position changes. Frequently, in order to play a *legato* melodic line while sustaining chords or other voices within the same hand, the pianist has to play unusual or uncomfortable fingerings, such as passing the third finger over the fourth finger. A good performance edition can provide effective fingering suggestions for these awkward passages. It is best to encounter these challenges first in shorter, easier pieces with a slow, sustained tempo and limited range.

Students may have trouble navigating these awkward fingerings while also controlling such factors as balance, melodic contour, and long phrasing.

Repertoire: Position Shifts in Passagework through Awkward Fingering
Schumann: *Album for the Young*, Op. 68, No. 22—Roundelay

Position Shifts through Hand Crossings

Position Shifts through Hand Crossings (One Hand Crossing)

Elementary-level method books sometimes introduce hand crossings at the mid-elementary level, usually through octave transposition and hand-over-hand arpeggios. The context of the hand crossings can affect its difficulty level. An important aspect of hand crossings is the aural and tonal control needed to connect the musical lines, since the ear often has trouble connecting musical lines through different ranges. Pieces will be easier if the crossing hand can return consistently to the original note or position, or if it can cross consistently to the same note or position. If the crossing hand is playing a melodic passage, the pianist's aural connection with that line can make the crossings easier. The presence of rests after crossings can be very helpful for returning to the starting position. Inconsistent patterns and positions will be the most challenging.

Repertoire: Position Shifts through Hand Crossings (One Hand Crossing)
Burgmüller: *25 Progressive Pieces*, Op. 100, No. 24—The Swallow
Burgmüller: *18 Characteristic Studies*, Op. 109, No. 9—Morning Bell
Gillock: *Lyric Preludes in Romantic Style*—Humming Bird (B section, mm. 9–14)
Grieg: *Lyric Pieces*, Op. 47, No. 6—Norwegian Dance

Position Shifts through Hand Crossings (Both Hands Alternately Crossing)

Many of Gillock's *Lyric Preludes in Romantic Style* require numerous hand crossings. When only one hand crosses while the other hand remains in position, the pianist has an easier time maintaining core stability. When both hands alternate crossings in different positions, a wider range is frequently involved. Playing through the wider ranges of the keyboard requires the pianist to rock on their sitz bones to either side in order to keep hands and arms aligned with the keyboard as much as possible. Both hands should anticipate the next positions, moving quickly and steadily without any hesitation. Failure to anticipate when to cross usually results in a sudden, uncontrolled motion to reach the correct position, which often creates unwanted accents and a lack of control of both tone quality and dynamics. In pieces with numerous hand crossings, the wider range means the pianist might have to memorize these pieces to be able to look at their hands.

Repertoire: Position Shifts through Hand Crossings (Both Hands Alternately Crossing)
Gillock: *Lyric Preludes in Romantic Style*—A Witch's Cat
Gillock: *Lyric Preludes in Romantic Style*—Fountain of Diana
Gillock: *Lyric Preludes in Romantic Style*—Moonlight Mood
Gillock: *Lyric Preludes in Romantic Style*—Phantom Rider
Gillock: *Lyric Preludes in Romantic Style*—Procession of the Mandarin
Gillock: *Lyric Preludes in Romantic Style*—Seascape

Awkward Positions

Interlocking Hands

Some pieces require both hands to play in the same range on top of each other, with fingers intertwined in awkward positions. When playing these types of passages, pianists should first analyze the passage to determine which hand should be on top. Although the same hand should usually remain on top, sometimes a change may be preferable. Pianists should raise the wrist of the hand that is playing on the top, moving further into the keys closer to the fallboard while keeping the wrist of the opposite hand low and further out on the keys. Teachers and students should pay careful attention to become aware of any tension in the hand, arm, or neck that these awkward positions may create.

Repertoire: Interlocking Hands
Gillock: *Lyric Preludes in Romantic Style*—Procession of the Mandarin
Schumann: *Album for the Young*, Op. 68, No. 17—The Little Morning Wanderer

Hands Crossed for Extended Periods

Another awkward position occurs when pianists must keep their hands crossed for an extended period. When this arrangement occurs in the middle range of the keyboard, pianists can maintain their general sitting position but will still need to adjust their arms and hands to keep them aligned with the keyboard as much as possible. When playing with crossed hands in the higher or lower ranges of the keyboard, pianists should rock on their sitz bones to either side to achieve the most comfortable position possible. As with interlocking hand positions, pianists must determine which hand should be on top. An excellent preparation for this type of playing is to practice major scales in this configuration, playing them twice so that each hand plays both on the top and on the bottom. Pianists will usually prefer one arrangement over the other but should practice the exercise both ways to train the body and brain to integrate the different coordination.

Repertoire: Hands Crossed for Extended Periods of Time
Gillock: *Lyric Preludes in Romantic Style*—Serenade

Both Hands Positioned in High or Low Ranges for an Extended Period

When students have to play pieces in either the high or low ranges of the keyboard for an extended period, they may develop tension in one or both legs, since shifting to one side or the other changes their center of gravity and can throw off their balance. Often students do not pay any attention to how these awkward positions affect all of their playing until problems occur. By finding comfortable positions with balanced weight distribution before starting to play, and monitoring any development of tension, students can become more comfortable playing in the more extreme ranges of the keyboard.

Repertoire: Both Hands Positioned in High or Low Ranges for an Extended Period

Grieg: *Lyric Pieces*, Op. 43, No. 6—To the Spring
Grieg: *Lyric Pieces*, Op. 57, No. 6—Homesickness
Schumann: *Album for the Young*, Op. 68, No. 23—Horseman's Song

Chords with Awkward Fingering

Students should learn standard fingerings when they begin playing chords during the middle-elementary level, even if they have larger hands. Chord fingerings are based upon the five-finger pattern as well as the intervallic changes in chord inversions, although there can always be exceptions to the standard fingerings depending upon the musical context. Standard triad fingerings in both hands are the following:

> Right hand: root position 1-3-5, first inversion 1-2-5, second inversion 1-3-5
> Left hand: root position 5-3-1, first inversion 5-3-1, second inversion 5-2-1

Composers in the nineteenth century began to expand their harmonic vocabulary to include sonorities with added notes for unexpected harmonic excursions and/or expressive effects. Intermediate-level students will begin to encounter larger chords with complicated fingerings that challenge both their reading abilities and physical comfort, since many of these chords will put their hands in awkward positions. Students will need to adapt their hand positions to find the most comfortable way to play these chords; teachers should use caution when assigning this repertoire to students with small hands.

Repertoire: Chords with Awkward Fingering
Grieg: *Lyric Pieces*, Op. 12, No. 6—Norwegian Melody
Schumann: *Album for the Young*, Op. 68, No. 17—The Little Morning Wanderer
Schumann: *Album for the Young*, Op. 68, No. 19—Little Romance
Schumann: *Album for the Young*, Op. 68, No. 22—Roundelay
Schumann: *Album for the Young*, Op. 68, No. 30—***
Schumann: *Album for the Young*, Op. 68, No. 32—Sheherazade

Schumann: *Album for the Young*, Op. 68, No. 33—Vintage Times
Schumann: *Album for the Young*, Op. 68, No. 42—Figured Chorale
Schumann: *Album for the Young*, Op. 68, No. 43—New Year's Eve

Passagework

Fast Scalar Passagework

Many intermediate-level students love to play fast as often as they can. Speed and facility must begin with the coordinated, free, and efficient technique previously discussed. Students who play with tension in their hands, arms, or shoulders will have trouble playing quickly, especially if they also use unnecessary force to play loudly. As previously discussed, fingers are the pianist's articulators, but they cannot be solely responsible for producing tone and volume. Playing quickly is also difficult if students are playing with a strong finger stroke on one note at a time. Forcing faster speeds with this technical approach usually leads to physical tension.

Fast playing is easily possible if pianists perceive notes within larger pulse groupings, which then inspire larger physical gestures. Students can use a metronome to increase speed one increment at a time until they can cut the metronome speed in half to transition to the next larger pulse grouping. Students are often surprised that they can easily play faster merely by grouping notes into larger pulse groupings.

Fast passagework depends upon secure, confident fingering that has become automatic through careful practicing. Passagework that primarily consists of scalar patterns is easier since the pianist is already familiar with scale fingerings. If passagework does not become smooth and effortless through practice, students need to re-evaluate fingering choices and hand positions that may be causing problems. An excellent practice technique to ensure secure fingerings is "additive" practicing. Students play the passage, starting with the first note only and adding one note at a time on successive repetitions. If any repetition does not feel comfortable, students should repeat that chunk multiple times until they feel ready to add the next note.

Repertoire: Fast scalar passagework
Burgmüller: *18 Characteristic Studies*, Op. 109, No. 2—The Pearls
Burgmüller: *18 Characteristic Studies*, Op. 109, No. 10—Velocity (with some chromaticism)

Passagework with Rapid Hand Contraction and Extension

Passagework that requires rapid hand contraction and extension requires careful attention to fingering within constantly shifting hand positions. Students must carefully analyze fingering groups, practicing chunks very slowly to grasp both mentally and physically where the hand contractions and extensions are needed. Failure to do this prior to practicing the piece can yield much frustration with fingering and hand positions. Students must conquer the challenges of the passagework prior to attempting to play both hands at the same time.

Repertoire: Passagework with Rapid Hand Contraction and Extension
Burgmüller: *25 Progressive Pieces*, Op. 100, No. 8—Gracefulness
Burgmüller: *25 Progressive Pieces*, Op. 100, No. 9—The Chase
Burgmüller: *25 Progressive Pieces*, Op. 100, No. 17—The Chatterbox
Burgmüller: *18 Characteristic Studies*, Op. 109, No. 5—The Spring
Burgmüller: *18 Characteristic Studies*, Op. 109, No. 15—Sylphs
Gillock: *Lyric Preludes in Romantic Style*—Forest Murmurs
Grieg: *Lyric Pieces*, Op. 38, No. 6—Elegie
Grieg: *Lyric Pieces*, Op. 43, No. 1—Butterfly
Grieg: *Lyric Pieces*, Op. 54, No. 5—Scherzo
Gurlitt: *Album for the Young*, Op. 140, No. 10—The Little Norwegian

Blocked and Broken Chords/Intervals

Left-hand Broken-chord Patterns without Traveling

Piano repertoire includes many passages with many different broken-chord patterns. The practice technique of playing broken-chord patterns as blocked chords should be introduced to students at the mid-elementary level once they begin to learn chords. Blocking broken-chord patterns facilitates fingering patterns and more importantly helps the student to hear broken chords as harmonic progressions. Passages that remain within close-position chord progressions will be easier to perform than passages in which the broken chords change hand positions. Once students are comfortable playing blocked-chord progressions, they can return to playing broken-chord passages as written. The use of rotation makes most broken-chord patterns easier to play and results in more tonal and rhythmic consistency when combined with continuous, fluid arm movements. Students must determine the appropriate movements for each broken-chord passage, including the Alberti-bass patterns that move in alternating directions.

Repertoire: Left-hand Broken-chord Patterns without Traveling
Burgmüller: *25 Progressive Pieces*, Op. 100, No. 12—The Farewell
Burgmüller: *25 Progressive Pieces*, Op. 100, No. 16—Sorrow
Gurlitt: *Album for the Young*, Op. 140, No. 14—Hunting Song
Gurlitt: *Album for the Young*: Op. 140, No. 18—Serenade

Broken-chord Patterns with Traveling

Broken-chord passages that include position shifts become much more challenging. Students should first practice traveling using blocked chords in continuous horizontal movements. Once students are comfortable doing this, they can play the passages as written, adding rotation for the broken chords while grouping these patterns in continuous movements.

Repertoire: Left-Hand Broken-chord Patterns with Traveling
Grieg: *Lyric Pieces*, Op. 12, No. 7—Album-leaf
Tchaikovsky: *Album for the Young*, Op. 39, No. 15—Italian Song
Tchaikovsky: *Album for the Young*, Op. 39, No. 23—The Handorgan Man

Repertoire: Right-hand Broken-chord Patterns with Traveling
Gurlitt: *Album for the Young*, Op. 140, No. 10—The Little Norwegian
Gurlitt: *Album for the Young*, Op. 140, No. 12—In the Church

Repertoire: Broken Intervals/Chords in Both Hands
Burgmüller: *25 Progressive Pieces*, Op. 100, No. 11—The Young Shepherdess
Grieg: *Lyric Pieces*, Op. 43, No. 1—Butterfly
Schumann: *Album for the Young*, Op. 68, No. 12—Knight Rupert

Repertoire: Line-within-a-line Broken Intervals
Burgmüller: *25 Progressive Pieces*, Op. 100, No. 7—The Clear Stream
Burgmüller: *25 Progressive Pieces*, Op. 100, No. 13—Consolation
Burgmüller: *18 Characteristic Studies*, Op. 109, No. 7—Lullaby
Gurlitt: *Album for the Young*, Op. 140, No. 5—Murmuring Brook
Gurlitt: *Album for the Young*, Op. 140, No. 11—Longing
Schumann: *Album for the Young*, Op. 68, No. 3—Humming Song
Schumann: *Album for the Young*, Op. 68, No. 5—Little Piece

Repertoire: Broken-Chord Patterns with Widely Spaced Intervals and/or Rapid Position Changes
Burgmüller: *25 Progressive Pieces*, Op. 100, No. 6—Progress
Burgmüller: *18 Characteristic Studies*, Op. 109, No. 5—The Spring
Burgmüller: *18 Characteristic Studies*, Op. 109, No. 7—Lullaby
Burgmüller: *18 Characteristic Studies*, Op. 109, No. 11—Serenade
Burgmüller: *18 Characteristic Studies*, Op. 109, No. 14—Song of the Gondolier
Grieg: *Lyric Pieces*, Op. 57, No. 2—Gade
Grieg: *Lyric Pieces*, Op. 68, No. 3—At Your Feet
Schumann: *Album for the Young*, Op. 68, No. 12—Knight Rupert
Schumann: *Album for the Young*, Op. 68, No. 14—Little Study
Tchaikovsky: *Album for the Young*, Op. 39, No. 14—Polka

Octaves and Large Stretches

Large Stretches in One or Both Hands

An intermediate-level student's age and piano ability can range widely, especially if students begin piano instruction at a young age and still have relatively small hands. Intermediate-level repertoire often requires a full octave hand span, which may still be uncomfortable for some students. Some students may be able to reach an octave but have trouble playing additional notes within the octave. If the student must play both notes of the octave concurrently, redistribution may be possible so that the octave interval does not fall within the same hand. If redistribution is not possible, students can either roll the octave or possibly leave out one of the notes depending upon the context. As with other repertoire requiring hand extensions, students should release their hand extension as soon as possible to avoid building up tension and potentially causing an injury. Students with small hands may be able to play broken octaves through rotation combined with lateral movement of the arms, but teachers may need to avoid pieces with octaves altogether until students can play them comfortably.

Repertoire: Large Stretches in One or Both Hands
Burgmüller: *18 Characteristic Studies*, Op. 109, No. 5—The Spring
Burgmüller: *18 Characteristic Studies*, Op. 109, No. 7—Lullaby
Burgmüller: *18 Characteristic Studies*, Op. 109, No. 14—Song of the Gondolier
Burgmüller: *18 Characteristic Studies*, Op. 109, No. 15—Sylphs
Grieg: *Lyric Pieces*, Op. 38, No. 6—Elegie
Grieg: *Lyric Pieces*, Op. 43, No. 1—Butterfly
Grieg: *Lyric Pieces*, Op. 57, No. 2—Gade
Schumann: *Album for the Young*, Op. 68, No. 35—Mignon

Repertoire: Large Chords in One or Both Hands, Including Octaves with Added Pitches
Burgmüller: *18 Characteristic Studies*, Op. 109, No. 16—Parting
Grieg: *Lyric Pieces*, Op. 43, No. 6—To the Spring
Grieg: *Lyric Pieces*, Op. 65, No. 5—Ballad
Grieg: *Lyric Pieces*, Op. 68, No. 1—Sailor's Song
Grieg: *Lyric Pieces*, Op. 68, No. 5—At the Cradle
Schumann: *Album for the Young*, Op. 68, No. 25—Echoes from the Theater
Schumann: *Album for the Young*, Op. 68, No. 29—Strange Man
Schumann: *Album for the Young*, Op. 68, No. 31—Song of War
Schumann: *Album for the Young*, Op. 68, No. 41—Norse Song

Octave Passages

Intermediate-level students are not ready to play rapid octaves until they have gained significant technical skills, so the presence of rapid octaves usually moves the repertoire into the advanced level. If octave passages are not very long and do not go extremely fast, they can provide a good opportunity for intermediate-level students to begin practicing them. Students should use wrist motion for rapid octave passages rather than the slower forearm motion. Students can prepare for these passages by playing a C major scale using octaves in either hand and then both hands, ascending and descending. Initially restricting these passages to white keys will make them easier. Once students can play these octaves comfortably on white keys, they can begin to play them in major keys that include a limited number of black keys, as the addition of black keys changes the feel of the keyboard topography.

Repertoire: Octave Passages
Burgmüller: *18 Characteristic Studies*, Op. 109, No. 15—Sylphs
Burgmüller: *18 Characteristic Studies*, Op. 109, No. 17—March
Grieg: *Lyric Pieces*, Op. 62, No. 5—Phantom
Grieg: *Lyric Pieces*, Op. 65, No. 2—Peasant's Song
Grieg: *Lyric Pieces*, Op. 68, No. 3—At Your Feet
Schumann: *Album for the Young*, Op. 68, No. 29—Strange Man
Schumann: *Album for the Young*, Op. 68, No. 31—Song of War

Broken Octaves

Broken octaves may be easier for intermediate-level students, since they can rely on rotation combined with lateral movement as needed to play the octaves without having to play both notes at the same time.

Repertoire: Broken Octaves
Burgmüller: *18 Characteristic Studies*, Op. 109, No. 12—Awakening in the Woods

Burgmüller: *18 Characteristic Studies*, Op. 109, No. 13—The Storm
Chaminade: *Album for the Young*, Book 2, Op. 126, No. 9—Patrouille
Schumann: *Album for the Young*, Op. 68, No. 36—Italian Sailor's Song

Note

1 Heinrich Neuhaus, *The Art of Piano Playing*, trans. K. A. Leibovitch (New York: Praeger, 1973), 100.

7
Articulation

Elementary-level piano method books introduce keyboard touch in different ways. Some methods advocate for starting with a non-*legato* touch with larger arm and wrist movements, while others default to a *legato* touch or simply leave this decision up to the teacher. Young students can make larger hand or arm detached movements more easily than *legato* individual finger movements. Students with small hands may find it difficult to play *legato* until they begin to develop some finger independence.

    As piano study develops, students soon learn the Italian terms *legato* (smoothly connected) and *staccato* (short or detached). *Staccato* playing usually first appears consistently throughout an entire piece, while *legato* playing first appears through long phrase lines. The variety of articulation markings gradually expands to include shorter slurs and mixtures of *legato* and *staccato*, as well as accents, *tenuto* markings, and combinations of symbols. Students often perceive *staccato* and *legato* as opposite singular options, rather than a spectrum of different and subtle gradations with significant impact on interpretation and character. Students should interpret articulation markings within the context of all of the other musical elements. An important point to remember is that articulation should not fracture a musical phrase into individual notes or small groups of notes, creating "vertical" rather than linear playing.

Legato

The piano is a percussion instrument, with sound produced by the striking of the hammer against the string, and therefore it cannot produce the true *legato* that other instrumentalists and singers can achieve. It is possible, though, to create *legato* by overlapping notes in an attempt to cover the hammer stroke of each previous note. The degree of *legato* can actually vary quite a bit, from barely connected to the significantly overlapped *legato* so essential to creating an expressive, *cantabile* melody. Supple hands/wrists and arms with weight released into the keys must be combined with solid fingers to play a beautiful *legato*.

Legato Fingering

Legato fingering is the primary and preferred foundation for playing *legato*. While it may seem obvious that fingering that directly connects pitches promotes *legato* playing, students often do not pay attention to fingering, especially if it calls for awkward shifts, finger substitutions, or unexpected fingerings. Students often think they can rely on the pedal to create a *legato* sound, but there is a distinct difference if the pianist combines *legato* fingering with good pedaling. An important step in mastering *legato* playing is for students to hear and feel the differences between *legato* with only finger action, *legato* using only the damper pedal, and *legato* combining finger action with the damper pedal.

In the initial stages of learning a new piece, students often pedal without much thought or aural attention. By practicing without the pedal until they have mastered other musical elements, they will perhaps be more aurally attentive to the pedaling. Practicing a *legato* melody first without the pedal allows students to listen to whether or not they are truly playing *legato* with their fingers.

<u>Repertoire: Awkward Fingerings Required for *Legato* Playing (finger crossovers, substitutions, etc.)</u>
Grieg: *Lyric Pieces*, Op. 12, No. 1—Arietta
Grieg: *Lyric Pieces*, Op. 38, No. 6—Elegie
Grieg: *Lyric Pieces*, Op. 43, No. 2—Solitary Traveler
Grieg: *Lyric Pieces*, Op. 43, No. 3—In My Native Country
Grieg: *Lyric Pieces*, Op. 62, No. 2—Gratitude

Grieg: *Lyric Pieces*, Op. 65, No. 2—Peasant's Song
Grieg: *Lyric Pieces*, Op. 68, No. 5—At the Cradle
Schumann: *Album for the Young*, Op. 68, No. 19—Little Romance
Schumann: *Album for the Young*, Op. 68, No. 22—Roundelay
Schumann: *Album for the Young*, Op. 68, No. 26—***

Variety of *Legato* Overlap

The amount of overlap in *legato* playing can significantly influence the character of the music. Teachers should demonstrate varying degrees of overlap to help students gain an aural awareness of the differences. Scales and other technique exercises provide excellent material for students to work on consistent articulation. When practicing basic technique exercises, pianists should use a clean, clear *legato* without much overlap. Common problems of *legato* playing include too much *legato* overlap and/or inconsistent overlap, resulting from a lack of aural attentiveness.

Once students can play technique exercises with a consistent, clean *legato*, they should explore the variety of touches called for in repertoire of different historical periods. Baroque music often suggests a non-*legato* keyboard touch. Classical repertoire may have a non-*legato* touch or a barely connected one for *legato* playing. A slow, Romantic-period *cantabile* melody that expresses deep feeling needs more overlapping *legato*, while a less-intense singing melody can have less overlap. Impressionistic music and some modern pieces call for even more overlapping and blending of sounds.

Two-note Slurs

A common articulation pattern is the two-note slur. With few exceptions, two-note slurs should have the dynamic shape of a *diminuendo*, with both notes approached as one sound that goes from more to less rather than as two notes with two different dynamic levels. Students can achieve this nicely using a flexible wrist that drops more weight into the key on the first note and lifts up and toward the fallboard on the second note. It is important to make sure that students are not playing the second note with a separate motion, since that might produce the opposite dynamic shape from the one desired. Successions of two-note slurs should maintain this dynamic shape within the flow of a longer phrase; each two-note slur should not sound like a "restart." The first note of any slur grouping should fit dynamically within the overall shape of the phrase. In addition, pianists should slightly separate the second note of the slur from the note following it. Two-note slurs and other short slurs are prevalent throughout the Romantic-period repertoire.

Repertoire: Two-note Slurs
Burgmüller: *25 Progressive Pieces*, Op. 100, No. 10—Tender Flower
Burgmüller: *25 Progressive Pieces*, Op. 100, No. 24—The Knight Errant
Burgmüller: *18 Characteristic Studies*, Op. 109, No. 7—Lullaby
Chaminade: *Album for the Young*, Book 2, Op. 126, No. 3—Rigaudon
Gurlitt: *Album for the Young*, Op. 140, No. 13—The Little Wanderer
Schumann: *Album for the Young*, Op. 68, No. 12—Knight Rupert
Tchaikovsky: *Album for the Young*, Op. 39, No. 2—A Winter Morning

Creating the Illusion of *Legato*

When pianists encounter pieces with multiple musical requirements that they cannot accomplish simultaneously, they must determine which musical elements to prioritize. Sometimes it is not physically possible to play a passage *legato*. The pianist can employ a variety of different solutions for this problem, depending upon the context. For example, in a series of thirds or other doubled intervals, it may be possible to play one voice *legato* while the other voice cannot be *legato* due to the use of the same finger on consecutive notes. Pianists can create the illusion of *legato* for both voices if they are able to play the top notes *legato*, since this is where aural attention is focused. Pianists should use smooth transitions between notes to attempt to play as *legato* as possible. Effective dynamic shaping also promotes the illusion of *legato*.

Finger Slides

Finger slides from black notes to white notes using the same finger can actually sound quite *legato*. This is not usually a preferred fingering, but sometimes it is the only option. This fingering will sound more *legato* if the pianist carefully controls the dynamic shape of these two notes.

Pedal-assisted *Legato* when Finger *Legato* Is Not Possible

Sometimes there are isolated transitions between notes or chords in which *legato* is impossible. Using long sustained pedals in these sections is not desirable, since it would cause too much blurring. Here is where a sophisticated and highly coordinated use of the pedal with the fingers is desirable to add just a little "pedal glue." The performer must be very careful not to hold the pedal any longer than necessary and to consider using a shallower pedal depth to avoid too much contrast between the tone quality of the pedaled and un-pedaled notes. Large leaps may be impossible to connect with the fingers, so the damper pedal must be used to connect these notes.

Staccato

The notation for *staccato* can be a dot, or in earlier keyboard music, a symbol that looks similar to an apostrophe. Pianists should play *staccato* notes shorter than their note value, usually by about 50 percent. In slower tempos and/or with longer note values marked *staccato*, the note or chord might be longer than anticipated.

Staccato has perhaps even more variety of possible character expressions than *legato*. Finger *staccato*, used for very rapid notes, can produce articulation ranging from delicate to crisp or biting. Hand or wrist *staccato* is used for playing more than one note at a time *staccato*, including double notes, chords, and octaves. Forearm *staccato* is a percussive touch used mostly in louder, powerful passages.

While these different approaches do not function independently of each other, it is important to determine the primary technique needed to achieve maximum efficiency, freedom, and character. For example, when students begin to play passages with extended *staccato* notes or chords, they may try to do this with only their forearms rather than their hand/wrist or fingers.

This results in a labored sound and causes fatigue or even pain. Attempts to play fast *staccato* passages with larger hand or arm movements may also result in frustration, since the fingers can play short notes much faster than the hand or the arm can move. At all times, when performing detached touches, performers must maintain flexibility and freedom in arms and hands to avoid fatigue, tension, and pain. Another challenge in playing detached notes is to maintain consistency and control of the note lengths throughout. Practicing scales and other technique exercises with varying types of *staccato* touches provides an excellent foundation for exploration of the variety of possible articulations found within the repertoire.

<u>Repertoire: *Staccato*</u>
Burgmüller: *25 Progressive Pieces*, Op. 100, No. 23—The Return (wrist)
Burgmüller: *18 Characteristic Studies*, Op. 109, No. 6— The Merry Maiden (wrist)
Burgmüller: *18 Characteristic Studies*, Op. 109, No. 11—Serenade (mixed)
Burgmüller: *18 Characteristic Studies*, Op. 109, No. 12—Awakening in the Woods (mixed)
Grieg: *Lyric Pieces*, Op. 68, No. 2—Grandmother's Minuet (finger)
Grieg: *Lyric Pieces*, Op. 71, No. 3—Puck (mixed)
Schumann: *Album for the Young*, Op. 68, No. 7—Hunting Song (mixed)
Schumann: *Album for the Young*, Op. 68, No. 8—Wild Rider (mixed)
Schumann: *Album for the Young*, Op. 68, No. 36—Italian Sailor's Song (wrist)
Tchaikovsky: *Album for the Young*, Op. 39, No. 3—The Hobby-Horse (wrist)

Accent Marks (>)

When musicians refer to accent marks, they are usually talking about the horizontal wedge accent that indicates an extra emphasis, usually through dynamics. Students may interpret this accent as simply meaning to play a note or chord loudly, but it is important to keep this accent within the dynamic context. For example, a wedge accent within a *forte* dynamic level would receive more emphasis than a wedge accent within a *mezzo-forte* dynamic level. In general, successive notes or chords with wedge accents also imply a small amount of space between them.

Marcato or *Martellato* (^)

The *marcato* accent implies a shorter, sharper accent than the horizontal wedge accent. Its use might suggest a more dramatic or intense character and implies more forearm involvement combined with quick finger motions.

Tenuto (—)

A *tenuto* marking is often defined as holding notes for their full value, although it can have various meanings depending upon the context. It may also imply a slight lengthening or emphasis of the note in an expressive context. Sometimes *tenuto* markings are included in sections that are otherwise marked *staccato* or accented to remind the performer that these notes should maintain their full value.

Combination of Articulation Markings

Any of the common articulation markings may be combined, perhaps causing confusion for students. A thorough analysis of all of the musical elements can help the pianist to gain an understanding of the articulations needed in these settings. One example of this is the *portato* notation, which is a non-*legato* touch somewhat between *legato* and *staccato*. It is often notated as *staccato* notes underneath a slur or as notes with both a *staccato* dot and a *tenuto* dash. ƒƒƒƒ This articulation creates a special effect, and it is very dependent upon the musical context. In single-note melodies, *portato* can emphasize individual pitches and usually has some differences in the degree of detachment. *Portato* may suggest pedaling of each individual note or chord with slight breaks in between.

Different Touches Needed Simultaneously between Hands

Pianists are often required to perform multiple articulations at the same time, or to play articulated notes in one hand while holding notes in the other hand. This requires quite a bit of control and coordination, as well as careful, slow practicing to master. Students can prepare for this by playing technique exercises with different articulations between the two hands. A simple exercise would be to play all *staccato* notes in one hand and all *legato* notes in the other hand simultaneously, and then reverse them. The number of possible patterns is virtually unlimited. Practicing articulations utilizing familiar technical exercises allows the pianist to concentrate fully on the articulation.

Repertoire: Different Touches Needed Simultaneously between Hands
Beach: *Children's Album*, Op. 36, No. 5—Polka
Burgmüller: *25 Progressive Pieces*, Op. 100, No. 2—Arabesque
Burgmüller: *25 Progressive Pieces*, Op. 100, No. 11—The Young Shepherdess (B section)
Burgmüller: *25 Progressive Pieces*, Op. 100, No. 15—Ballade
Burgmüller: *18 Characteristic Studies*, Op. 109, No. 4—The Gypsies
Chaminade: *Album for the Young*, Book 1, Op. 123, No. 5—Gavotte
Schumann: *Album for the Young*, Op. 68, No. 10—The Happy Farmer
Schumann: *Album for the Young*, Op. 68, No. 26—***
Tchaikovsky: *Album for the Young*, Op. 39, No. 13—Folk-Song
Tchaikovsky: *Album for the Young*, Op. 39, No. 14—Polka

Articulations that Conflict with the Meter

Composers often use articulation groupings that go across the bar lines or do not fit the meter. When this occurs, students can easily lose their sense of pulse, performing the start of any slurred groupings with an accent regardless of where they occur within the measure. This can wreak havoc on both the metrical pulse and the rhythmic continuity. Two practice options can help to remedy this: (1) students can perceive the pulse and meter properly by speaking the passage on neutral syllables using the proper metrical grouping inflection, and (2) they can remove all articulation markings and play the passage according to the basic meter, using either all *legato* or all *staccato* touches depending upon the piece. Once they can do both of these consistently, they should then be able to add the articulation markings back into the passage while continuing to maintain the proper sense of meter.

Repertoire: Articulations that Conflict with the Meter
Burgmüller: *25 Progressive Pieces*, Op. 100, No. 5—Innocence
Burgmüller: *25 Progressive Pieces*, Op. 100, No. 6—Progress (B section)
Grieg: *Lyric Pieces*, Op. 54, No. 2—Norwegian March
Schumann: *Album for the Young*, Op. 68, No. 39—Wintertime II
Tchaikovsky: *Album for the Young*, Op. 39, No. 4—Mamma
Tchaikovsky: *Album for the Young*, Op. 39, No. 8—Waltz
Tchaikovsky: *Album for the Young*, Op. 39, No. 22—Song of the Lark

Variety of Articulation Touches Needed within One Piece

Teachers should assign repertoire that includes a variety of different articulation markings in a variety of textures and contexts, so that students have an opportunity to learn the subtleties of each of these markings and the different ways to approach them. Mastery of repertoire with consistent articulations should precede pieces that require a variety of touches within one piece.

Repertoire: Variety of Articulation Touches Needed within One Piece
Beach: *Children's Album*, Op. 36, No. 2—Gavotte
Beach: *Children's Album*, Op. 36, No. 5—Polka
Burgmüller: *25 Progressive Pieces*, Op. 100, No. 14—Austrian Dance
Burgmüller: *18 Characteristic Studies*, Op. 109, No. 3—The Shepherd's Return
Burgmüller: *18 Characteristic Studies*, Op. 109, No. 4—The Gypsies
Burgmüller: *18 Characteristic Studies*, Op. 109, No. 9—Morning Bell
Burgmüller: *18 Characteristic Studies*, Op. 109, No. 15—Sylphs

Burgmüller: *18 Characteristic Studies*, Op. 109, No. 17—March
Chaminade: *Album for the Young*, Book 2, Op. 126, No. 6—Scherzo-Valse
Grieg: *Lyric Pieces*, Op. 12, No. 2—Waltz

Increasing Complexity of Articulation

As with other musical elements, the increase in complexity of articulation requires significant finger independence and slow practicing. Teachers should use caution when assigning repertoire with too much challenging articulation if the student has not already mastered basic articulation demands.

8

Fingering

Pedagogical repertoire usually includes appropriate fingering for the average-size hand that is likely to yield good technical and musical results. While fingering may need to be altered because it does not fit individual hands, students should consider the notated fingering as a solid starting point. Unfortunately, many students do not pay attention to fingering at all or may not follow it consistently. Alert teachers can catch a student not paying attention to fingerings and gently but firmly insist on consistently good fingering. Teachers must watch the student's hands especially when hearing new pieces, since teachers are more likely to be looking at the music notation instead.

If a student has reached the intermediate level and is still not consistently following good fingering, the student should regularly sight-read a lot of elementary-level repertoire to focus specifically on fingering. They should progress steadily through graded repertoire levels until they reach their current playing level. Students who do not use good fingering will have trouble playing accurately and consistently, which will thwart their security and confidence as well.

Intermediate-level repertoire may not have as much notated fingering as elementary method books and supplementary repertoire do, even in pieces with careful editing. Students need to understand basic fingering principles so that they can learn how to choose their own fingering. They may not readily perceive logical fingering choices that are not marked in the score. The most important principle to remember when selecting fingering is that it must not only be physically comfortable but must also serve the music.

Fingering Principles

Individual Finger Sizes and Proportions

All individuals have hands and fingers that are slightly different in size and proportions. A fingering that works well for one person might not work for another, especially if they have very small or very large hands, or if their finger length proportions are unusual. Pianists who do not have normal anatomy in their hands and/or fingers will obviously have to adjust fingerings based on their own unique challenges.

Suggested/Edited Fingerings

Less-experienced pianists should first attempt the fingerings written in the score and should pay careful attention to fingerings while sight-reading. In some editions, the editor may have included the composer's original fingering in Italics or provided multiple fingering options, usually notated on separate lines. The selection of some fingerings may not initially be comprehended, but an analysis of the entire piece can help students better understand them. Passages that have exact repeats should use the same fingerings, and these finger numbers likely will need to be added to the score, since publishers rarely repeat fingerings in subsequent repeated passages. Notating some or all of these fingerings will help to ensure that students are playing consistent fingerings in repeated passages. Some passages may be similar but not exact, and editors often attempt to use the same fingerings through slightly different patterns if possible. Alternate fingerings are always possible if they maintain the desired musical result, but changing fingerings must be a conscious decision rather than merely a lack of attention.

Often students have problems playing fingerings that feel unusual or unexpected. They may default to another less-desirable fingering, possibly without even realizing it. Teachers should guide students to be sensitive to the musical effect of one fingering as opposed to another. This may motivate students to be consistently careful and sophisticated in their fingering choices. Continued familiarity with repertoire, as well as maturing technique and musicianship, will help students grow in their ability to select their own fingerings.

Common Fingering Notation Practices

Pianists should mark important fingering in the score in pencil. Mark fingering for the right hand above the treble clef and fingering for the left hand below the bass clef to avoid confusion with rhythmic counting numbers that are usually written in between the two staves. When more than one finger number is needed, the lowest-numbered finger should be written closest to the staff on both clefs. It is not necessary or desirable to mark in fingering for every pitch. Important fingerings are those on the first note played within a piece/movement/section, in places where hand-positions change, or for unexpected fingering patterns. These are the most common places where fingerings are marked, but pianists should add whatever fingerings are helpful to ensure consistency.

Five-finger Pattern Positions

The five-finger pattern is the foundation of good fingering. Most pianists' hands function well in this position, which is both comfortable and secure. When hand-position changes are necessary, pianists should usually attempt to select fingering that allows them to stay in the next position for as long as possible before shifting again. Stepwise patterns imply the use of adjacent fingers. When possible, fingering should fit other intervals as found within the five-finger pattern: for example, using fingers 1 and 3 would be appropriate for an interval of a third.

Redistribution

When it is not possible for a pianist to reach a larger chord or interval in one hand, one or more notes can be played with the other hand. This practice, known as redistribution, is always a possibility as long as the pianist can maintain the desired musical result. For example, it might be technically possible to redistribute notes in a particular passage, but redistribution might make it difficult to maintain proper voicing or clarity of texture.

Finger Crossings

Finger crossings are one method of traveling on the keyboard. Normally this is accomplished by using more lower-numbered fingers, such as in the typical white key scale fingering of 1-2-3 followed by the thumb crossing under to continue. In some unusual passages, finger 4 might cross over finger 5 to achieve a *legato* line, especially if lower-numbered fingers are already playing other notes at the same time. While this feels different and awkward at first, it is a successful way of ensuring finger *legato* in complicated textures.

Hand Extension and Contraction

Hand extensions and contractions are another method used to travel on the keyboard. Generally, as the hand extends in one direction, it should also contract from the opposite direction instead of trying to maintain an extended position. Continuing to keep the hand extended for a long period can result in fatigue or strain, especially if the pianist has small hands. Fluid lateral motion combined with appropriate contraction and extension can help to maintain physical comfort and freedom. In rapid hand contractions or extensions, the pianist can maintain stability by keeping one finger in position as an "anchor" or pivot while the rest of the hand moves.

Finger Substitutions on Sustained Notes

Pianists can use finger substitutions on sustained notes to help facilitate *legato* connections or smooth traveling. Finger substitutions are usually marked with a dash in between the two finger numbers, so 4-3 would mean playing the note with the fourth finger and then shifting to the third without rearticulating the note.

Finger Substitutions on Repeated Notes

Repeated notes often imply changes of fingers for consistency and fluency, even if there are only two notes. Fingering patterns on repeated notes often move from higher-numbered fingers to lower ones: for example, four repeated notes might use the fingering 4-3-2-1 and three would use the fingering 3-2-1. Depending on the passage, other finger patterns might be preferable, such as alternating between two fingerings or even going from lower-numbered fingers to higher ones.

<u>Repertoire: Finger Substitutions on Repeated Notes</u>
Burgmüller: *25 Progressive Pieces*, Op. 100, No. 10—Tender Flower
Burgmüller: *25 Progressive Pieces*, Op. 100, No. 11—The Young Shepherdess
Burgmüller: *25 Progressive Pieces*, Op. 100, No. 17—The Chatterbox
Burgmüller: *25 Progressive Pieces*, Op. 100, No. 20—Tarantelle
Gurlitt: *Album for the Young*, Op. 140, No. 3—The Sky is Bright
Tchaikovsky: *Album for the Young*, Op. 39, No. 17—German Song
Tchaikovsky: *Album for the Young*, Op. 39, No. 18—Neapolitan Song
Tchaikovsky: *Album for the Young*, Op. 39, No. 20—The Witch

Avoiding Thumbs on Black Keys

It is normally preferable to avoid using thumbs on black keys. Playing a black key with the thumb requires the whole hand to move far up into the keys, potentially making the hand cramped and making it difficult to cross fingers over the thumb. Sometimes, however, playing a black key with the thumb is the best or only option, depending upon what comes before or after that particular note.

Fingerings and Tempo

Pianists should test fingerings at the anticipated performance tempo early in the process of learning repertoire, since fingering that seems fine at a slow tempo might not work well at a faster tempo. Short, fast bursts of groups of notes can help the pianist determine if the chosen fingerings will work when the pianist is not yet ready to play entire passages up to tempo.

Temporary Fingering Changes for Practice

Temporary changes of fingering may be required when using a variety of different practice techniques. Fingering changes force pianists to listen more acutely, as their kinesthetic memory is disturbed and therefore their aural memory has to compensate. Playing a chord split between the two hands that is usually played with one hand can help a student better hear voicing. Separating a melody out from its context can allow for a smoother fingering that yields a better *legato* aural model. Blocking harmonies or intervals facilitates hearing and simplifies textures. After practicing with temporary fingering changes, the pianist should quickly return to playing the passage as written, while maintaining their improved aural awareness.

More Than One Note Played by One Finger

Sometimes in hand extensions, the pianist needs to play two notes with one finger at the same time, usually the thumb. This typically happens with either two white notes or two black notes. For example, if the hand needs to play a G octave with another note added next to the thumb, such as G and A, the thumb should be used to play both the G and the A. Turning the thumb sideways makes this easier to do.

Alternate Fingerings for Very Loud Dynamics

When very loud pitches are necessary, pianists can use the strong third finger to play the note and support or brace it with the thumb behind the distal interphalangeal joint. They can also gather multiple fingers together vertically to form another type of braced support.

Playing with the Hand

It is also possible to turn the hand in a vertical position to play a loud note with the side of the hand rather than a finger. This is more common when playing low bass notes very loudly and resonantly. Performers can also play various clusters of notes using the entire hand or palm.

Glissandos can be performed with several fingers at a time in a more vertical position.

9

Pedaling

Anton Rubinstein referred to the damper pedal as the "soul of the piano." Skillful pedaling is an absolute necessity for any pianist. Artistic and creative pedaling is essential for advanced pianism, usually taking years of experience to master. Unfortunately, poor pedaling technique significantly compromises many performances. While various aspects of performance preparation should become automatic, such as notes, rhythms, fingering, and general technical approaches, other variables such as tempo, balance, and pedaling need constant monitoring. All pedaling must begin with careful listening, and the development of sophisticated aural skills is an essential task for the intermediate-level pianist. References to pedaling in this chapter refer to the damper pedal unless otherwise indicated.

Elementary-level method books typically introduce basic damper pedaling at the middle-elementary level. Various approaches to pedaling at this level include the following:

1. One long pedal

The student depresses the damper pedal for the entire piece, often playing notes of the whole-tone scale to create an Impressionistic soundscape. A pedal marking may or may not be included, but if there is a marking, it is usually the bracket type extended for the entire piece.

2. Individual chord pedaling

Figure 9.1 Overlapping pedaling example (author owned).

In Figure 9.1, the notation seems to indicate that the pianist should use the damper pedal for several isolated chords, without any overlapping or connected pedaling. The pedal marking is usually the bracket type but can be confusing, since the chords may be notated as a quarter note followed by rests while the pedal is deployed. The presence of visual rests when the sound should continue can be confusing, and the visual gaps between the brackets might suggest breaks in the sound. I would not recommend introducing pedaling to students with this notation.

3. Overlapping or syncopated pedaling ⎯⎯⎯⎯⎯∧⎯⎯⎯⎯⎯∧⎯⎯⎯⎯

A few method books present overlapping pedaling using the continuous line with the inverted "v" to indicate when to change the pedal. This notation is the most appropriate, since the visual notation matches the desired aural experience and also matches the physical movement of the foot.

Subsequent repertoire pieces may include pedal indications, but do not necessarily include any discussion of pedaling techniques. There is rarely much information in method books about how the foot should pedal, when to use the pedal, or the critical importance of listening to pedaling. As pedal markings gradually disappear from the notation throughout students' progression, students will have to make their own pedaling choices through their own hearing strategies. Teachers can provide guidance, but this is also an opportunity for students to develop their own pedaling creativity. A number of pedaling guides provide helpful and thorough information, such as *The Pianist's Guide to Pedaling* by Joseph Banowetz and *Artistic Pedal Technique: Lessons for Intermediate and Advanced Pianists* by Katherine Faricy. Teachers can use resources such as these to ensure that they are covering important foundational pedaling information. Mastering the fundamentals of pedaling provides a baseline from which students can explore and develop the infinite possibilities of artistic pedaling.

Pedaling Fundamentals

The pedal should be controlled with the foot only, not with the leg. As students begin to use the damper pedal more, they may realize that they have been sitting too close to the piano if their leg feels uncomfortable. The heel should remain in contact with the floor, and the ball of the foot should rest on the pedal close to the end of the toes, with minor adjustments for each individual preference and foot size. Students who pedal using only their toes have less control of the pedal. Students should wear supportive shoes with appropriate soles that allow them to have more of a physical awareness of pedaling. Individuals who wear extremely high heels may experience more difficulty with pedaling. All pedals have a small range of motion or "play" in the "top" of the pedal dip before the dampers actually start lifting off the strings; students must find where this point is on each piano, depending upon the pedal regulation. If the pedal is needed at any point in a piece, the foot should remain in constant contact with the pedal to maintain control of pedaling and to avoid extraneous shoe-tapping noises.

The Three Pedals

Damper Pedal

On both grand and upright pianos, the pedal to the right is the damper pedal, normally played with the right foot. Depressing the pedal raises the dampers from the strings; releasing the pedal lowers them. Sometimes the pedal is referred to as the "sustaining" pedal, not to be confused with the *sostenuto* pedal. The damper pedal can sustain notes, connect notes, blend notes together, provide more volume and resonance to notes, change the tonal color of notes, and create dynamic changes on notes. The pedal can be depressed to an almost unlimited variety of depths, producing many different sonorities. Students must master foundational pedaling as a prelude to understand other subtle possibilities and variations of pedaling.

Una Corda Pedal

Sometimes referred to as the "soft pedal," the *una corda* pedal is located to the far left and played with the left foot. On a modern grand piano, depressing the *una corda* pedal shifts the keyboard action to the right, causing the hammers to strike the strings at a different point on the hammer felt. On a properly regulated piano, this should result in both a softer dynamic level and a change in tone quality. This pedal originally got its name because the shifting of the pedal on early instruments resulted in the hammer striking one string instead of two. On a modern grand piano, most notes have three strings, and the action does not shift enough for the hammer to strike just one string. The important thing to remember when using this pedal is that the hammers are striking the string in different places on the hammer felt than without using this pedal.

On an upright piano, using the *una corda* pedal creates a similar effect by moving the hammers closer to the strings, resulting in a shorter distance to the string and therefore less velocity for the hammer. While the dynamic level may decrease on an upright piano, the tone color may not change as dramatically as it does on a grand piano. A loud or raucous instrument may prompt the pianist to put the *una corda* pedal down to limit the harsh sound. Pianists collaborating with others may be asked to use the *una corda* to achieve a better balance with the other performers. The *una corda,* however, is not simply a crutch to play softer; its purpose is to produce special effects of dynamics and color in the sound. Like the damper pedal, the *una corda* pedal has a wide range of pedal depth.

Sostenuto Pedal

The *sostenuto* pedal, the middle pedal of the three on a modern grand piano, is a more specialized pedal usually played with the left foot. Depressing the *sostenuto* pedal captures and holds up only the dampers for the notes already depressed, sustaining them until the pedal is released. The *sostenuto* pedal can be used in combination with the damper pedal. The result is that some pitches can be sustained by the *sostenuto* pedal while notes played after the *sostenuto* pedal is depressed are changed by the damper pedal as normal.

Since the *sostenuto* pedal did not appear until around 1844, pianists do not normally use it with music composed prior to that time. Some pianists use the *sostenuto* pedal for sustaining long pedal points underneath changing harmony, as in the *Consolation in D-flat Major*, No. 3 (S. 172) by Franz Liszt and the *Prelude in C-sharp Minor*, Op. 3, No. 2 by Sergei Rachmaninoff. Contemporary composers also use this pedal for a variety of special sound effects, such as the creation of harmonics. To produce harmonics, the pianist silently depresses selected notes so that the hammers do not strike the strings to produce any sound and then engages the *sostenuto* pedal. Playing other notes while the pedal stays down results in some very interesting harmonics and sonorities.

Upright pianos may not have a middle pedal at all, or if there is one, it may not function as a true *sostenuto*. It may be a partial *sostenuto* affecting a smaller range of notes, usually only in the bass. The middle pedal may also be a "practice pedal" that puts a buffer between the hammers and the strings so that the sound is substantially muffled. The pianist can move this pedal into a slot that keeps it in this position indefinitely so that the pianist does not have to physically keep it down.

Pedal Markings and Instructions

Although composers attempt to provide specific instructions through a variety of pedal markings, these markings can sometimes be confusing to the pianist. If a composer has made the choice to include pedal markings in the score, the pianist should first attempt them as written, as they provide insight into the composer's artistic intentions. Although pedaling is an aural process and not a visual one, pedal markings can assist pianists in making good pedaling choices, particularly for those with less pedaling experience.

Bracket ⌊_____⌋

The bracket pedal symbol frequently appears in pedagogical music. The shape of the sign corresponds to the relative positions of the pedal: going down, sustained, going up. When multiple brackets are written one after another in the music, even though these brackets may not be connected visually, they should usually be interpreted to indicate overlapping, continuous pedaling with brief pedal changes.

Extended Line

A variation on the bracket marking is the use of a continuous extended line with an inverted V inserted whenever the pedal should be changed. This marking is preferable to the bracket, since the visual continuity of the extended line matches the continuous aural expectation.

Ped. Sign with Asterisk 𝓟𝓮𝓭. ✻

Composers frequently use the *Ped.* marking to show when to depress the pedal and the asterisk to indicate when to release the pedal. These markings generally appear in intermediate- or advanced-level repertoire. Since it is not possible to place the *Ped.* marking and the asterisk on top of each other, these markings can generate the same confusion as the bracket markings when indicating a pedal change amid overlapping, continuous pedaling. The visual notation appears to indicate a break between the asterisk and the next *Ped.*, which is usually not the case. A general guideline is for the pianist to focus on changing the pedal at the *Ped.* sign and use interpretive judgment for determining whether the asterisk suggests an overlapping pedaling or a break before the next pedal.

Absence of Pedal Markings

Often a composer does not include any pedal markings or may instead give a general indication to use the pedal. A teacher can help students understand when and how to use the pedal in these works. A comprehensive pedagogical approach that includes all style periods and multiple types of pieces can help students gain important knowledge regarding pedaling in advanced-level repertoire.

Pedal Techniques

Aural Pedaling

One of the problems with how pedaling is often introduced in elementary method books is that it appears to be a visual rather than aural skill. Following the desired learning approach of sound before sight and experience before explanation, pedaling should be introduced initially by rote with a primary focus on the sounds that the pedal can produce. Young pianists should be encouraged to explore the pedals on their own and actually may have already done so. Many students enjoy this aural experience, and it can facilitate much intuitive learning about pedaling.

One-finger Pedal Exercise

Once students need to start pedaling consistently, the teacher should introduce a one-finger pedal exercise that relies on listening rather than visual markings to determine when to change the pedal. The student should play a C major scale slowly (using only the second finger so that they cannot connect the notes with their fingers), pedaling each note and changing the pedal when they hear the next note blur with the previous one. This approach helps the student gain the proper coordination between hands and feet without any other notational or technical distractions. By observing this exercise, teachers can tell immediately if a student is having trouble with coordinating the pedaling and to what extent the pedaling is aurally motivated. The objective should be a clean, clear, *legato* pedal change. Once students can hear the sound that results from a proper pedal change in coordination with their foot movement, they will be ready to learn when to change the damper pedal within repertoire pieces.

Speed of Pedaling

As students are learning to pedal using the one-finger pedal exercise, teachers can guide them to listen carefully to the differences in sound created by varying the speed of the pedal change. A quicker change of pedal facilitates a clean and clear *legato*, while a slower pedal change can yield a richer and more expressive overlapped *legato*. Dynamics greatly affect the speed of the pedal change: louder sounds, especially in thicker textures, need a slightly longer time to clear between pedal changes.

Legato Fingering

Pianists should use *legato* fingering when pedaling, and not merely rely on the pedal to connect notes. The combination of *legato* fingering with the use of the damper pedal is especially important for performing a singing melody and any other lyrical lines.

When and How to Pedal

How does a student learn when the pedal should be used if the composer has not given any indication in the score? The damper pedal is normally used for the following:

1) Single notes. The pedal can enhance the tone quality of even a single note, due to the production of overtones. When the dampers lift off the strings, the strings corresponding to the notes in the overtone series above the performed note or notes will vibrate sympathetically if the piano has good tuning. This results in a more resonant tone quality.
2) Long notes. The pedal can be used to help sustain chords or notes longer than if the pedal is not used.
3) Blocked chords. The damper pedal can be used to connect chords smoothly, as in hymn or chorale-style textures. The pianist should change the pedal with each new harmony, which can happen quite quickly with a fast harmonic rhythm. Pianists sometimes do not change the pedal when there are only one or two altered notes, such as through implied chord changes using passing tones. Although there are many exceptions to this principle, it is generally better to change the pedal throughout any implied chord changes. Pianists should still try to use as much *legato* fingering as possible.

4) Broken chords. The pedal can be used to connect and blend any broken-chord passages. As with blocked chords, the pedal should be changed when the implied harmony changes.
5) Bell-tones. Pedaling a single note while playing the note *staccato* results in a "bell-tone" effect, in which the sound blooms quickly and then dies away. This is particularly helpful for creating a very loud, resonant sound.
6) Two-note slurs. The pedal can be used to clarify the shape and articulation of two-note slurs and other small articulation gestures.
7) Loud dynamics. The pedal can increase the volume of both single notes and fuller chords. Holding the pedal down for an extended period allows sound to accumulate and therefore overall volume to increase.
8) Special effects. Sometimes a composer wants a deliberately blurry sound or other special effects that can be produced by the pedal, with its ability to produce a variety of sounds.

Generally, avoid using the pedal in:

1) Passages with mixed articulations. Using the pedal during passages that have many different articulations will blur the articulation.
2) Arpeggios in melodic passages. Sometimes in two-part textures, a melodic line incorporating arpeggiated figures would seem to indicate the use of the pedal. However, using the pedal in these passages would result in the creation of harmony rather than a melody, and thus it should be avoided.
3) Rests. Rests in music usually provide much-needed breaths in the sound, so the pianist should generally not pedal through them. There are exceptions to this principle, though, depending upon the composer and the musical context.

Historical Style Period Considerations

Once students gain some basic understanding of and coordination with pedaling, they can begin to explore pedaling considerations related to the various historical style periods and individual composers. In music of the

Renaissance, Baroque, and Classical periods, the pedal is used sparingly, and usually not to the full depth. Significant musical maturity and experience are required for a pianist to comprehend the subtle uses of the pedal in these historical style periods. Romantic-period music typically involves extensive use of pedaling that is more intuitive, so it may be easier for pianists to master pedaling in this style first. Impressionistic music as well as other repertoire with thicker or more complicated textures require a very skillful use of the pedal with much control over many musical elements and should be delayed until after a student can properly pedal Romantic-period repertoire. Contemporary music of the twentieth century and beyond can vary widely, with many different pedaling needs.

Pedaling Influences and Variables

As with all musical elements, pedaling decisions require careful aural attention and should not be made independently of any other performance aspects. Many elements influence pedaling, only some of which the pianist can monitor and control. Some of the fixed elements of the instrument over which the pianist has little control are the quality of regulation and consistency, and the dynamic range and tonal palette. The pianist has no control over the size of the piano (and possibly its placement) as well as the size and acoustics of the room. The pianist cannot control the performances of other musical collaborators, if any are involved. Examples of elements that the pianist can control include their own dynamic ranges and levels, voicing and balance of the texture, musical character, and articulation. Although pianists should thoughtfully prepare and practice pedaling choices, pedaling always needs constant monitoring and adjustment during performances. Watching an expert pianist's pedaling is quite fascinating, since the foot appears to be in constant motion, sculpting every note with just the right application of pedaling. The ultimate guide to pedaling decisions is the ear.

Pedaling Curriculum

Consistent and Regular Overlapping Pedal Changes

Students should master basic overlapping pedaling by rote using the one-finger pedal exercise first and then study pieces in which appropriate pedaling is very patterned and consistent. An example of this consistency would be a regular change of pedal at the downbeat of each measure. Repertoire should be selected that allows the student to use a full basic overlapping pedal technique, with the focus being on a clean pedal change coordinated through careful listening. Students who still need more practice with consistent pedaling can study many similar examples in elementary-level repertoire.

Repertoire: Consistent and Regular Overlapping Pedal Changes
Beach: *Children's Album*, Op. 36, No. 3—Waltz
Burgmüller: *18 Characteristic Studies*, Op. 109, No. 7—Lullaby
Burgmüller: *18 Characteristic Studies*, Op. 109, No. 11—Serenade
Chaminade: *Album for the Young*, Book 2, Op. 126, No. 2—Aubade
Chaminade: *Album for the Young*, Book 2, Op. 126, No. 7—Élégie
Schumann: *Album for the Young*, Op. 68, No. 14—Little Study
Schumann: *Album for the Young*, Op. 68, No. 35—Mignon

Frequent but Patterned Pedal Changes

Once a student has mastered slower, consistent overlapping pedaling, the student is ready to play pieces that require a more sophisticated pedaling technique. This includes pieces that require frequent pedal changes, especially pieces with chordal textures. It would be best to first play pieces with frequent pedal changes at slower tempos, to allow the student to hear the changes clearly and master the physical coordination. Frequent pedal changes that are consistent and patterned will be easier than those in which pedal changes are inconsistent with different rhythms and patterns.

Repertoire: Frequent but Patterned Pedal Changes in Slower Tempos
Gillock: *Lyric Preludes in Romantic Style*—A Faded Letter
Gillock: *Lyric Preludes in Romantic Style*—Autumn Sketch

Repertoire: Frequent but Patterned Pedal Changes in Faster Tempos
Burgmüller: *25 Progressive Pieces*, Op. 100, No. 7—The Clear Stream (pedal with chord changes)
Burgmüller: *18 Characteristic Studies*, Op. 109, No. 1—Confidence (pedal more consistently than is notated)
Burgmüller: *18 Characteristic Studies*, Op. 109, No. 8—Agitato (pedal more consistently than is notated)
Gurlitt: *Album for the Young*, Op. 140, No. 11—Longing (pedal each beat)
Schumann: *Album for the Young*, Op. 68, No. 41—Norse Song (pedal each chord)

Frequent Pedal Changes in Inconsistent or Un-patterned Settings

Pieces with complicated, inconsistent textures, especially with multiple voices with different rhythms, require a very sophisticated pedaling technique. This type of pedaling is essential for the performance of mature and musically challenging repertoire by composers such as Schumann and Brahms. As with most performance requirements, learning these skills at slower tempos makes them much easier. In addition to the complexities of simply performing the notes, rhythms, voice leading, and balance between the individual parts, the addition of challenging pedaling greatly increases the difficulty. Students should be well into the upper-intermediate level and progressing into early advanced repertoire before attempting these types of pieces.

Repertoire: Frequent Pedal Changes in Inconsistent or Un-patterned Settings in Slower Tempos
Schumann: *Album for the Young*, Op. 68, No. 15—Spring Song
Schumann: *Album for the Young*, Op. 68, No. 16—First Loss

Schumann: *Album for the Young*, Op. 68, No. 30—***
Schumann: *Album for the Young*, Op. 68, No. 34—Theme
Schumann: *Album for the Young*, Op. 68, No. 38—Northern Song
Schumann: *Album for the Young*, Op. 68, No. 39—Wintertime II
Schumann: *Album for the Young*, Op. 68, No. 43—New Year's Eve

Repertoire: Frequent Pedal Changes in Inconsistent and Un-patterned Settings in Faster Tempos
Schumann: *Album for the Young*, Op. 68, No. 19—Little Romance
Schumann: *Album for the Young*, Op. 68, No. 22—Roundelay
Schumann: *Album for the Young*, Op. 68, No. 26—***

Partial or Shallow Pedaling

It is not always desirable to depress the pedal completely. In partial pedaling, sometimes referred to as "half pedaling," "quarter pedaling," or "shallow" pedaling, the dampers do not completely disengage from the strings. This still allows for some pedaling connection and blending but with a less resonant sound. Shallow pedaling can be extremely helpful when there is a need for continuity, but there is enough counterpoint in the texture to lose clarity if a fully depressed pedal is used. A skillful pianist can find many gradations in the depth of the pedal, each of which can contribute to a variety of sound colors.

Shallow pedaling is not usually indicated in musical scores, so it requires training with a teacher for the student to understand when it can be helpful. It is particularly helpful in Classical period pieces, such as when used with an Alberti-bass line to create a tonal foundation without obscuring the melodic line. In passages like these, using a completely depressed pedal would produce a thick texture that is not consistent with the period aesthetic. Shallow pedaling is not restricted to the Classical period—it can be used anytime to create a lighter, less resonant, or perhaps more ethereal sound. Shallow pedaling may allow the pianist to use longer pedals without excessive blurring in the sound. In polyphonic textures where there are moving voices, the use of shallow pedaling can provide the clarity needed while still allowing the pianist to avoid having to pedal every note.

Repertoire: Partial or Shallow Pedaling
Burgmüller: *25 Progressive Pieces*, Op. 100, No. 3—Pastorale
Burgmüller: *25 Progressive Pieces*, Op. 100, No. 21—Angels' Voices
Burgmüller: *25 Progressive Pieces*, Op. 100, No. 24—The Swallow
Burgmüller: *18 Characteristic Studies*, Op. 109, No. 2—The Pearls
Burgmüller: *18 Characteristic Studies*, Op. 109, No. 5—The Spring
Burgmüller: *18 Characteristic Studies*, Op. 109, No. 13—The Storm
Gillock: *Lyric Preludes in Romantic Style*—Forest Murmurs
Schumann: *Album for the Young*, Op. 68, No. 30—***
Schumann: *Album for the Young*, Op. 68, No. 32—Sheherazade

Intermittent and/or Direct Pedaling

Another important use of the pedal is direct pedaling, in which the pianist depresses the pedal at the same time that the notes are depressed. This type of pedaling is frequently used for chords or single notes that need to be strong and articulated. Direct pedaling should not be introduced until a pianist is completely comfortable with the coordination of basic overlapping pedaling first, in order to avoid confusing the two techniques.

Repertoire: Intermittent and/or Direct Pedaling
Burgmüller: *18 Characteristic Studies*, Op. 109, No. 3—The Shepherd's Return
Burgmüller: *18 Characteristic Studies*, Op. 109, No. 4—The Gypsies
Burgmüller: *18 Characteristic Studies*, Op. 109, No. 5—The Spring
Burgmüller: *18 Characteristic Studies*, Op. 109, No. 6—The Merry Maiden
Burgmüller: *18 Characteristic Studies*, Op. 109, No. 15—Sylphs
Burgmüller: *18 Characteristic Studies*, Op. 109, No. 17—March
Schumann: *Album for the Young*, Op. 68, No. 20—Rustic Song

Schumann: *Album for the Young,* Op. 68, No. 23—Horseman's Song (pedal more than notated)
Schumann: *Album for the Young,* Op. 68, No. 28—Remembrance
Schumann: *Album for the Young,* Op. 68, No. 33—Vintage Times

Finger Pedaling

Finger pedaling is not related to the use of the damper pedal, although it can substitute for it, and provides greater flexibility than the foot pedals can. Often used in thin textures, finger pedaling usually involves holding some of the bass notes in the left hand as a way of providing sound continuity without getting a thick, blurred sound. Sometimes finger pedaling is indicated by double-stemmed note values, but often it is a decision made by the performer. This type of pedaling is common in the two-part textures of the Classical period, although it is possible in the Romantic period as well. Finger pedaling can provide some of the same effects as shallow pedaling (See Figure 9.2).

Figure 9.2 Gurlitt: *Album for the Young,* Op. 140, No. 3, mm. 13–16 (author owned).

Repertoire: Finger Pedaling
Burgmüller: *18 Characteristic Studies,* Op. 109, No. 14—Song of the Gondolier
Burgmüller: *18 Characteristic Studies,* Op. 109, No. 15—Sylphs
Gurlitt: *Album for the Young,* Op. 140, No. 3—The Sky is Bright
Tchaikovsky: *Album for the Young,* Op. 39, No. 4—Mamma

Flutter Pedaling

Flutter pedaling occurs when the pianist moves the foot up and down in a rapid motion without completely releasing the pedal. Flutter pedaling serves to eliminate some of the previously accumulated sound or prevent too much blurring of the sound while retaining some continuity. Intermediate-level students may have trouble with this pedaling, since it requires significant aural and technical control.

10

Musical Expression

All of the musical elements discussed thus far in this book contribute to the expressiveness of a piece. The composer crafts fixed elements, such as the pitches, rhythmic patterns, harmony, and form, and also notates flexible indications that the performer manipulates, such as the dynamics and articulation. Performers synthesize these elements with a sense of musical phrasing, tempo, harmonic tension/resolution, and tone color to be able to play more expressively. This chapter explores how these elements contribute to musical expression and offers teaching approaches to support students' expressive development.

Form and Musical Analysis

Exploring the expressive content of any piece should begin with musical analysis, starting with a foundational understanding of the form. At the early-elementary level, students begin understanding form by identifying whether musical material is the same or different. Through the intermediate level, students should be able to determine same and different with more nuance. Differences in musical material might include the following:

1) Two or more phrases that are significantly different from each other, labelled by the letters A, B, C, D.
2) Two or more phrases that are generally the same but with some differences, labelled as A^1, A^2, A^3, A^4.

3) Two or more phrases that begin exactly the same but end differently, as in a period structure in which the first phrase (antecedent) ends inconclusively and the second phrase (consequent) ends conclusively.

Form Curriculum

Form competencies for intermediate-level students should include the following:

1) Understand and identify standard forms common in intermediate-level piano music such as binary, ternary, theme and variations, and through-composed. (Common forms such as the sonata/sonatina and fugue are not prevalent in intermediate-level Romantic-period repertoire.)
2) Strengthen awareness of form through an understanding of cadences by practicing cadential patterns and typical chord progressions in all major and minor keys.
3) Identify various parts of a form such as the introduction, thematic content, interpolations or transitions, and coda.
4) Identify phrases within sections of a piece or movement and create an appropriate phrase hierarchy within each section or movement.

Common Musical Forms

Binary Form (AB)

Binary form is a two-part form (AB) that composers have been using for centuries. The A section usually modulates to the dominant key if the piece is in a major mode or to the relative major key if the piece is in a minor mode. The B section begins in the new key and then modulates back to the first key. Both sections are usually repeated, so the form is actually AABB. The clarity of the harmonic structure defines each section, and both sections often have clear phrasing within them.

Ternary Form (ABA)

Ternary form is the most common musical form found in Romantic-period music. The middle section often provides great contrast, and the return of the

A section has numerous opportunities for differences in musical expression. The final A section has been transformed in some way by the contrasting B section, so it must be played differently. This is where imagery or metaphors can provide inspiration: for example, the second A section could be a reflective and restful return home after an exciting excursion or a triumphant celebration over intervening struggles.

Theme and Variations

A theme and variations form consists of a simple theme, often in a homophonic texture, followed by a number of variations that retain the same general structure and harmonic content of the theme. The variations are often like musical etudes, with each one exhibiting a specific technique, pattern, or texture. Sometimes composers will change one or more of the variations to a different mode. Variations can be sectional, with pauses between them, or continuous, flowing from one to the next without any breaks. In sectional variations, the pacing or timing between the variations requires much consideration: variations that are dramatic with great energy need to be followed by longer pauses, while other variations can continue to move forward fluidly. Variations of similar characters can also be played as sub-groups.

Through-Composed

Through-composed pieces usually do not have any clearly repeated musical material, often consisting instead of the repetition of a specific musical figuration. One of the most common genres in this form is the prelude. Because this form often does not have a typical melody, a major challenge is to delineate phrasing through slight pauses. Planning dynamics in a through-composed piece can also be challenging.

Identifying Various Parts of a Composition

Various parts of a composition serve different functions and therefore have different expressive goals. In a typical composition, a composer might begin with an introduction, present melodic material (often referred to as "themes") in clearly delineated phrases, possibly insert transitional musical material or interpolations in between phrases or sections, and conclude with a coda.

A basic introduction may consist of an ostinato or other common accompaniment pattern that establishes the character, tonality, and rhythmic flow of the piece but does not necessarily present any thematic material. Students should not give these introductions too much musical expression, since they usually do not present any thematic material. These introductions usually flow seamlessly into the first important thematic phrase, at which time the student should demonstrate an obvious difference in the musical texture.

Another type of introduction might present a declamatory or dramatic statement, which should be dynamically stronger and brighter in tone quality, setting the tone of the piece from the beginning. These introductions would need a more significant transition to the main thematic section, possibly through a pause on a note or a rest. The pianist has to perform any introduction based upon its inherent character and purpose within the form of the piece.

Composers present thematic material in various formats. Sometimes phrases follow a clearly defined period structure of antecedent and consequent. Composers may also create a series of phrase chains with inconclusive cadences that eventually conclude with a resolution to the tonic. Musical material that comes in between thematic phrases is often referred to as an interpolation or a transition.

Finally, composers often conclude pieces with a coda. Because material in the coda is usually moving toward conclusion rather than leading toward something new, pianists must align their musical expressiveness within the musical purpose of the coda.

Phrasing

Once students have determined the basic form of a piece, they should identify the phrasing within each section or movement. The typical arch-shaped lyrical phrase usually begins softer, moves toward the climax, and tapers off until its conclusion. Chapter 2 discusses phrasing as related to melody: phrase climaxes often occur on the highest note, on a strong beat, and/or on a longer note value compared to those around it. The simultaneous joining of two or all three of these criteria strengthens the possibility that the phrase shape may reach its climax at that point. A significant harmonic arrival at the same time further strengthens the climax. An important tool for projecting phrasing clearly is to conclude one phrase before the start of the next one, finishing musical ideas before starting new ones. Inexperienced students who have not yet mastered the art of timing can be encouraged to take a breath physically at the end of each phrase to begin sensing this artistic concept.

Cadential Patterns and Chord Progressions

An understanding of form includes an understanding of functional harmony. Many students will be able to recognize phrases intuitively, especially through the analogy that a phrase is like a musical "sentence," but they still need to have a comprehensive understanding of the principles behind their intuition. Identifying clear cadences is one way for students to be able to identify phrases. Elementary-level students should have already learned primary chord progressions and cadences in all major (I-IV-I-V7-I) and minor (i-iv-i-V7-i) keys, but these can be expanded to include longer chord progressions such as I-vi-IV-ii6-I$^6_4$-V7-I and i-VI-iv- ii°6-i$^6_4$-V7-i. Teachers should guide students to apply knowledge from these keyboard skills to their repertoire pieces.

Structurally Significant Notes

Within each phrase, not every note has the same importance. Teachers who are familiar with Schenkerian analysis will understand that certain pitches within a phrase are more structurally important than others, functioning as a skeleton for the whole phrase. Students should shape phrases by emphasizing the structurally important notes. In Burgmüller's *Gracefulness*, Op. 100, No. 8, the important structural notes are the eighth notes on each downbeat, while the notes in between merely decorate the structural notes. A helpful practice technique is to alter the score temporarily to play just the structural notes to hear the basic skeleton of the phrase. When returning to playing the phrase as written, students should demonstrate a new perception of the phrase.

Personal Emotional Connection

Once students understand the basic phrasing of a piece, they should be encouraged to feel personally the ebb and flow of each phrase, with a clear physical sensation of climax arrivals and resolutions. All humans have the innate ability to respond to the artistic communication of emotions, moods, and experiences. Experiencing musical events through an emotional connection can help students better communicate expressively to listeners. It is not enough merely to play the details found in the musical notation or try to play phrases as others play them.

While some students may have a deep personal connection with their playing, they may hesitate to project this in public performances. Teachers can encourage students and give them many opportunities for performances to help them feel comfortable communicating their emotions. Teachers should caution students, however, against simply playing phrases merely as they "feel" them; students should be able to combine their natural feeling for the music with established considerations of form and other musical parameters.

Phrase Hierarchy

To create a unified section or movement while still maintaining individual phrase shapes, it is helpful to view different phrases of a section within a hierarchy of importance. As pianists learn to play more expressively, they often start shaping every phrase with the same dynamic levels, leading to too much similarity. Instead, pianists should experiment with numerous ways to shape phrases, altering musical contours, climax points, dynamic levels, timing, or character. The first phrase of the piece often should not have as much dramatic shaping as phrases later in the piece, so pianists should save the most expressive playing for the more climactic moments. Repeated phrases can be played differently with each iteration for effective contrast and sense of direction. Pianists should understand that musical lines having the greatest dynamic shaping will be the ones that the listener gravitates toward, so expressiveness should be stronger in the melody and more limited in the accompaniment. It can be helpful to remind students that regarding musical shaping, sometimes *less* shaping is preferred, and just because you *can* shape every phrase significantly does not mean you *should*.

Once hierarchy between phrases has been established, it should be applied on a larger scale, related to large sections and even movements of a work. Multimovement pieces require pianists to think about how these movements relate to each other and how much time they should pause in between movements.

Phrase Groups with Multiple Inconclusive Phrases

Conclusive phrases end with a return to the tonic, while inconclusive phrases usually end on the dominant. In Romantic-period repertoire, composers frequently create a restless or unfulfilled emotional character through a chain of inconclusive phrases. Inconclusive phrase groupings may include shorter phrases followed by one longer concluding phrase, with the final phrase often possessing the climactic arrival point for the entire section. Delaying significant arrival points often heightens the sense of melodic climax and strengthens the eventual return to the tonic.

Repertoire: Phrase Groups with Multiple Inconclusive Phrases
Burgmüller: *18 Characteristic Studies*, Op. 109, No. 13—The Storm
Gillock: *Lyric Preludes in Romantic Style*—Forest Murmurs
Grieg: *Lyric Pieces*, Op. 38, No. 6—Elegie
Grieg: *Lyric Pieces*, Op. 43, No. 6—To the Spring
Grieg: *Lyric Pieces*, Op. 54, No. 4—Notturno
Grieg: *Lyric Pieces*, Op. 71, No. 3—Puck
Schumann: *Album for the Young*, Op. 68, No. 15—Spring Song
Schumann: *Album for the Young*, Op. 68, No. 21—***
Schumann: *Album for the Young*, Op. 68, No. 35—Mignon
Tchaikovsky: *Album for the Young*, Op. 39, No. 1—Morning Prayer

Asymmetrical Phrasing

Asymmetrical phrases have irregular phrase lengths in contrast to symmetrical phrasing. Counting the number of measures in each phrase is one easy but revealing way to help students become aware of asymmetrical phrases. Asymmetrical phrasing occurs in many Romantic-period pieces, specifically nationalistic works, as composers from individual countries and cultures began to take an interest in expressing their own styles. This music typically includes the use of simple folk melodies that have irregular phrase lengths.

Repertoire: Asymmetrical Phrasing
Grieg: *Lyric Pieces*, Op. 47, No. 6—Norwegian March (B section)
Schumann: *Album for the Young*, Op. 68, No. 43—New Year's Eve
Tchaikovsky: *Album for the Young*, Op. 39, No. 11—Russian Song (6 measures)
Tchaikovsky: *Album for the Young*, Op. 39, No. 13—Folk-Song—(3 and 6 measures)
Tchaikovsky: *Album for the Young*, Op. 39, No. 23—The Handorgan Man (12 measures: 2+3+3+4)

Interpolations

Composers may insert non-thematic musical material in between phrases that is often figurational and may have a different texture. Pianists should perform these sections differently so that it is clear to the listener that they are transitional rather than thematic.

Repertoire: Interpolations
Beach: *Children's Album*, Op. 36, No. 5—Polka (mm. 50–53)
Burgmüller: *18 Characteristic Studies*, Op. 109, No. 3—The Shepherd's Return (mm. 36–39)
Chaminade: *Album for the Young*, Book 1, Op. 123, No. 1—(untitled) (mm. 9–12)
Chaminade: *Album for the Young*, Book 1, Op. 123, No. 5—Gavotte (mm. 31–34)
Gillock: *Lyric Preludes in Romantic Style*—Fountain of Diana (arpeggiations between phrases)
Gillock: *Lyric Preludes in Romantic Style*—October Morning (*pp* chords)

Phrases Consisting of Continuous Short Motives

In addition to the standard arch, phrases can take other shapes. Phrases in pieces that are less lyrical in character may consist of a series of short motives rather than singing melodies. Often these motives involve articulation that makes the perception of long phrases challenging. Motives consisting of dotted rhythms are particularly difficult, since students tend to pause on the dotted notes rather than playing the dotted-rhythm patterns within a larger pulse grouping. Following the practice principle of temporarily altering the score to improve musical perception, the articulations can be removed and dotted rhythms can be changed to even rhythms to facilitate the hearing of a longer line. Practicing these pieces with altered elements helps students continue to maintain hearing the longer phrases internally once they return to playing the passage as written.

Repertoire: Phrases Consisting of Continuous Short Motives
Burgmüller: *18 Characteristic Studies*, Op. 109, No. 8—Agitato
Gillock: *Lyric Preludes in Romantic Style*—Autumn Sketch
Grieg: *Lyric Pieces*, Op. 62, No. 1—Sylph
Gurlitt: *Album for the Young*, Op. 140, No. 6—Catch Me!
Schumann: *Album for the Young*, Op. 68, No. 12—Knight Rupert
Schumann: *Album for the Young*, Op. 68, No. 23—Horseman's Song
Tchaikovsky: *Album for the Young*, Op. 39, No. 14—Polka

Phrasing that Moves across Rests

Phrasing that moves across rests causes many of the same problems as phrases consisting of short motives. Because it may be difficult to alter these passages to be able to physically connect the musical line temporarily, one practice technique would be to vocally sing the phrase, connecting all of the breaks to hear a more continuous line. Once this phrase continuity has been experienced, the student will be more able to maintain it when the rests have been restored to the piece.

Repertoire: Phrasing that Moves across Rests
Burgmüller: *25 Progressive Pieces*, Op. 100, No. 18—Inquiétude
Burgmüller: *25 Progressive Pieces*, Op. 100, No. 25—The Knight Errant
Burgmüller: *18 Characteristic Studies*, Op. 109, No. 11—Serenade
Burgmüller: *18 Characteristic Studies*, Op. 109, No. 15—Sylphs
Grieg: *Lyric Pieces*, Op. 62, No. 1—Sylph

Gurlitt: *Album for the Young*, Op. 140, No. 7—The Festive Dance
Gurlitt: *Album for the Young*, Op. 140, No. 15—Will-o-the-Wisp
Tchaikovsky: *Album for the Young*, Op. 39, No. 2—A Winter Morning
Tchaikovsky: *Album for the Young*, Op. 39, No. 5—March of the Tin Soldiers
Tchaikovsky: *Album for the Young*, Op. 39, No. 8—Waltz

Long Musical Phrases

Because elementary-level students have been accustomed to playing short four-measure phrases, the intermediate level is an important developmental period for learning to play longer phrases. Playing a longer phrase requires focused aural attention through the entire musical phrase shape. Many of the repertoire pieces in the collections referenced in this book include eight-measure phrases. Suggested phrase lengths are provided for each piece in the musical annotations in Part II.

Dynamics

Continuing to follow the important principle of sound before sight and experience before explanation, teachers should first introduce dynamics aurally to students at the elementary level. The teacher can perform a piece on the piano or play an audio recording with a range of dynamic levels, then lead the student to discover different dynamics by rote and through improvisational exploration at the keyboard. The student can then experiment with dynamics in a more structured way by adding dynamics to familiar technical exercises such as basic scales. Once students can hear and produce different dynamics, they are ready to connect aural dynamic levels with the dynamic markings and symbols in repertoire notation.

Dynamic Markings

Piano students first encounter notated dynamics in their elementary-level piano method books through abbreviations for Italian terms that identify sound volume, such as *forte* and *piano*. Elementary-level students often think of dynamic markings as indicating isolated sound levels always played in the same way. This is not uncommon, as students at this level usually do not have the ability to consistently produce and control many levels of dynamics, nor do they have the musical maturity to interpret or understand sophisticated dynamic expressiveness.

The intermediate level is an appropriate time to broaden a student's concept of dynamics. An important foundational principle is that dynamic levels are always contextual and relative. A *forte* dynamic is different when played by a flutist, brass player, woodwind trio, chamber orchestra, or marching band. While there are only a limited number of dynamic level markings, there is an infinite number of gradations within each level, as a *forte* dynamic may be different depending upon its context.

If students do not differentiate parts of a musical texture dynamically, the texture will be unclear. A single dynamic marking defines a volume level for the total sonority, but not for every part of the texture. The melody, for example, should sound louder than the accompaniment. Students should listen to the entire sonority rather than isolating dynamic levels for the individual parts.

Understanding dynamics also means understanding the many variables that influence sound volume. A brighter tonal color usually sounds louder than a muted or darker tone color. The acoustics of the instrument, the room size and configuration as well as the various items in it, and the number of people present all contribute to the perception of dynamics.

Dynamics Curriculum

Goals related to performing dynamics for intermediate-level pianists should include the following essential skills:

1) Perform a wide range of dynamic levels while maintaining a consistently good tone quality.
2) Perform smooth dynamic shaping through phrases of different lengths.
3) Perform sudden dynamic changes at various levels.
4) Balance dynamics within chords to voice (bring out) individual chord tones, usually the top notes.

5) Balance homophonic textures that have the melody in either hand.
6) Balance and control contrapuntal textures to maintain linear voice leading.
7) Maintain balance through shifting textures and range changes.

Producing Different Dynamic Levels

Rarely do method books provide instructions on how to produce different dynamic levels at the piano. Students often use muscular force or push into the keys to make loud sounds. Many pianists rely primarily on individual finger strokes to play louder, often using high finger motions. Fingers articulate the notes, but since there are no muscles in the fingers, they do not have the "strength" to play independent of the rest of the body. Trying to achieve *forte* playing with fingers alone can lead to a lot of physical tension and a high potential for injuries. Excessive physical tension or "holding" in any part of the body can create a constricted sound.

Paradoxically, students also may develop tension when trying to play softer, holding back in the arms and shoulders to avoid producing too much sound. In addition, failure to maintain a good hand position with stable finger joints can result in a weak, unfocused sound, especially at softer dynamic levels.

Instead, pianists can create different dynamics through speed of attack into the keys, which clearly aligns with how to produce a sound on the piano. Speed of attack should also be coordinated with arm weight and release. Varying the amount of arm weight released into the key can produce different sound colors and dynamic levels. Intermediate-level students should focus on producing variety in dynamics primarily through speed of attack before later applying more subtle changes of arm weight to achieve a wider dynamic range and tonal palette. The coordinated, relaxed, and balanced use of fingers, hands/wrists, forearms, and the entire body is essential for producing and sustaining different volume levels while maintaining a good sound quality.

Changes of Dynamics

As with other musical competencies and skills, regular practicing of dynamic control should begin within the easiest musical settings or exercises that allow the student to focus solely on the dynamics. This could include pacing of *crescendo* and *diminuendo* by repeating a single note, gradually becoming louder then softer. Next, the student can practice the same dynamic changes on a five-note scale ascending and descending, followed by *crescendo* and *diminuendo* on a major scale ascending and descending in one octave. Students should initially avoid a slow tempo so that the sound does not decay significantly between notes.

To practice controlling the speed of attack of the first note, students should practice playing isolated notes or chords using different dynamic levels. An effective activity might involve the teacher randomly calling out various dynamic levels to determine how well the student can adapt to quickly playing different volume levels. This exercise can also help students develop more specificity about dynamic levels at the start of phrases or after rests.

Sudden Dynamic Changes

Another challenge for the intermediate-level pianist is to rapidly change from one dynamic level to another. A standard four-measure phrase with a clear arch shape that builds slowly to the climax at a moderate tempo will be easier to master than one with more rapid dynamic changes. Students can practice dynamic changes at moderate tempos and then practice quicker changes of dynamics within both slower and faster tempos once they gain greater control. In addition to the ability to produce sound at varying dynamic levels, students must master the ability to balance different dynamic levels between hands and within one hand.

Repertoire: Sudden Dynamic Changes
Burgmüller: *25 Progressive Pieces*, Op. 100, No. 25—The Knight Errant
Burgmüller: *18 Characteristic Studies*, Op. 109, No. 4—The Gypsies
Burgmüller: *18 Characteristic Studies*, Op. 109, No. 14—Song of the Gondolier
Burgmüller: *18 Characteristic Studies*, Op. 109, No. 15—Sylphs
Burgmüller: *18 Characteristic Studies*, Op. 109, No. 16—Parting
Gillock: *Lyric Preludes in Romantic Style*—Phantom Rider
Grieg: *Lyric Pieces*, Op. 12, No. 4—Dance of the Elves (Elfin Dance)
Schumann: *Album for the Young*, Op. 68, No. 7—Hunting Song

Schumann: *Album for the Young*, Op. 68, No. 19—Little Romance

Repertoire: Wide Dynamic Ranges
Burgmüller: *18 Characteristic Studies*, Op. 109, No. 4—The Gypsies
Burgmüller: *18 Characteristic Studies*, Op. 109, No. 9—Morning Bell
Burgmüller: *18 Characteristic Studies*, Op. 109, No. 13—The Storm
Burgmüller: *18 Characteristic Studies*, Op. 109, No. 17—March
Gillock: *Lyric Preludes in Romantic Style*—Phantom Rider
Grieg: *Lyric Pieces*, Op. 12, No. 8—National Song (Song of the Fatherland)
Grieg: *Lyric Pieces*, Op. 54, No. 2—Norwegian March
Grieg: *Lyric Pieces*, Op. 54, No. 5—Scherzo
Grieg: *Lyric Pieces*, Op. 71, No. 3—Puck

Repertoire: Long *Crescendo* or *Diminuendo*
Burgmüller: *25 Progressive Pieces*, Op. 100, No. 20—Tarantelle
Grieg: *Lyric Pieces*, Op. 43, No. 6—To the Spring
Grieg: *Lyric Pieces*, Op. 54, No. 2—Norwegian March
Grieg: *Lyric Pieces*, Op. 54, No. 4—Notturno
Grieg: *Lyric Pieces*, Op. 57, No. 2—Gade
Grieg: *Lyric Pieces*, Op. 71, No. 3—Puck
Tchaikovsky: *Album for the Young*, Op. 39, No. 3—The Hobby-Horse
Tchaikovsky: *Album for the Young*, Op. 39, No. 19—The Nurse's Tale

Repertoire: Mixture of Dynamics Requirements
Burgmüller: *18 Characteristic Studies*, Op. 109, No. 5—The Spring
Burgmüller: *18 Characteristic Studies*, Op. 109, No. 7—Lullaby
Burgmüller: *18 Characteristic Studies*, Op. 109, No. 8—Agitato
Burgmüller: *18 Characteristic Studies*, Op. 109, No. 9—Morning Bell
Burgmüller: *18 Characteristic Studies*, Op. 109, No. 10—Velocity
Burgmüller: *18 Characteristic Studies*, Op. 109, No. 11—Serenade
Burgmüller: *18 Characteristic Studies*, Op. 109, No. 12—Awakening in the Woods
Burgmüller: *18 Characteristic Studies*, Op. 109, No. 17—March
Grieg: *Lyric Pieces*, Op. 12, No. 3—Watchman's Song (Intermezzo section)

Tempo *Rubato* and Pacing

Tempo *Rubato*

Romantic-period music makes extensive use of tempo *rubato*, which means to "rob" or "steal" time. Tempo *rubato* implies a give-and-take approach to timing, with some beats compressed and others elongated. Tempo *rubato* should not be arbitrary; it should express the various elements of the piece at all structural levels.

Multiple Tempo Changes in One Piece

Expressive pieces may have different sections, each with their own character. This often involves changes in tempo, key/mode, melodic content, rhythmic patterns, dynamic levels, character, articulation, texture, and pedaling. A *fermata* over a note or rest often assists the performer in the transition to a new section. The pianist has to make decisions such as how long to hold the *fermata*, whether there should be a complete pedal break before the new section if the *fermata* is on a note, and how long the silent pauses should be. This understanding of pacing requires maturing artistry; it is difficult to teach this skill, since pacing implies a distinct sense of what feels right as a result of much experience.

An initial approach to pacing involves the pianist determining an appropriate metronome marking for each section and practicing each section consistently at that tempo. Students can practice making a complete stop and then taking time to audiate a measure or two of the new section, followed by playing a few measures and then checking the tempo with the metronome. Once students can start the new section consistently close to the desired tempo, they can then experiment with the length of pauses between the sections, and whether or not a break in sound/pedaling is appropriate.

An important point to remember is that pacing depends upon all of the musical elements, but especially upon the amount of energy generated in the previous section. A climax with more energy and sound usually means that a longer transition to the next section is needed, especially if the next section is much softer and slower.

Sometimes the pause between sections needs to have a significant "breath" before the next section commences. Students can sometimes be uncomfortable with a prolonged pause but should be aware that silence is an essential part of musical expression. Students can practice listening to repertoire that includes multiple sections to pinpoint aurally the start of each section after a pause, then practice doing the same thing within their own repertoire.

<u>Repertoire: Multiple Tempo Changes in One Piece</u>
Chaminade: *Album for the Young*, Book 2, Op. 126, No. 11—Conte de Fées
Chaminade: *Album for the Young*, Book 2, Op. 126, No. 12—Valse Mignonne
Grieg: *Lyric Pieces*, Op. 38, No. 7—Waltz
Grieg: *Lyric Pieces*, Op. 57, No. 6—Homesickness
Grieg: *Lyric Pieces*, Op. 68, No. 4—Evening in the Mountains
Schumann: *Album for the Young*, Op. 68, No. 9—Folk Song
Schumann: *Album for the Young*, Op. 68, No. 39—Wintertime II

Harmony

Harmonic activity that is predictable fosters a calm, stable, and peaceful character. Predictable harmonic activity includes normal chord progressions with clear cadences, moderate harmonic rhythm, and the use of diatonic chords. Unpredictable or unexpected harmonic activity creates interest and intensity. Unexpected harmonic activity might include chord progressions that move far away from, or do not return to, the tonic, unusual or abrupt modulations, deceptive cadences, unexpected key relationships, secondary dominant- and diminished-seventh chords, dissonant or chromatic chords, or rapid changes in the harmonic rhythm.

Tension/Resolution

An important expressive device is the creation of tension/resolution. An increase in musical tension within a phrase heightens the sense of musical climax. While tension/resolution involves many elements, tension usually strengthens with the arrival of cadential patterns and relaxes when the phrase reaches a conclusion. Teachers can help students analyze the harmonic structure of a piece to discern points of musical tension. Students should continue the sense of musical tension through climax points with a growing intensity, without letting the musical tension and energy sag or diminish.

Repertoire: Tension/Resolution
Burgmüller: *25 Progressive Pieces*, Op. 100, No. 12—The Farewell
Burgmüller: *18 Characteristic Studies*, Op. 109, No. 9—Morning Bell
Burgmüller: *18 Characteristic Studies*, Op. 109, No. 13—The Storm
Grieg: *Lyric Pieces*, Op. 12, No. 1—Arietta
Grieg: *Lyric Pieces*, Op. 54, No. 4—Notturno
Grieg: *Lyric Pieces*, Op. 65, No. 5—Ballad
Grieg: *Lyric Pieces*, Op. 68, No. 3—At Your Feet
Gurlitt: *Album for the Young*, Op. 140, No. 13—The Little Wanderer
Schumann: *Album for the Young*, Op. 68, No. 15—Spring Song
Tchaikovsky: *Album for the Young*, Op. 39, No. 21—Sweet Dreams

Tone Color

A prerequisite for expressive playing is the ability to produce and maintain a good sound quality, which the typical intermediate-level student has not usually mastered. Students who cannot control sound may have trouble successfully manipulating either dynamic levels or tonal colors.

Piano tone color is a somewhat ambiguous concept that can be difficult to describe, but often a comparison between different instruments can help students hear differences in timbres. This is an excellent reason for students to become aware of the unique tonal qualities of the instruments of the orchestra. This concept obviously depends upon students having heard the different instruments of the orchestra often enough to retain an aural image of their sound. While all instruments are capable of a variety of unique sonorities, their basic tone quality differs from one instrument to another. Teachers can help students develop a list of descriptive adjectives similar to the following:

Brass: bright, brilliant, resonant, clean, clear
Strings: warm, rich, ethereal, transparent, delicate, shimmering
Woodwind reeds: mournful, penetrating, raspy, quirky, mellow
Flutes: airy, warm, delicate, sweet, brilliant

The challenge is in trying to convey these sonorities on the piano; how does a pianist play in a penetrating, shimmering, or transparent way? The best approach is to guide students to experiment with different ways of tone production to discover sonorities that have similar effects to different instruments. Students can then apply these to their repertoire through the process of orchestration, which involves correlating different musical materials with different orchestral timbres.

Visual art can also be an inspiration for tone color. Colors are images that can inspire variations or shadings in sound, such as royal blue for a melody with pale blue for the accompaniment, yellow for a bright sound, or white for a bleak, empty sound. Note that these are only images, not actual colors, although an extremely small percentage of people who have synesthesia can connect sounds with actual colors.

While the concept of tone color may be challenging to describe, pianists whose playing demonstrates tonal colors possess a significant asset in the attainment of expressiveness and variety.

Musical Character

The development of musical expression should begin during the elementary level through repertoire that overtly demonstrates different musical characters. Young students combine their vivid imaginations with an uninhibited exploration of their world, so pieces should focus on their experiences with people, animals, things, places, or events. Eventually, teachers should help students discover character elements within pieces that do not have explicit nonmusical connections. Character involves the fusion of all musical elements rather than any individual one.

Some indications in the score of different musical characters might include the following:

1) Peaceful: *legato* articulation, consistent slower tempo, melody in a limited range, even note values, use of pedaling, softer dynamics, predictable diatonic harmony.
2) Majestic: thick texture with large chords in both hands, a slower or broad tempo, loud dynamics, use of pedaling.
3) Passionate: a *cantabile* melody with many vocal leaps, significant use of tempo *rubato*, rhythmically active accompaniment, frequent dynamic changes within a wide dynamic range, unpredictable chromatic harmony with modulations and inconclusive cadences.
4) Quirky: use of many different rhythmic patterns with a variety of different articulations, broken-chord accompaniment patterns, chromatic harmony, moderate tempo.
5) Restless or uncertain: unpredictable harmonic progressions that avoid the tonic, fast tempo, disjunct melody, sudden dynamic changes, fast or changing harmonic rhythm.

By analyzing the musical elements to establish the overall musical character of a piece, students can associate the character with previous personal or musical experiences, leading to more imaginative and inspired expressiveness.

Variety of Repertoire

The intermediate level is an important period in which students should study many short compositions from all historical-style periods to explore their essential musical elements, leading to the possibility of more meaningful musical expression. Ideally, students have already had some experience with this repertoire, including both original style period pieces and similar contemporary pedagogical works, since there is a large amount of it available at the upper elementary level.

Mastering the musical elements requires significant patience from both students and their teachers, as students are typically more interested in playing repertoire that is more technically difficult rather than exploring greater musical sophistication within less challenging pieces. Teachers need a steady persistence combined with judicious repertoire choices to keep intermediate-level students engaged in all areas of their piano development.

Listening

Some students have a great deal of natural musical ability. They seem to be musically intuitive and easily develop into expressive performers. Can students who are less talented also learn to play expressively? Yes, and teachers are responsible for giving students the analytical tools they need to do this. How do students learn to play with sensitivity? As with all music learning, an aural image should precede all other instruction whenever possible: students learn to play with expression by listening to other performers play with expression. Since listening to "live" music can be an experience that transcends other listening options, students need to have as many opportunities as possible to hear excellent pianists in person. While live performances are preferable, virtually all students have the opportunity to hear great musicians perform online at any time. While modern technology supplies recorded performances of some of the greatest pianists in the history of Western music, students who are studying piano regularly should also hear their own teachers' playing frequently.

Teacher Modeling

The history of piano teaching informs us that the practice of teacher modeling dates back several centuries. The one-to-one student-teacher relationship is one of the most important means by which students learn to play expressively. Teachers, therefore, must maintain their own performance skills to be able to demonstrate excellent performances of their students' repertoire. It is not enough, however, for teachers to perform a piece and expect students to be able to replicate their playing merely by hearing it. One effective method is for teachers to guide students to hear the differences between better or weaker performances by demonstrating pieces in different ways. Teachers also frequently coach repertoire details by working through a piece measure by measure. This method, however, does not always transfer to other repertoire, leaving students dependent upon the teacher to show them how to play every piece. Teachers must supplement their modeled performances with verbal instructions, which can take multiple formats.

Imagery and Emotion

One verbal instructional method that teachers employ is to suggest a nonmusical image or metaphor as an inspiration for expression, such as comparing a piece to a beautiful sunny day at the beach or to a stark winter landscape. Unfortunately, while students may find this type of imagery interesting, they probably do not have the cognitive skills to translate it into any specific performance instructions. When the teacher's imagery or metaphor is unclear, students may become frustrated trying to understand what they are supposed to do, both in the lesson and subsequently during the practice week. Sadly, frustrated students can quickly become unmotivated students.

Another method used by teachers to teach musical expression is to encourage students to feel certain emotions in order to play their pieces more expressively. Students may become confused, however, by instructions such as "play this piece more sadly." Even more concerning is when the student mistakenly concludes that they can only play the piece well if they feel sad while playing it, which is an unreasonable expectation. Students can more easily understand verbal instructions that focus on the emotional character of the piece rather than trying to manipulate their personal emotions. The teacher should clearly make the distinction that a piece with a sad character does not require the student to feel emotionally sad to play it well. Metaphors and imagery are more prevalent in lessons and masterclasses with advanced students, since they usually have had enough musical experience to be able to translate these images into specific musical tools. Intermediate-level students, however, need much more concrete guidance. Students can thrive when teachers clearly communicate expressive tools by pairing imagery with specific technical and musical instructions, so that students learn to associate interpretive concepts with specific skills.

Early Musical Experiences

The seeds of musical expressiveness should be cultivated from the beginning of piano instruction through how teachers introduce pitch and rhythm. Students should learn pitch and rhythmic patterns aurally first within a musical context by singing songs and listening to all types of music. Teachers can model musical expressiveness while singing with their students through phrasing, dynamic levels, tempo changes, and a variety of tonal colors. Intuitive students can keenly sense and respond to these sounds, but all students will benefit from exposure to expressive performances.

Teachers then connect these musical patterns to tonal and rhythmic syllables within tonal and metrical contexts. Pitches should always be experienced within the context of a key and rhythms need to be comprehended within a beat-function system. When these syllables are connected to their notation symbols, students may mistakenly begin to isolate individual pitches and note values, which does not promote expressive performance. One way to continue strengthening musical connections is for students to sing melodies from their piano pieces using included texts or neutral syllables, and to articulate rhythmic patterns within metrical groupings before playing them. Teachers should take every opportunity to help students understand that pitches are only meaningful when considered in the context of melody, harmony, rhythm, texture, form, articulation, sonority, and character, or a combination of these.

Musical Expression Strategies

Teachers can create various activities to help students explore musical expression and musical character. Some examples of these are the following:

1. Phrase shapes

Sing lyrics in beginning repertoire (or on a neutral syllable if there are no lyrics) using all expressive markings to discern phrases and their shapes. Move expressively to music using scarves to show musical gestures.

2. Harmony

Walk while listening to the teacher play various harmonic progressions. Each time that the harmony returns to the tonic, return to the same location. Turn in a different direction when the harmony does not progress as expected.

3. Tension/resolution

Stretch and relax a rubber exercise band in response to the teacher playing a piece demonstrating tension/resolution. Discuss the elements of the music that define these points of tension/resolution.

4. Expressive markings

Make a map using only the expressive markings of a piece, including separate lines for dynamics, tempo, tone color, texture, character, and so on. Play the piece while looking at the map instead of the music notation.

5. Dynamics

Tap rhythmic patterns of a piece, demonstrating all dynamic changes. Try playing an expressive piece that normally uses tempo *rubato* completely in rhythm, using only dynamics rather than tempo changes to convey expression.

6. Tempo *rubato*

Conduct a teacher playing a piece to direct the teacher to make expressive tempo changes or move while the teacher plays a piece in order to feel the fluidity and pacing of tempo *rubato*.

7. Articulation

Create a story about a place or event using multiple expressive words. Experiment with creating a number of different nuances through different ways of speaking each word. Speak rhythmic syllables with different articulations.

8. Orchestration

Use the instrumental sounds of a digital keyboard to orchestrate different sections of a piece, then play it on the piano, trying to portray differences in the expressive details.

9. Moods, emotions

Listen to a variety of short pieces, assigning colors to them that define the character of the piece. Explain why the colors were chosen.

10. Characters

While listening to recorded examples, choose from cards supplied by the teacher with different character terms (e.g., playful, mysterious) on them to match different sections of the piece. Listen to a piece and draw icons or pictures to represent different characters while the piece is being performed.

Musical Expression Curriculum

In summary, intermediate-level students should develop the ability to do the following to develop more expressive playing:

1. Project the architecture of a piece at all levels from the overall form to the individual phrases.
2. Produce and control a wide dynamic palette.
3. Pace the rhythmic flow through various sections and/or tempo changes.
4. Produce and manipulate various tonal colors and sonorities through technique and artistic pedaling.
5. Discern and project the musical character, mood, or emotion of a piece through the exploration of all of its musical elements.

Since musicians communicate character through the fusion of multiple musical elements rather than individual ones, teachers should guide students to be able to talk about elements and their influence on musical character. A reference summary of some of these elements is listed below.

Compositional Elements

- Melody: Pitch, range, shape (contour), conjunct/disjunct, phrases, cadences, vocal or instrumental character, countermelody, line within a line

- Rhythm: Steady/unsteady beat, even/uneven rhythms, short/long note values, mixture of note values, rate of change of note values, duple/triple meter, pulse groupings, upbeats/downbeats, syncopation, polyrhythms, tempo *rubato*
- Texture: Monophonic, homophonic, polyphonic, full/thin, number of lines, complexity between the hands, accompaniment patterns
- Harmony: Major/minor mode, consonant/dissonant, tonal/atonal, diatonic/chromatic, expressive "color chords," drone bass or pedal point, ground bass, harmonic rhythm, tension/resolution
- Form: Repetition/contrast, phrase structure, cadences, imitation, ostinato patterns, coda; binary (AB), ternary (ABA), rondo (ABACABA), through-composed, theme and variations
- Genre: Prelude, fugue, sonatina/sonata, etude, character piece, dance (waltz, polonaise, allemande, courante, sarabande, gigue, minuet, etc.), fantasy or fantasia, theme and variations, concerto

Performance Elements

- Dynamics: Range, terraced, inflection, gradual/sudden, *crescendo/diminuendo*, voicing/balance, phrase shaping
- Articulation: *Legato, staccato*, non-*legato*, *portato*, accent, *marcato, tenuto*
- Tone color: Tone color/sonority, instrumentation/orchestration, pedaling
- Character and Expression: Peaceful, happy, bouncy, joyful, sad, reflective, anxious, driving, determined, celebratory, dignified, strong, elegant, ethereal, transparent, brilliant, resonant, clear, warm, rich, delicate, shimmering, mournful, mellow, penetrating, sweet, quirky, raspy, airy, and so forth.

With the introduction of each new repertoire piece, teachers should help students examine the expressive possibilities available through each of the musical elements. The more students explore these elements, the more easily they will begin to understand them.

The development of expressive playing is of the highest importance, since this is what will communicate with listeners more than anything else.

While technique may dazzle, the most inspiring performances are those in which the performer combines great technical skill with expressive musical communication. Helping students become independent musicians who can discern musical ideas for themselves can promote their lifelong love for music and continue the tradition of musical excellence.

Part II

Repertoire Annotations

Difficulty Levels
EI = early intermediate
MI = middle intermediate
LI = late intermediate
A = advanced
JM = Jane Magrath difficulty level ratings

Range reference
C1 is the lowest C on the piano

Amy Beach—*Children's Album*, Op. 36

Op. 36, No. 1: *Minuet*
Level: MI

1. Keyboard Skills/Technique/Mobility—great variety of articulation and quick hand-position changes.
2. Notation—range is G3-B-flat5; entire piece uses two treble clefs.
3. Tempo/Meter/Rhythm—(no tempo marking); 3/4; rhythmic patterns through the division of the beat.
4. Texture—homophonic: right-hand, single-line melody with occasional added voice and left-hand, single-line accompaniment with occasional added voices or chords.
5. Form—ABA-CC-ABA; eight-measure phrases.
6. Harmony—A section: F major; B section: F major, on a dominant C pedal point; C section: B-flat major; varied harmonic rhythm.
7. Melody—right-hand, single-line melody with occasional added voices, including parallel thirds and parallel sixths.
8. Articulation—extensive variety of articulation: numerous two-note slurs; *staccatos*; *portatos*.
9. Dynamics—*pp-f*, with extensive *crescendo* and *diminuendo*.
10. Musical Expression/Character—graceful minuet.
11. Pedaling—intermittent, direct pedaling, especially for the two-note slurs.

Op. 36, No. 2: *Gavotte*
Level: MI

1. Keyboard Skills/Technique/Mobility—great variety of articulation and quick hand-position changes.

2. Notation—range is D4-D6; entire piece uses two treble clefs.
3. Tempo/Meter/Rhythm—(none); **C**; rhythmic patterns through the division of the beat.
4. Texture—A section: monophonic: split between the two hands; B section: homophonic: right-hand melody with active left-hand accompaniment; C, D sections: right-hand melody with left-hand drone accompaniment.
5. Form—AA-BB-CC-D-AB; eight-measure phrases.
6. Harmony—A, B sections: D minor; C, D sections: D major; varied harmonic rhythm.
7. Melody—disjunct, articulated melody with occasional added voices.
8. Articulation—A, B sections: great variety of articulation on every note, including *staccatos*, two-note slurs, and *tenutos*; C, D sections: short slurs interspersed with *staccato* sections.
9. Dynamics—*pp-f*, with *crescendo* and *diminuendo* and sudden dynamic changes.
10. Musical Expression/Character—A, B sections: sneaky, scary; C, D sections: dance-like.
11. Pedaling—none.

Op. 36, No. 3: Waltz
Level: MI

1. Keyboard Skills/Technique/Mobility—long musical phrases with vocal leaps; melody often quite close to the accompaniment, making voicing difficult.
2. Notation—range is G3-B-flat5; entire piece uses two treble clefs.
3. Tempo/Meter/Rhythm—*Cantabile*; $\frac{3}{4}$; rhythmic patterns through the division of the beat.
4. Texture—homophonic: right-hand, lyrical, single-line melody with easy, limited-range, waltz-bass accompaniment.
5. Form—AA^1-BB^1-AA^1; eight-measure phrases.
6. Harmony—A section: C major; B section: E minor; moderate harmonic rhythm.

7. Melody—right-hand, single-line, lyrical melody with extensive vocal leaps.
8. Articulation—*legato,* with short slurs and *portatos.*
9. Dynamics—*pp-f,* with *crescendo* and *diminuendo.*
10. Musical Expression/Character—elegant waltz.
11. Pedaling—shallow, overlapping pedaling in long lyrical sections; careful, intermittent pedaling to define the short slurs.

Op. 36, No. 4: *March*
Level: MI

1. Keyboard Skills/Technique/Mobility—rapidly changing hand positions; very active left-hand accompaniment and great diversity of patterns between the two hands.
2. Notation—range is A3-D6; entire piece uses two treble clefs.
3. Tempo/Meter/Rhythm—(none); ₵; rhythmic patterns through the subdivision of the beat; extensive dotted-rhythm patterns making longer phrases more difficult.
4. Texture—homophonic: right-hand, single-line melody with occasional added voices and left-hand, single-line accompaniment with occasional added voices.
5. Form—Introduction AA^1-BB^1-A^2; four- and seven-measure phrases.
6. Harmony—A section: D major; B section: A major; fast harmonic rhythm.
7. Melody—right-hand melody with dotted-rhythm patterns and frequently changing number of voices.
8. Articulation—extensive two-note slurs and diverse articulation between the two hands.
9. Dynamics—*p-f,* with *crescendo* and *diminuendo* and sudden dynamic changes.
10. Musical Expression/Character—jaunty, happy.
11. Pedaling—none; careful, intermittent pedaling could be used to enhance the tone quality and define the slurs.

Op. 36, No. 5: *Polka*
Level: MI

1. Keyboard Skills/Technique/Mobility—great variety of articulation in the melody.
2. Notation—range is G3-C6; entire piece uses two treble clefs.
3. Tempo/Meter/Rhythm—*Scherzando*; $\frac{2}{4}$; rhythmic patterns through the subdivision of the beat; some notated tempo *rubato*.
4. Texture—homophonic: right-hand, single-line melody with mixed-texture accompaniment of single notes and chords.
5. Form—ABBACA; four- and eight-measure phrases.
6. Harmony—A section: G major; B section: C major; C section: modulatory; varied harmonic rhythm.
7. Melody—right-hand, single-line melody with occasional added voices and a great variety of articulation.
8. Articulation—short slurs, *staccatos*, *tenutos*, accents.
9. Dynamics—*pp-f*, with *crescendo* and *diminuendo*.
10. Musical Expression/Character—humorous polka dance.
11. Pedaling—occasional direct pedaling to enhance the short-slur sections.

Johann Burgmüller— *25 Progressive Pieces*, Op. 100

<u>Op. 100, No. 1: *Sincerity*</u>
Level: EI, JM3

1. Keyboard Skills/Technique/Mobility—right-hand passagework, with some two-voice sections requiring finger independence.
2. Notation—range is C3-C6; use of two treble clefs.
3. Tempo/Meter/Rhythm—*Allegro Moderato*; **C** ; rhythmic patterns through the division of the beat; notated tempo *rubato* at the ends of phrases.
4. Texture—A section: homophonic: right-hand, single-line melody with left-hand, chordal accompaniment; B section: homophonic, with moving parts in both hands and some right-hand two-part writing.
5. Form—AABB + coda; four- and eight-measure phrases.
6. Harmony—C major; slow harmonic rhythm.
7. Melody—right-hand, lyrical, eighth-note passagework.
8. Articulation—long *legato* lines.
9. Dynamics—*p-f*, with *sf* and extensive *crescendo* and *diminuendo*.
10. Musical Expression/Character—peaceful, sincere.
11. Pedaling—limited, shallow pedaling to support the melody and join the chords together smoothly.

<u>Op. 100, No. 2: *Arabesque*</u>
Level: EI, JM3-4

1. Keyboard Skills/Technique/Mobility—rapid sixteenth-note patterns with frequent hand-position and range changes.

2. Notation—range is A2-E6.
3. Tempo/Meter/Rhythm—*Allegro scherzando*; $\frac{2}{4}$; rhythmic patterns through the subdivision of the beat.
4. Texture—A section: homophonic: right-hand, scalar, sixteenth-note patterns accompanied by intermittent *staccato* chords; B section: polyphonic: right-hand, lyrical melody accompanied by left-hand sixteenth-note patterns.
5. Form—Introduction ABA + coda; four- and eight-measure phrases.
6. Harmony—A minor, with brief modulations to C major and D minor; moderate harmonic rhythm.
7. Melody—A section: short, scalar sixteenth-note passages separated by rests; B section: long lyrical line with vocal leaps.
8. Articulation—short and long slurs, *staccato* chords.
9. Dynamics—*p-f* with *sf*.
10. Musical Expression/Character—dramatic, exciting.
11. Pedaling—on *sf* for resonance and volume.

<u>Op. 100, No. 3</u>: *Pastorale*
Level: EI, JM4

1. Keyboard Skills/Technique/Mobility—passagework with hand contraction and extension; left-hand sustained notes with additional repeated notes requiring finger independence.
2. Notation—range is G2-D7; use of two treble clefs.
3. Tempo/Meter/Rhythm—*Andantino*; $\frac{6}{8}$; rhythmic patterns through the division of the beat.
4. Texture—A section: homophonic: right-hand, single-line melody with left-hand, *legato*, repeated-chord accompaniment; B section: homophonic: right-hand, single-line melody with left-hand sustained chords and additional repeated notes.
5. Form—Introduction AABA¹ + coda; four-measure phrases.
6. Harmony—G major; slow harmonic rhythm.
7. Melody—right-hand, single-line, vocal melody; grace notes and short ornaments; long melodic notes may cause fading sound challenges.

8. Articulation—*legato*, with shorter slurs.
9. Dynamics—*pp-mf*, with *crescendo* and *diminuendo*.
10. Musical Expression/Character—peaceful, serene.
11. Pedaling—shallow, overlapping pedaling.

Op. 100, No. 4: *The Little Party*
Level: MI, JM5

1. Keyboard Skills/Technique/Mobility—parallel thirds in both hands; right-hand parallel sixths.
2. Notation—range is C3-E6; limited use of two treble clefs.
3. Tempo/Meter/Rhythm—*Allegro ma non troppo*; **C** ; rhythmic patterns through the division of the beat.
4. Texture—homophonic: right-hand melody with parallel intervals in both hands and an active accompaniment.
5. Form—Introduction ABA; four-measure phrases.
6. Harmony—A section: C major; B section: on the dominant; moderate harmonic rhythm.
7. Melody—parallel thirds and sixths with various articulations; both ascending and descending musical phrases, with climaxes sometimes on the first note.
8. Articulation—short slurs, *marcato* accents, *staccato* passages.
9. Dynamics—*p-f*, with *sf* and sudden dynamic changes.
10. Musical Expression/Character—lively, celebratory.
11. Pedaling—none.

Op. 100, No. 5: *Innocence*
Level: MI, JM4

1. Keyboard Skills/Technique/Mobility—passagework with numerous position shifts; quick finger changes on repeated notes.
2. Notation—wide range: F2-C7.
3. Tempo/Meter/Rhythm—*Moderato*; $\frac{2}{4}$; rhythmic patterns through the subdivision of the beat.

4. Texture—homophonic: A section: right-hand, single-line, lyrical melody with *legato*, repeated-chord accompaniment; B section: *leggiero* melody with varied articulations and *legato*, broken-interval accompaniment.
5. Form—AABB; four- and eight-measure phrases.
6. Harmony—F Major; slow harmonic rhythm.
7. Melody—A section: flowing, scalar sixteenth notes with position shifts through quick hand extension and contraction; B section: scalar passagework with quick finger changes on repeated notes.
8. Articulation—A section: *legato*; B section: extensive articulation with short slurs and *staccatos*.
9. Dynamics—*p-f*, with long *crescendo* and *diminuendo*.
10. Musical Expression/Character—graceful, dainty.
11. Pedaling—intermittent, direct pedaling to enhance tone quality on longer notes and two-note slurs.

Op. 100, No. 6: *Progress*
Level: MI, JM4

1. Keyboard Skills/Technique/Mobility—fast passagework in both hands alternating with broken intervals; position shifts through quick hand contraction and extension.
2. Notation—range is C3-E6.
3. Tempo/Meter/Rhythm—*Allegro*; **C** ; rhythmic patterns through the subdivision of the beat.
4. Texture—A section: polyphonic; B section: sequential imitative counterpoint between the hands and a challenging polyphonic section.
5. Form—AABA; four-measure phrases.
6. Harmony—A section: C major; B section: A minor, modulatory; varied harmonic rhythm.
7. Melody—fast passagework in both hands with scalar runs and broken intervals.
8. Articulation—*legato* passagework; accents and *staccatos* in broken-interval passages; numerous two-note slurs in each hand that do not correspond with normal metric strong and weak beats.

9. Dynamics—*p-f*, with *crescendo* and *diminuendo*.
10. Musical Expression/Character—lively, energetic, exciting.
11. Pedaling—none.

Op. 100, No. 7: *The Clear Stream*
Level: MI, JM4

1. Keyboard Skills/Technique/Mobility—A section: right-hand, frequently changing, broken-chord patterns with line-within-a-line melody on the bottom; B section: left-hand, lyrical melody with right-hand, triplet pattern accompaniment.
2. Notation—range is G2-A5.
3. Tempo/Meter/Rhythm—*Allegro Vivace*; **C**; triplet rhythmic patterns.
4. Texture—homophonic: A section: right-hand broken chords with line-within-a-line melody on the bottom and left-hand, simple ostinato accompaniment; B section: single-line, left-hand melody with right-hand, triplet pattern accompaniment.
5. Form—ABA, four-measure phrases.
6. Harmony—A section: G major; B section: D major; varied harmonic rhythm.
7. Melody—A section: right-hand, broken chord patterns with line-within-a-line melody on the bottom; B section: left-hand, long *legato* line.
8. Articulation—*legato*.
9. Dynamics—*pp-p*, with extensive *crescendo* and *diminuendo*.
10. Musical Expression/Character—"murmuring."
11. Pedaling—overlapping pedaling with the chord changes.

Op. 100, No. 8: *Gracefulness*
Level: MI, JM5

1. Keyboard Skills/Technique/Mobility—notated ornamental turns in both hands followed immediately by leaps to new positions.

2. Notation—wide range: F2-F8.
3. Tempo/Meter/Rhythm—*Moderato*; 3/4 ; rhythmic patterns through the thirty-second-note level.
4. Texture—homophonic: A section: right-hand, single-line melody with left-hand, repeated-chord accompaniment; B section: right-hand melody on top of chords with left-hand, mixed-texture accompaniment.
5. Form—AABA; four-measure phrases.
6. Harmony—A section: F major; B section: C major; slow harmonic rhythm.
7. Melody—A section: right-hand, *legato* arpeggios connected by notated turns; B section: right-hand, limited-range melody on top of chords.
8. Articulation—*leggiero* touch throughout with repeated *portato* chords in each hand.
9. Dynamics—*p-f*, with *crescendo* and *diminuendo*.
10. Musical Expression/Character—dance-like.
11. Pedaling—none, due to clarity required.

Op. 100, No. 9: *The Chase*
Level: MI, JM7

1. Keyboard Skills/Technique/Mobility—repeated chords with rapid position shifts on inversions; broken octaves with repeated notes requiring fast hand contraction and extension.
2. Notation—range is A2-C6; use of two treble clefs.
3. Tempo/Meter/Rhythm—*Allegro Vivace*; 6/8 ; rhythmic patterns through the division of the beat.
4. Texture—homophonic: A section: left-hand melody with parallel horn fifths and right-hand, broken-octave accompaniment; B section: right-hand melody with parallel thirds; C section: right-hand, single-line, lyrical melody with left-hand, broken-chord accompaniment.
5. Form—Introduction ABACA + coda; four- and eight-measure phrases.
6. Harmony—A section: C major; B section: G major; C section: A minor; moderate harmonic rhythm.

7. Melody—A section: left-hand melody with parallel horn fifths; B section: right-hand, *legato* melody with parallel thirds; C section: single-line, lyrical melody.
8. Articulation—finger *staccato* notes, wrist *staccato* chords, two-note slurs, phrasing with long slurs, accents.
9. Dynamics—*p-f*.
10. Musical Expression/Character—lively, "hunting horn" piece.
11. Pedaling—overlapping pedaling in the lyrical sections.

Op. 100, No. 10: *Tender Flower*
Level: MI, JM6

1. Keyboard Skills/Technique/Mobility—quick finger substitutions on repeated notes; wide stretches; hand contraction and extension.
2. Notation—range is E3-F-sharp6.
3. Tempo/Meter/Rhythm—*Moderato*; C ; rhythmic patterns through the division of the beat; notated tempo *rubato* at the ends of phrases.
4. Texture—homophonic: right-hand, single-line melody with left-hand, single-line accompaniment with occasional chords.
5. Form—AA-BA-BA; four-measure phrases.
6. Harmony—A section: D major; B section: A major; slow harmonic rhythm.
7. Melody—right-hand, *legato* passagework of scales and arpeggios with quick finger substitutions on repeated notes; a few short ornaments.
8. Articulation—numerous two-note slurs alternating with long *legato* passages; accents.
9. Dynamics—*p-mf*.
10. Musical Expression/Character—delicate.
11. Pedaling—limited, shallow pedaling in the *legato* sections.

Op. 100, No. 11: *The Young Shepherdess*
Level: MI, JM6

1. Keyboard Skills/Technique/Mobility—broken arpeggios in inversions in both hands; quick finger changes on repeated notes; parallel thirds; diverse articulation between the two hands.

2. Notation—range is C3-G6; use of two treble clefs.
3. Tempo/Meter/Rhythm—*Allegretto*; 2/4; rhythmic patterns through the subdivision of the beat.
4. Texture—homophonic: A section: right-hand melody with left-hand, intermittent, chordal accompaniment; B section: left-hand melody with *legato*, right-hand, parallel-thirds accompaniment.
5. Form—Introduction AABB + coda; four-measure phrases.
6. Harmony—A section: C major; B section: A minor, modulatory; slow harmonic rhythm.
7. Melody—A section: right-hand, arpeggiated melody; B section: left-hand, arpeggiated melody.
8. Articulation—numerous short slurs with *staccatos*.
9. Dynamics—*p-f*, with *crescendo* and *diminuendo*.
10. Musical Expression/Character—happy, dancing maiden.
11. Pedaling—some limited, direct pedaling on chords.

Op. 100, No. 12: *The Farewell*
Level: MI, JM5-6

1. Keyboard Skills/Technique/Mobility—right-hand, single-line passagework; wide stretches in the melody; quick finger changes on repeated notes.
2. Notation—range is A2-G6; use of two treble clefs.
3. Tempo/Meter/Rhythm—*Allegro moderato agitato*; **C**; extensive use of triplets.
4. Texture—homophonic: A section: right-hand, single-line passagework with left-hand, quarter-note accompaniment with occasional chords; B section: right-hand, lyrical melody with left-hand, broken-chord, triplet accompaniment.
5. Form—Introduction ABA + coda; four- and eight-measure phrases.
6. Harmony—A section: A minor; B section; C major; varied harmonic rhythm.

7. Melody—A section: right-hand, perpetual-motion passagework etude; B section: lyrical melody with large leaps.
8. Articulation—*legato,* with some *staccatos* and accents.
9. Dynamics—*p-f*, with some *sf*.
10. Musical Expression/Character—energetic, dramatic.
11. Pedaling—overlapping pedaling may be used in the B section.

Op. 100, No. 13: *Consolation*
Level: MI, JM6

1. Keyboard Skills/Technique/Mobility—line-within-a-line melody in both hands requiring finger independence; duets between the two hands.
2. Notation—range is C3-C6; use of two treble clefs.
3. Tempo/Meter/Rhythm—*Allegro moderato*; **C** ; rhythmic patterns through the division of the beat; notated tempo *rubato*.
4. Texture—A section: homophonic; B section; polyphonic.
5. Form—Introduction AABB + coda; four-measure phrases.
6. Harmony—C major; varied harmonic rhythm.
7. Melody—broken-chord passages with line-within-a-line melody on the top in the right hand and on the bottom in the left hand.
8. Articulation—*legato*.
9. Dynamics—*p-f*.
10. Musical Expression/Character—intimate, sweet.
11. Pedaling—careful, shallow, overlapping pedaling changing on most beats.

Op. 100, No. 14: *Austrian Dance*
Level: MI, JM4

1. Keyboard Skills/Technique/Mobility—finger independence required in both hands; passagework with rapid hand contraction and extension; quick finger changes on repeated notes.
2. Notation—range is G2-C6; use of two treble clefs; dotted lines show the placement of grace notes on the beat.

3. Tempo/Meter/Rhythm—*Mouvement de Valse*; 3/4 ; rhythmic patterns through the division of the beat.
4. Texture—homophonic: right-hand passagework with waltz-bass accompaniment.
5. Form—Introduction ABCAB, with each section repeated; eight-measure phrases.
6. Harmony—A section: G major; B section: E minor, G major; C section: C major; moderate harmonic rhythm.
7. Melody—right-hand, instrumental melody with frequent directional changes; grace notes and short ornaments.
8. Articulation—extensive mixed articulations of both *staccato* and *legato*.
9. Dynamics—*p-f*; dynamic levels change with each section.
10. Musical Expression/Character—Austrian waltz.
11. Pedaling—none, due to the extensive articulation; finger pedaling requiring finger independence.

Op. 100, No.15: *Ballade*
Level: MI, JM4

1. Keyboard Skills/Technique/Mobility—awkward left-hand passagework, fast parallel passagework between the two hands.
2. Notation—range is C2-C7.
3. Tempo/Meter/Rhythm—*Allegro con brio*; 6/8 ; rhythmic patterns through the subdivision of the beat.
4. Texture—A section: left-hand, single-line melody with right-hand, *staccato*, repeated-chord accompaniment; B section: right-hand, single-line, lyrical melody with left-hand, intermittent, chordal accompaniment.
5. Form—Introduction ABA + coda; eight-measure phrases.
6. Harmony—A section: C minor; B section: C major; slow harmonic rhythm.
7. Melody—A section: left-hand figuration melody; B section: right-hand singing melody.
8. Articulation—wrist *staccato* repeated chords against *legato* passagework, two-note slurs, *marcato* accents.

9. Dynamics—*p-f*, with *sf*.
10. Musical Expression/Character—dramatic, passionate.
11. Pedaling—direct pedaling on *forte* chords; B section: overlapping pedal.

Op. 100, No. 16: *Sorrow*
Level: MI, JM5

1. Keyboard Skills/Technique/Mobility—passages of broken intervals and rapidly changing chords.
2. Notation—range is D3-D6; use of two treble clefs.
3. Tempo/Meter/Rhythm—*Allegro moderato*; 𝐂 ; rhythmic patterns through the subdivision of the beat; notated tempo *rubato*.
4. Texture—homophonic: A section: right-hand, single-line melody with broken-chord accompaniment; B section: mixed textures, including chromatic chords split between the two hands.
5. Form—AABB; four-measure phrases.
6. Harmony—G minor; varied harmonic rhythm.
7. Melody—A section: right-hand, single-line melody that shifts to the left hand; long notes may create fading sound challenges; B section: right-hand melody on top of chords, shifting to a single-line melody.
8. Articulation—primarily *legato*, with some *staccato* chordal sections.
9. Dynamics—*p-f*, with *sf*.
10. Musical Expression/Character—painful, sorrowful.
11. Pedaling—intermittent pedaling to sustain long notes and blend broken intervals.

Op. 100, No. 17: *The Chatterbox*
Level: MI, JM6

1. Keyboard Skills/Technique/Mobility—rapid finger changes on repeated notes; rapid hand contraction and extension; parallel thirds.
2. Notation—range is C2-F6.
3. Tempo/Meter/Rhythm—*Allegretto*; $\frac{3}{8}$; rhythmic patterns through the subdivision of the beat.

4. Texture—homophonic: A section: single-line melody with intermittent, chordal accompaniment; B section: melody with parallel thirds.
5. Form—Introduction AABA + coda; four- and eight-measure phrases.
6. Harmony—A section: F major; B section: on the dominant.
7. Melody—A section: instrumental melody with wide leaps and rapid repeated notes; B section: lyrical melody with parallel thirds.
8. Articulation—*staccato* repeated notes, *legato* passagework.
9. Dynamics—*p-f*, with *crescendo* and *diminuendo*.
10. Musical Expression/Character—A section: jumpy, excited; B section: pleading.
11. Pedaling—limited to the B section to connect the *legato* parallel-third passages.

Op. 100, No. 18: *Inquiétude*
Level: JM5

1. Keyboard Skills/Technique/Mobility—rapidly alternating hands, with frequent right-hand position shifts.
2. Notation—range is E2-B5.
3. Tempo/Meter/Rhythm—*Allegro agitato*; $\frac{2}{4}$; rhythmic patterns through the subdivision of the beat.
4. Texture—homophonic: fragmented melody with detached chordal accompaniment.
5. Form—ABA + coda; four-measure phrases.
6. Harmony—A section: E minor: B section: G major; varied harmonic rhythm.
7. Melody—right-hand, rapid, fragmented passagework.
8. Articulation—left-hand *staccato* chords, right-hand short slurs.
9. Dynamics—*p-f*, with *crescendo* and *diminuendo*.
10. Musical Expression/Character—agitated, anxious.
11. Pedaling—none

Op. 100, No. 19: *Ave Maria*
Level: MI, JM5

1. Keyboard Skills/Technique/Mobility—*legato* chordal playing; mixed textures requiring finger independence within each hand and between the two hands.
2. Notation—range is A2-E5; use of two treble clefs.
3. Tempo/Meter/Rhythm—*Andantino*; $\frac{3}{4}$; rhythmic patterns through the division of the beat.
4. Texture—homophonic: A, B sections: chordal; A^1 section has varied accompaniments.
5. Form—AA-B-A^1 + coda; eight-measure phrases.
6. Harmony—A section: A major; B section: E major, modulatory; varied harmonic rhythm.
7. Melody—right-hand, limited-range, lyrical melody on top of chords with many repeated notes.
8. Articulation—*legato*.
9. Dynamics—*pp*, with *crescendo* and *diminuendo*.
10. Musical Expression/Character—reverent, contemplative.
11. Pedaling—overlapping pedaling with the chord changes.

Op. 100, No. 20: *Tarantelle*
Level: MI, JM6

1. Keyboard Skills/Technique/Mobility—parallel scalar passages with finger changes on repeated notes for rapid position shifts.
2. Notation—wide range: C3-F8; use of two treble clefs.
3. Tempo/Meter/Rhythm—*Allegro vivo*; $\frac{6}{8}$; rhythmic patterns through the division of the beat.
4. Texture—homophonic: introduction: parallel scalar passages doubled between the two hands; A section: right-hand, single-line melody with an accompaniment of blocked and broken chords.
5. Form—Introduction AA-BA^{1}BA^1-CC-A^{1}A^1 + coda; four- and eight-measure phrases.

6. Harmony—A, B sections: D minor; C section: D major; slow harmonic rhythm.
7. Melody—right-hand passagework with many leaps; grace notes requiring quick finger changes and other short ornaments.
8. Articulation—short slurs, *staccato* chords.
9. Dynamics—*p-f*, with some *sf* and *crescendo* and *diminuendo*.
10. Musical Expression/Character—driven, energetic.
11. Pedaling—limited to direct pedaling on the chords and/or *sf*.

Op. 100, No. 21: *Angels' Voices*
Level: MI, JM5

1. Keyboard Skills/Technique/Mobility—single line of triplets flowing between the two hands.
2. Notation—range is G2-C7; use of two treble clefs.
3. Tempo/Meter/Rhythm—*Allegro moderato*; **C**; consistent triplet rhythmic pattern throughout.
4. Texture—almost completely monophonic, with occasional accompaniment.
5. Form—AA-BABA + coda: four- and eight-measure phrases.
6. Harmony—A section: G major; B section: E minor; slow harmonic rhythm.
7. Melody—continuous, broken-chord, single musical line flowing between the two hands.
8. Articulation—*legato*.
9. Dynamics—*pp-p*, with *crescendo* and *sf*.
10. Musical Expression/Character—peaceful, tranquil, flowing.
11. Pedaling—overlapping.

Op. 100, No. 22: *Barcarolle*
Level: MI, JM6

1. Keyboard Skills/Technique/Mobility—extended introduction with multiple tempo changes and *fermatas*; right-hand, single-line melody

with wide leaps and rapid directional changes requiring hand extension and contraction.
2. Notation—range is A-flat2-C6; use of two treble clefs.
3. Tempo/Meter/Rhythm—*Andantino quasi allegretto*; $^6_8$; rhythmic patterns through the division of the beat; notated tempo *rubato*.
4. Texture—homophonic: right-hand, single-line melody with intermittent, chordal accompaniment.
5. Form—Introduction AB (interpolation) A^1 + coda; four- and eight-measure phrases.
6. Harmony—A-flat major; harmonic rhythm varies.
7. Melody—right-hand, single-line, lyrical melody with wide leaps and rapid directional changes.
8. Articulation—mostly *legato*, with some accents and *staccatos*.
9. Dynamics—*pp-sf*, with extensive *crescendo* and *diminuendo* and sudden dynamic changes.
10. Musical Expression/Character—happy, joyful.
11. Pedaling—intermittent, direct pedaling on the sustained chords.

Op. 100, No. 23: *The Return*
Level: MI, JM7

1. Keyboard Skills/Technique/Mobility—left-hand octave leaps with rapid hand contraction and extension, with right-hand, *legato*, parallel thirds and sixths; rapid, repeated, *staccato* chords with shifting chord configurations; finger independence required in the right hand to play sustained notes and *staccatos* simultaneously.
2. Notation—range is C2-A-flat5.
3. Tempo/Meter/Rhythm—*Molto agitato quasi presto*; $^6_8$; rhythmic patterns through the division of the beat.
4. Texture—homophonic: A section: right-hand melody on top of chords; B section: left-hand, *legato* melody with right-hand, *staccato*, chordal accompaniment.
5. Form—Introduction AA-BABA + coda; four- and eight-measure phrases.

6. Harmony—A section: E-flat; B section; C minor, modulatory; varied harmonic rhythm.
7. Melody—A section: right-hand, scalar melody on top of *staccato* chords; B section: left-hand, *legato*, arpeggiated melody with wide leaps.
8. Articulation—mixed textures of *staccato* in one hand and *legato* in the other hand; some accents.
9. Dynamics—*pp-sf*, with some sudden dynamic changes.
10. Musical Expression/Character—dramatic, agitated.
11. Pedaling—limited to the final chords.

Op. 100, No. 24: *The Swallow*
Level: MI, JM6-7

1. Keyboard Skills/Technique/Mobility—rapid, left-hand crossings to play bass and melody notes.
2. Notation—range is G2-D6.
3. Tempo/Meter/Rhythm—*Allegro non troppo*; **C** ; continuous sixteenth notes.
4. Texture—monophonic: passagework split between the two hands, with some places where the melody notes are sustained longer.
5. Form—AAB + coda; four-measure phrases, with a seven-measure coda.
6. Harmony—A section: G major; B section, B minor; varied harmonic rhythm.
7. Melody—fragmented melody played by the left-hand crossings.
8. Articulation—*legato*; left-hand crossing notes marked *staccato* create melodic bell-tones.
9. Dynamics—*pp-p*, with some *crescendo*.
10. Musical Expression/Character—happy, energetic.
11. Pedaling—consistent, overlapping pedaling with the chord changes.

Op. 100, No. 25: *The Knight Errant*
Level: MI, JM7

1. Keyboard Skills/Technique/Mobility: fast tempo with many quick hand-position shifts and detailed articulations; fast, scalar passagework alternating between the two hands and parallel, scalar passages in both hands.
2. Notation—wide range: C2–C7.
3. Tempo/Meter/Rhythm—*Allegro marziale*; 𝄴 ; rhythmic patterns through the subdivision of the beat with many dotted rhythms; alternation between the duple and triple division of the beat.
4. Texture—homophonic: A section: right-hand, disjunct melody alternating single notes with additional voice; B section: passagework doubled in octaves between the two hands alternating with chords; C section: right-hand, single-line, lyrical passagework with sustained chordal accompaniment; coda: multiple textures, including rhythmic patterns divided between the hands, right-hand, single-line melody with intermittent, chordal accompaniment, and scalar passages in both hands.
5. Form—AA-BA^1 BA^1-CC + extensive coda; four-measure phrases.
6. Harmony—A section: C major; B section: G major; C section: F major; extensive chromaticism; varied harmonic rhythm.
7. Melody—A, B sections: disjunct, fragmented melody; C section: right-hand, lyrical passagework; grace notes; coda: multiple textures.
8. Articulation—great variety of articulation, including all *staccato* sections, all *legato* sections, alternation of *legato* and *staccato* sections, and numerous short slurs.
9. Dynamics—*p*-*f*, with sudden dynamic changes.
10. Musical Expression/Character—A, B sections: quirky; C section: delicate; coda: dramatic, brilliant, exciting.
11. Pedaling—intermittent, direct pedaling on selected chords for resonance and volume.

Johann Burgmüller—
18 Characteristic Studies, Op. 109

Op. 109, No. 1: *Confidence*
Level: MI, JM7

1. Keyboard Skills/Technique/Mobility—right-hand broken chords with line-within-a-line melody on the top.
2. Notation—range is G2-E6; use of two treble clefs.
3. Tempo/Meter/Rhythm—*Allegro non troppo*; **C** ; rhythmic patterns through the division of the beat; notated tempo *rubato* at the ends of phrases.
4. Texture—homophonic: A section: right-hand broken chords with line-within-a-line melody on the top accompanied by a left-hand, lyrical countermelody; B section: right-hand, lyrical, quarter-note melody with left-hand, broken-chord accompaniment, switching to left-hand quarter notes and right-hand broken chords.
5. Form—AA-BABA + coda; eight-measure phrases.
6. Harmony—A section: C major; B section: C minor; fast harmonic rhythm.
7. Melody—A section: right-hand, lyrical, broken chords with line-within-a-line melody on the top in a limited range with many repeated notes; B section: right-hand, lyrical, quarter-note melody that switches to the left hand.
8. Articulation—*legato*, with short slurs and a few ornaments.
9. Dynamics—*pp-fz*, with extensive *crescendo* and *diminuendo*.
10. Musical Expression/Character—sweet, sincere, yearning.
11. Pedaling—rapid, overlapping pedaling, changing with the fast harmonic rhythm.

Op. 109, No. 2: *The Pearls*
Level: LI, JM7

1. Keyboard Skills/Technique/Mobility—right-hand, fragmented melody within a scalar passage with irregular fingerings extending high in the range; wide leaps and rapid range changes within the right-hand passagework; fast, scalar passages in octaves and tenths between the two hands; left-hand waltz bass with wide leaps; hands separated in a wide range on the keyboard.
2. Notation—wide range: G1-G7; all notes except the melody notes are in a smaller print size; extensive use of 8va.
3. Tempo/Meter/Rhythm—*Moderato*; $\frac{3}{4}$; extensive use of thirty-second notes.
4. Texture—homophonic: right-hand, line-within-a-line melody accompanied by a left-hand waltz bass; scalar passages in octaves and tenths between the two hands.
5. Form—AA-BA + coda; four- and eight-measure phrases.
6. Harmony—A section: C major; B section: G major; slow harmonic rhythm.
7. Melody—fragmented two-note slurs within scalar passagework; grace notes.
8. Articulation—*legato*, with two-note melodic slurs.
9. Dynamics—wide dynamic range: *ppp-ff*, with some *sfz*.
10. Musical Expression/Character—delicate, airy, transparent.
11. Pedaling—direct pedaling with the waltz-bass patterns.

Op. 109, No. 3: *The Shepherd's Return*
Level: LI, JM7

1. Keyboard Skills/Technique/Mobility—left-hand waltz bass with a wide range and slurred broken-chord patterns; right-hand, instrumental melody with varied articulations and many directional changes requiring rotation and shifting of arm weight; right-hand parallel thirds and parallel first-inversion chords; parallel unison passagework.

2. Notation—range is G1-B6.
3. Tempo/Meter/Rhythm—*Allegro*; ¾ ; rhythmic patterns through the division of the beat.
4. Texture—homophonic: right-hand melody with left-hand, waltz-bass accompaniment.
5. Form—Introduction AA-BA¹-CC (interpolation) A + coda; eight-measure phrases.
6. Harmony—A section: G major; B section: B minor; C section: C major; slow harmonic rhythm.
7. Melody—right-hand, instrumental melody with many directional changes; extensive use of ornamentation; some additional voices in parallel thirds and parallel first-inversion chords.
8. Articulation—an extensive variety of articulation: numerous two-note slurs, various accents, finger and wrist *staccato* notes/intervals/chords, and *legato* passagework.
9. Dynamics—*pp-f*, with *sf* and extensive *crescendo* and *diminuendo*.
10. Musical Expression/Character—waltz.
11. Pedaling—a variety of overlapping, waltz-bass, and direct pedaling.

Op. 109, No. 4: *The Gypsies*
Level: LI, JM8

1. Keyboard Skills/Technique/Mobility—technically difficult mixed texture with solid and broken octaves and broken-chord passages; wide range with rapid position changes.
2. Notation—wide range: C1-G7; use of two bass clefs.
3. Tempo/Meter/Rhythm—*Allegro non troppo*; ₵ ; rhythmic patterns through the division of the beat, plus sixteenth-note triplets.
4. Texture—homophonic: right-hand melody in mixed textures of single notes with additional voices, and on top of chords.
5. Form—ABBA¹-C-A² + coda; four-measure phrases.
6. Harmony—A section: C minor; B section: E-flat major; C section: C major; fast harmonic rhythm.

7. Melody—single notes with additional voices and on top of chords; wide range.
8. Articulation—an extensive variety of articulation: finger, wrist, and forearm *staccato* notes and chords, slurs, *portatos*, various accents.
9. Dynamics—wide dynamic range: *ppp-ff*, with *sf, fp*, and sudden dynamic changes.
10. Musical Expression/Character—dramatic, frightening.
11. Pedaling—limited, intermittent pedaling, some of which is notated.

Op. 109, No. 5: *The Spring*
Level: LI, JM8

1. Keyboard Skills/Technique/Mobility—right-hand, broken-chord patterns (including some broken octaves) requiring rotation; rapid hand contraction and extension; line-within-a-line melody with the melody in different places; left-hand wide stretches; mixed voicing requiring significant finger independence; parallel thirds.
2. Notation—range is C2-B6; all right-hand, non-melodic notes are in smaller print.
3. Tempo/Meter/Rhythm—*Andante grazioso*; $\frac{3}{4}$; extensive use of thirty-second notes; notated tempo *rubato*.
4. Texture—homophonic: right-hand, broken-chord passagework with line-within-a-line melody in various places; varied accompaniment of single notes or intervals.
5. Form—AA-BABA + coda.; eight-measure phrases.
6. Harmony—G major, with some chromaticism.
7. Melody—right-hand, broken-chord passagework with line-within-a-line melody in different places.
8. Articulation—*legato*, with left-hand short slurs and *staccatos*.
9. Dynamics—wide range: *ppp-f*, with *sf* and sudden dynamic changes.
10. Musical Expression/Character—shimmering.
11. Pedaling—challenging intermittent pedaling.

Johann Burgmüller—18 Characteristic Studies, *Op. 109*

Op. 109, No. 6: <u>*The Merry Maiden*</u>
Level: LI, JM8

1. Keyboard Skills/Technique/Mobility—right-hand, double-note etude with wide stretches.
2. Notation—wide range: C2–C7; both hands are sometimes notated on the same staff.
3. Tempo/Meter/Rhythm—Allegretto; 3/8; rhythmic patterns through the subdivision of the beat; continuous right-hand sixteenth notes.
4. Texture—homophonic: right-hand double notes with left-hand, mixed-texture accompaniment.
5. Form—Introduction AABB + coda; eight-measure phrases.
6. Harmony—C major: varied harmonic rhythm.
7. Melody—right-hand, instrumental melody on top of double-note patterns.
8. Articulation—*staccato*, with some short slurs.
9. Dynamics—*pp-f*, with *crescendo* and *diminuendo* and sudden dynamic changes.
10. Musical Expression/Character—happy, giddy.
11. Pedaling—intermittent pedaling as notated.

Op. 109, No. 7: <u>*Lullaby*</u>
Level: LI, JM 7

1. Keyboard Skills/Technique/Mobility—right-hand broken chords with line-within-a-line melody on the top; wide stretches in both hands; broken-chord patterns split between the hands.
2. Notation—range is C2-D6.
3. Tempo/Meter/Rhythm—*Andantino con moto*; 3/8; rhythmic patterns through the subdivision of the beat, plus some thirty-second notes.
4. Texture—homophonic: right-hand broken chords with line-within-a-line melody on the top and left-hand, broken-chord accompaniment; finger independence required within the right hand.
5. Form—AABB + coda; four- and eight-measure phrases.

6. Harmony—F major; slow harmonic rhythm.
7. Melody—right-hand, line-within-a-line triadic melody with wide leaps; notated ornamental turns and grace notes.
8. Articulation—*legato*, with numerous short slurs.
9. Dynamics—*pp-f*, with quick *crescendo* and *diminuendo*.
10. Musical Expression/Character—lullaby.
11. Pedaling—consistent overlapping pedaling.

Op.109, No. 8: *Agitato*
Level: LI, JM7

1. Keyboard Skills/Technique/Mobility—fast, sixteenth-note broken intervals alternating rapidly between the two hands.
2. Notation—range is E1-C6; both hands are sometimes notated on the same staff.
3. Tempo/Meter/Rhythm—*Allegro Vivace*; 𝐂 ; rhythmic patterns through the subdivision of the beat; the tempo needs to be fast enough for a one-measure pulse grouping.
4. Texture—monophonic: single line split between the two hands.
5. Form—AA-BA¹BA¹ + coda; eight-measure phrases.
6. Harmony—A section: E minor; B section: G major; varied harmonic rhythm.
7. Melody—fragmented melody on the top notes in the right hand, which is difficult to perceive because of the rests.
8. Articulation—numerous two-note slurs within each hand and some accents.
9. Dynamics—wide dynamic range: *p-ff*.
10. Musical Expression/Character—agitated.
11. Pedaling—shallow, overlapping pedaling, more than is notated.

Op. 109, No. 9: *Morning Bell*
Level: LI, JM7

1. Keyboard Skills/Technique/Mobility—Left-hand crossings to a consistent "bell-tone" note; right-hand finger independence needed for

multiple voices and awkward fingering needed for the *legato* melody; repeated intervals and chords.

2. Notation—range is E-flat1-D-flat6; rapid and frequent changes of clefs.
3. Tempo/Meter/Rhythm—*Andante sostenuto*; 3/4 ; note values through the subdivision of the beat.
4. Texture—homophonic: A section: three-part texture of melody, inner voice accompaniment, and bass line with hand crossings; B section: right-hand, overlapping, two-part polyphony with left-hand, repeated-chord accompaniment; C section: thicker texture with the melody in parallel thirds and sixths accompanied by left-hand chords.
5. Form—ABCA[1] + coda; eight-measure phrases.
6. Harmony—A section: A-flat major; B section: E-flat major; C section: A-flat major; varied harmonic rhythm; tension/resolution.
7. Melody—right-hand, lyrical melody with vocal leaps and a short, cadenza-like passagework section.
8. Articulation—extensive variety of articulations: short slurs, finger *staccatos*, various accents, *portatos*.
9. Dynamics—*pp-ff*, with *sf* and numerous sudden dynamic changes.
10. Musical Expression/Character—dramatic, passionate.
11. Pedaling—overlapping pedaling.

<u>Op. 109, No. 10: *Velocity*</u>
Level: MI, JM7

1. Keyboard Skills/Technique/Mobility—right-hand, instrumental passagework that sometimes moves beneath the *staccato*, repeated-chord accompaniment.
2. Notation—range is C2-G7; use of two bass clefs.
3. Tempo/Meter/Rhythm—*Vivo*; 6/8 ; rhythmic patterns through the subdivision of the beat.
4. Texture—homophonic: passagework with *staccato*, repeated-chord accompaniment.
5. Form—AABCA[1]+ coda; four- and eight-measure phrases.

6. Harmony—A section: C major; B section: C major and C minor; C section: A-flat major, modulatory; varied harmonic rhythm.
7. Melody—right-hand, single-line, instrumental passagework with chromaticism.
8. Articulation—*leggiero* melody with *staccato* accompaniment chords and short slurs.
9. Dynamics—*p-f*, with *sf* and sudden dynamic changes.
10. Musical Expression/Character—exciting, joyful.
11. Pedaling—limited, shallow, direct pedaling.

Op. 109, No. 11: *Serenade*
Level: LI, JM9

1. Keyboard Skills/Technique/Mobility—right-hand, *staccato* melody with broken-chord inner voices in both hands; left-hand has wide leaps from the bass notes to the broken chords.
2. Notation—range is A1-A6; extensive use of grace notes makes the score very cluttered.
3. Tempo/Meter/Rhythm—*Allegretto grazioso*; $\tfrac{6}{8}$; rhythmic patterns through the division of the beat; the minimum pulse grouping should be two beats per measure.
4. Texture—homophonic: right-hand, *staccato*, fragmented melody with broken-chord accompaniment in both hands.
5. Form—AA¹BB¹ + coda; four-measure phrases.
6. Harmony—A section: A minor; B section: C major; moderate harmonic rhythm.
7. Melody—right-hand, *staccato* melody requiring finger independence to play both the melody notes and broken chords.
8. Articulation—*staccato* melody and accompaniment, slurred grace-note broken chords, and various accents and *staccatos*.
9. Dynamics—*pp-f*, with *fp* and sudden dynamic changes.
10. Musical Expression/Character—dance-like.
11. Pedaling—consistent, shallow, overlapping pedaling with the bass notes.

Op. 109, No. 12: *Awakening in the Woods*
Level: LI, JM9

1. Keyboard Skills/Technique/Mobility—rapid broken octaves in both hands; rapid, repeated, wrist *staccato* chords; different articulations required between the two hands; quick position changes in both hands.
2. Notation—range is A1-A6; use of two treble clefs.
3. Tempo/Meter/Rhythm—*Allegro*; 𝄴; rhythmic patterns through the division of the beat.
4. Texture—homophonic: right-hand, *staccato*, broken-octave melody with left-hand, wrist *staccato*, repeated-chord accompaniment; the texture switches hands in the B section.
5. Form—Introduction ABAC + coda; eight-measure phrases.
6. Harmony—A section: F major; B section: D minor; C section: F minor; varied harmonic rhythm.
7. Melody—A section: right-hand melody in broken octaves; B section: left-hand melody in broken octaves; C section: melody in both hands.
8. Articulation—*staccato* eighth notes with a *leggiero* touch; some short slurs.
9. Dynamics—wide dynamic range: *pp-f*, with *sf* and sudden dynamic changes.
10. Musical Expression/Character—energetic, dramatic.
11. Pedaling—intermittent, direct pedaling to support *forte* and *sf* dynamics.

Op. 109, No. 13: *The Storm*
Level: MI, JM6-7

1. Keyboard Skills/Technique/Mobility—rapid broken octaves, broken intervals, and arpeggios; rapid hand contraction and extension; rapid sixteenth-note passages split between the two hands.
2. Notation—range is D1-F6; use of two bass clefs.
3. Tempo/Meter/Rhythm—*Allegro*; 𝄴; rhythmic patterns through the subdivision of the beat.

4. Texture—homophonic: instrumental, motivic passagework in various textures.
5. Form—AA-BB-A¹ + coda; four- and eight-measure phrases.
6. Harmony—A section: D minor; B section: F major, D minor; coda: D major.
7. Melody—primarily instrumental figuration, with some sections more "melodic."
8. Articulation—a variety of articulations: short slurs, accents, *marcatos*, *staccatos*.
9. Dynamics—*pp-ff*, with *sf* and many sudden dynamic changes.
10. Musical Expression/Character—stormy, agitated.
11. Pedaling—frequently changing, overlapping pedaling; some direct pedaling.

Op. 109, No. 14: *Song of the Gondolier*
Level: LI, JM8

1. Keyboard Skills/Technique/Mobility—difficult, left-hand, broken-chord accompaniment with rapid awkward position shifts and wide stretches; right-hand, single-line, lyrical melody with occasional additional voices; finger independence is required within each hand and between the two hands; the left-hand accompaniment stemming indicates finger pedaling.
2. Notation—range is A1-C-sharp6.
3. Tempo/Meter/Rhythm—*Andantino con moto*; $_8^6$; rhythmic patterns through the subdivision of the beat.
4. Texture—homophonic: right-hand, single-line melody with occasional added voices with left-hand, broken-chord accompaniment that includes finger pedaling.
5. Form—Introduction AABBC + coda; eight-measure phrases.
6. Harmony—A major, with some awkward chromatic sections; varied harmonic rhythm.
7. Melody—right-hand, scalar, vocal melody with some wide leaps; limited short trills and smaller ornaments.

8. Articulation—*legato*, with short slurs, *portatos*, and unusual *staccato* bass notes.
9. Dynamics—*pp-mf*, with *sf* and extensive *crescendo* and *diminuendo*; quick dynamic changes.
10. Musical Expression/Character—singing, graceful.
11. Pedaling—limited, shallow, direct pedaling; overlapping pedaling in section C and the coda.

Op. 109, No. 15: *Sylphs*
Level: LI, JM8

1. Keyboard Skills/Technique/Mobility—rapid, light, broken-chord patterns with wide stretches and quick range changes; octave passages; melody doubled in octaves between the hands with intermittent accompanying chords requiring finger independence within each hand.
2. Notation—range is B1-D7; use of two treble clefs; left-hand finger pedaling notated by stemming.
3. Tempo/Meter/Rhythm—*Vivo*; $\frac{3}{8}$; rhythmic patterns through the subdivision of the beat, with many sixteenth-note triplets.
4. Texture—homophonic: A section: right-hand, motivic, instrumental melody with chordal accompaniment; B section: lyrical melody doubled in octaves between the two hands with intermittent, chordal accompaniment.
5. Form—Introduction AB (interpolation) C-AB; eight-measure phrases.
6. Harmony—A section: G minor; B section: modulatory; C section: G major; moderate harmonic rhythm; tension/resolution.
7. Melody—right-hand, instrumental melody with broken-chord patterns and short, lyrical sections.
8. Articulation—extensive articulations and variety of differing articulations between the two hands: *staccatos*, short slurs, accents, *marcatos*.
9. Dynamics—*pp-f*, with *sf* and many sudden dynamic changes.
10. Musical Expression/Character—dance-like.
11. Pedaling—limited, shallow, intermittent pedaling and left-hand finger pedaling.

Op. 109, No. 16: *Parting*
Level: LI, JM8

1. Keyboard Skills/Technique/Mobility—left-hand, *marcato* melody, often doubled in octaves; large right-hand, rapid, repeated chords.
2. Notation—range is F1-G6.
3. Tempo/Meter/Rhythm—*Allegro agitato*; C ; rhythmic patterns through the division of the beat, with numerous triplets; notated tempo *rubato*.
4. Texture—homophonic: left-hand melody with right-hand, intermittent, chordal accompaniment.
5. Form—AA-BA¹BA¹ + coda; four- and eight-measure phrases.
6. Harmony—A section: E-flat; B section: C minor; fast harmonic rhythm.
7. Melody—left-hand, disjunct, chromatic melody, often doubled in octaves.
8. Articulation—a variety of articulations: *staccatos*, *marcatos*, combination markings, short slurs.
9. Dynamics—*p-ff*, with *sf* and extensive *crescendo* and *diminuendo*.
10. Musical Expression/Character—agitated, anxious.
11. Pedaling—quick, overlapping, and intermittent pedaling; more pedaling may be used than is notated.

Op. 109, 17: *March*
Level: LI, JM8

1. Keyboard Skills/Technique/Mobility—dotted-rhythm passagework spanning a wide range; rapid, repeated, *staccato* chords; rolled chords; arpeggios spanning a wide range; wide leaps in each hand; fast octave passages.
2. Notation—wide range: F1-E7.
3. Tempo/Meter/Rhythm—*Allegro maestoso*; C ; rhythmic patterns through the subdivision of the beat, plus thirty-second notes.

4. Texture—homophonic: right-hand, single-line melody that frequently alternates with the melody on top of chords; frequent range changes; left-hand, mixed-texture accompaniments.
5. Form—AA-BA¹BA¹-CC-ABA¹; eight-measure phrases.
6. Harmony—A, B sections: F major; C section: B-flat major; varied harmonic rhythm.
7. Melody—lively, instrumental, right-hand melody within various textures; some grace notes and short ornaments.
8. Articulation—great variety of articulation: short slurs, *staccatos*, *marcatos*, *tenutos* with *staccatos*, *portatos*.
9. Dynamics—*p-ff*, with *sf* and many sudden dynamic changes.
10. Musical Expression/Character—energetic, quirky march.
11. Pedaling—limited pedaling due to the extensive articulations.

Op. 109, No. 18: *Spinning Song*
Level: LI, JM8

1. Keyboard Skills/Technique/Mobility—right-hand, broken-chord, scalar passagework with difficult fingering, rapid hand contraction and extension, and wide leaps; left-hand, detached accompaniment alternating bass notes and chords; the B section has a brief, left-hand, lyrical melody.
2. Notation—wide range: D1-D7; extensive use of 8va; use of two bass clefs.
3. Tempo/Meter/Rhythm—*Allegro Moderato*; **C** ; rhythmic patterns through the subdivision of the beat, with extensive use of sixteenth-note triplets.
4. Texture—homophonic: right-hand, instrumental passagework with line-within-a-line melody notes in different places and left-hand, intermittent, chordal accompaniment.
5. Form—AABB + coda; four-measure phrases.
6. Harmony—D major; varied harmonic rhythm.
7. Melody—A section: right-hand, instrumental passagework covering a wide range; B section: brief, left-hand, lyrical melody.
8. Articulation—*legato*, with short slurs, *staccatos*, *marcatos*, accents.

9. Dynamics—*pp-ff*, with extensive *crescendo* and *diminuendo* and sudden dynamic changes.
10. Musical Expression/Character—whirling, spinning.
11. Pedaling—overlapping, intermittent, and direct pedaling.

Cécile Chaminade—*Album for the Young*, Book 1, Op. 123

Op. 123, No. 1: (untitled)
Level: EI

1. Keyboard Skills/Technique/Mobility—potentially challenging fingering due to textural shifting between single notes and intervals in both hands.
2. Notation—range is A2-G5; use of two treble clefs.
3. Tempo/Meter/Rhythm—*All° tranquillo*; $\mathbf{C}$; mostly quarter notes.
4. Texture—homophonic: chordal texture split between the two hands, with the melody on the top of the right hand.
5. Form—AA^{1}BA^2; eight-measure phrases.
6. Harmony—A section: C major; B section: G major; fast harmonic rhythm.
7. Melody—right-hand, lyrical melody with additional voice.
8. Articulation—*legato*, with short slurs.
9. Dynamics—*p-f*, with *crescendo* and *diminuendo*.
10. Musical Expression/Character—calm, serene, peaceful.
11. Pedaling—frequent, shallow pedaling.

Op. 123, No. 2: *Intermezzo*
Level: EI

1. Keyboard Skills/Technique/Mobility—potentially challenging fingering due to textural shifting between single notes and intervals in both hands.

2. Notation—range is G2-G6; use of two treble clefs; both hands on the same staff at the end.
3. Tempo/Meter/Rhythm—*Moderato*; $\frac{3}{4}$; rhythmic patterns through the subdivision of the beat; extensive dotted-eighth and sixteenth notes.
4. Texture—homophonic: chordal texture split between the two hands, with the melody on the top of the right hand.
5. Form—AA¹BA² + coda; eight-measure phrases.
6. Harmony—G major; fast harmonic rhythm.
7. Melody—right-hand, limited-range melody with an additional voice.
8. Articulation—sustained, with short slurs, accents, and a brief *marcato* section.
9. Dynamics—*p-f*, with *crescendo* and *diminuendo*.
10. Musical Expression/Character—sweet, graceful, with a few declamatory sections.
11. Pedaling—intermittent pedaling, primarily to enhance the two-note slurs and provide resonance on the chords.

Op. 123, No. 3: *Canzonetta*
Level: EI

1. Keyboard Skills/Technique/Mobility—extensive left-hand contraction and extension.
2. Notation—range is G2-B5; use of two treble clefs.
3. Tempo/Meter/Rhythm—*Allegretto*; **C**; rhythmic patterns through the division of the beat.
4. Texture—homophonic: right-hand, single-line, lyrical melody with intermittent additional voice and active left-hand accompaniment.
5. Form—A-BA¹-BA¹; eight-measure phrases.
6. Harmony—A section: C major; B section: G major; fast harmonic rhythm.
7. Melody—right-hand, single-line, lyrical melody with intermittent additional voice; long notes may cause fading sound challenges.
8. Articulation—*legato*, with short slurs that may be interpreted as longer phrases.

9. Dynamics—*mf-f*, with *diminuendo* to softer dynamic levels.
10. Musical Expression/Character—sweet, gentle.
11. Pedaling—none, or possibly frequent, shallow, overlapping pedaling.

Op. 123, No. 4: *Rondeau*
Level: EI

1. Keyboard Skills/Technique/Mobility—potential fingering challenges due to textural shifts in the number of voices in the right hand.
2. Notation—range is F2-C6.
3. Tempo/Meter/Rhythm—*Allegro*; $^6_8$; rhythmic patterns through the division of the beat.
4. Texture—homophonic: A section: right-hand, single-line melody with inconsistent additional voices; B section: limited octave doubling of the melody between the two hands.
5. Form—AB (interpolation) A¹; four- and eight-measure phrases.
6. Harmony—A section: F major; B section: A minor, C major; varied harmonic rhythm.
7. Melody—Right-hand, single-line melody with intermittent additional voices.
8. Articulation—short slurs and accents; non-slurred sections imply detached touches.
9. Dynamics—*mf-f*, with limited *crescendo* and *diminuendo*.
10. Musical Expression/Character—gigue, dance-like.
11. Pedaling—limited, intermittent pedaling to enhance the slurs.

Op. 123, No. 5: *Gavotte*
Level: MI

1. Keyboard Skills/Technique/Mobility—quick range changes; significant diversity between the two hands.
2. Notation—range is A2-C6; use of two treble clefs.
3. Tempo/Meter/Rhythm—*Allegretto*; $^2_4$; rhythmic patterns through the subdivision of the beat.

4. Texture—A section: polyphonic; B section: homophonic.
5. Form—AA¹-BB¹ (interpolation) A²; four- to eight-measure phrases.
6. Harmony—A section: A minor, C major; B section: C major; B¹ modulates back to A minor; fast harmonic rhythm.
7. Melody—A section: single-line, scalar, instrumental melody; grace notes; B section: chords split between the two hands; A² melody starts in the left hand, switches to the right hand, then switches back to the left hand for the coda.
8. Articulation—variety of articulations: short slurs, *staccatos*, varied accents, *tenutos*; diverse articulations between the two hands.
9. Dynamics—*p-f*, with *crescendo* and *diminuendo* and sudden dynamic changes.
10. Musical Expression/Character—gavotte, folk dance.
11. Pedaling—limited, intermittent pedaling, primarily on the chords.

Op. 123, No. 6: *Gigue*
Level: EI

1. Keyboard Skills/Technique/Mobility—two-part texture with significant diversity of patterns between the two hands.
2. Notation—range is C2-G5; extensive use of two treble clefs.
3. Tempo/Meter/Rhythm—*Allegro*; $\frac{6}{8}$; rhythmic patterns through the division of the beat.
4. Texture—polyphonic, with active single musical lines in each hand.
5. Form—A-BA¹C-BA¹C; eight- and nine-measure phrases, with thematic similarity between the phrases.
6. Harmony—A section: C major; B section: mostly "on" the dominant G; C section: C major; varied harmonic rhythm.
7. Melody—active, right-hand melody with scalar passages and broken intervals.
8. Articulation—*legato*, with many short slurs.
9. Dynamics—wide dynamic range: *p-ff*, with *crescendo* and *diminuendo*.
10. Musical Expression/Character—sweet, happy.
11. Pedaling—none, due to the active left hand.

Op. 123, No. 7: *Romance*
Level: EI

1. Keyboard Skills/Technique/Mobility—potential fingering challenges due to textural shifts between single notes and intervals in both hands.
2. Notation—range is C2-A5; use of two treble clefs.
3. Tempo/Meter/Rhythm—*Andante*; 2/4 ; rhythmic patterns through the subdivision of the beat, plus thirty-second notes.
4. Texture—homophonic: right-hand, single-line melody with left-hand accompaniment; both hands have inconsistent number of voices.
5. Form—A-BC-BC + coda; five- and eight-measure phrases.
6. Harmony—A section: F major; B, C sections: modulatory, returning back to F major; varied harmonic rhythm.
7. Melody—right-hand, single-line melody with inconsistent number of voices; grace notes.
8. Articulation—*legato*, with short slurs.
9. Dynamics—*p-f*, with *crescendo* and *diminuendo*.
10. Musical Expression/Character—sweet, gentle.
11. Pedaling—A section: limited, intermittent, shallow pedaling; B section: shallow, overlapping pedaling.

Op. 123, No. 8: *Barcarolle*
Level: EI

1. Keyboard Skills/Technique/Mobility—significant diversity of musical patterns between the two hands; right-hand, single-line melody with inconsistent number of additional voices and left-hand, single-line accompaniment with occasional additional voice.
2. Notation—range is E2-F-sharp5.
3. Tempo/Meter/Rhythm—*Allegretto*; 6/8 ; rhythmic patterns through the division of the beat.
4. Texture—homophonic: right-hand melody with inconsistent number of additional voices and active, left-hand accompaniment with occasional additional voice; B section: the melody briefly switches to the left hand.

5. Form—A-BA¹-BA¹ + coda; four-measure phrases.
6. Harmony—A section: A major; B section: F-sharp minor; moderate harmonic rhythm.
7. Melody—right-hand, lyrical, disjunct melody with inconsistent number of voices.
8. Articulation—*legato*, with numerous short slurs and accents.
9. Dynamics—*p-f*, with *crescendo* and *diminuendo*.
10. Musical Expression/Character—sweet, joyful.
11. Pedaling—none, or possibly intermittent, shallow pedaling due to the active left hand.

Op. 123, No. 9: *Orientale*
Level: EI

1. Keyboard Skills/Technique/Mobility—frequent, left-hand range changes.
2. Notation—range is B1-D6; use of two treble clefs.
3. Tempo/Meter/Rhythm—*Mouvement modéré de valse*; $\frac{3}{4}$; rhythmic patterns through the division of the beat.
4. Texture—homophonic: right-hand, single-line melody with left-hand, patterned, chordal accompaniment.
5. Form—ABA¹ + coda; four-measure phrases, plus a seven-measure coda.
6. Harmony—E minor; moderate harmonic rhythm.
7. Melody—right-hand, single-line, lyrical melody in the Dorian mode.
8. Articulation—*legato*, with some accents and *portatos*.
9. Dynamics—*pp-f*, with some *diminuendo*.
10. Musical Expression/Character—waltz.
11. Pedaling—shallow pedaling, primarily on the left-hand two-note slurs.

Op. 123, No. 10: *Tarentelle*
Level: MI

1. Keyboard Skills/Technique/Mobility—fast tempo with diversity of patterns between the two hands; left-hand, widely spaced, broken-chord patterns; difficult right-hand fingering with rapid position shifts.

2. Notation—range is A1-B5; use of two treble clefs; both hands notated in octaves on the same staff at the end.
3. Tempo/Meter/Rhythm—*Vivo*; 6/8 ; rhythmic patterns through the division of the beat.
4. Texture—homophonic: A section: right-hand, single-line melody with active left-hand accompaniment; B section: chords alternating with mixed-textures.
5. Form—AA¹-BA²A³-BA²A³ + coda; eight-measure phrases.
6. Harmony—A section: A minor; B section: C major; fast harmonic rhythm.
7. Melody—A section: right-hand, scalar melody with intermittent additional voice; B section: melody on top of chords.
8. Articulation—many short slurs, accents, and *tenuto* markings.
9. Dynamics—*p-ff*, with sudden dynamic changes.
10. Musical Expression/Character—whirling dance, wild, dramatic.
11. Pedaling—B section: direct pedaling on the *marcato* chords and overlapping pedaling on the *tenuto* chords.

Op. 123, No. 11: *Air de Ballet*
Level: EI

1. Keyboard Skills/Technique/Mobility—right-hand, lyrical melody with chordal accompaniment.
2. Notation—range is D2-A5; use of two treble clefs.
3. Tempo/Meter/Rhythm—*Movement de valse*; 3/4 ; rhythmic patterns through the division of the beat; notated tempo *rubato*.
4. Texture—homophonic: A section: right-hand, single-line, lyrical melody with intermittent, chordal accompaniment; B section: right-hand melody with inconsistent number of voices and left-hand, continuous, chordal accompaniment; C section: left-hand melody with occasional added voice and right-hand, *staccato* accompaniment chords.
5. Form—A-BC-B¹C; eight-measure phrases.
6. Harmony—D major; many chords have added pitches; variable harmonic rhythm.

7. Melody—A section: right-hand, single-line, lyrical melody with many vocal leaps; B section: right-hand melody with additional voices; C section: left-hand, single-line melody.
8. Articulation—*legato*, with many short slurs and accents.
9. Dynamics—*p-f.*
10. Musical Expression/Character—elegant waltz.
11. Pedaling—A section: intermittent pedaling, primarily on the long notes; B section: overlapping pedaling; C section: intermittent pedaling, primarily on the long notes.

Op. 123, No. 12: *Marche Russe*
Level: EI

1. Keyboard Skills/Technique/Mobility—right-hand finger independence required due to difficult fingering for quickly changing dotted-eighth note patterns with parallel intervals.
2. Notation—wide range: A1-E-flat6; use of two treble clefs and two bass clefs.
3. Tempo/Meter/Rhythm—*Moderato*; **C** ; dotted-eighth and sixteenth-note patterns.
4. Texture—homophonic: chordal texture with melody on top of the chords; some unison octave doubling between the two hands.
5. Form—ABA¹ + coda; four-measure phrases.
6. Harmony—A section: D minor, F major; B section: F major, A major.
7. Melody—right-hand melody on top of chords; coda: left-hand melody.
8. Articulation—*tenutos*, accents, and many two-note slurs.
9. Dynamics—wide dynamic range: *pp-ff.*
10. Musical Expression/Character—Russian march.
11. Pedaling—some intermittent, overlapping pedaling on the *tenuto* chords; direct pedaling on the accented notes.

Cécile Chaminade—*Album for the Young*, Book 2, Op. 126

<u>Op. 126, No. 1: *Idylle*</u>
Level: EI

1. Keyboard Skills/Technique/Mobility—wide stretches in the right-hand, *legato* melody.
2. Notation—range is G2-B5; use of two treble clefs.
3. Tempo/Meter/Rhythm—*Allegretto*; $\frac{6}{8}$; rhythmic patterns through the division of the beat; some notated tempo *rubato*.
4. Texture—homophonic: right-hand, lyrical melody with left-hand, broken-chord accompaniment.
5. Form—ABA; eight-measure phrases.
6. Harmony—A section: C major; B section: G major; varied harmonic rhythm.
7. Melody—right-hand, lyrical melody with wide vocal leaps and occasional added voice.
8. Articulation—*legato*, with short slurs and accents.
9. Dynamics—*p-f*, with *crescendo* and *diminuendo*.
10. Musical Expression/Character—tranquil, pastorale.
11. Pedaling—pedaling as notated by the composer; B section includes finger pedaling.

<u>Op. 126, No. 2: *Aubade*</u>
Level: MI

1. Keyboard Skills/Technique/Mobility—left-hand, lyrical melody with intermittent, right-hand accompaniment.

2. Notation—range is B1-F-sharp4; use of two treble clefs.
3. Tempo/Meter/Rhythm—*Andante tranquillo*; ¢ ; rhythmic patterns through the subdivision of the beat.
4. Texture—homophonic: left-hand, single-line, lyrical melody with right-hand, intermittent, chordal accompaniment; C section: right-hand melody on top of *legato* chords.
5. Form—ABCA; eight-measure phrases.
6. Harmony—A section: E major; B section: modulatory, B major; C section: E major; unpredictable harmonic progressions.
7. Melody—left-hand, single-line, lyrical melody.
8. Articulation—*legato*, with accents and many short slurs.
9. Dynamics—*pp-f*, with *crescendo* and *diminuendo*.
10. Musical Expression/Character—sweetly; a morning song.
11. Pedaling—overlapping pedaling as notated.

Op. 126, No. 3: Rigaudon
Level: MI

1. Keyboard Skills/Technique/Mobility—difficult fingering patterns due to rapidly changing hand positions and shifts in the number of voices within each hand.
2. Notation—range is A1-A5.
3. Tempo/Meter/Rhythm—*Allegretto très rythmé*; 2/4 ; rhythmic patterns through the subdivision of the beat; notated tempo *rubato* at the ends of phrases.
4. Texture—homophonic: A section: chordal texture split between the two hands, with the melody on top of the right hand and inconsistent number of voices in both hands; B section: right hand has some single-line melody sections.
5. Form—ABA¹; four-measure phrases.
6. Harmony—A section: A minor; B section: C major; fast harmonic rhythm.
7. Melody—right-hand melody with inconsistent number of voices.
8. Articulation— an extensive diversity of articulation between the two hands: short slurs, accents, *staccatos*, and *portatos*.

9. Dynamics—*p-f*, with sudden dynamic changes.
10. Musical Expression/Character—lively rustic dance.
11. Pedaling—intermittent, direct, and overlapping pedaling as notated.

Op. 126, No. 4: <u>Eglogue</u>
Level: MI

1. Keyboard Skills/Technique/Mobility—challenging fingering due to constantly shifting chords, hand positions, and number of voices.
2. Notation—range is D2-G5.
3. Tempo/Meter/Rhythm—*Andantino*; $\frac{6}{8}$; rhythmic patterns through the division of the beat, with many dotted-eighth and sixteenth-note patterns.
4. Texture—homophonic: right-hand, lyrical melody on top of chords split between the two hands; intermittent, short, scalar passages in both hands.
5. Form—ABA¹; four- and eight-measure phrases.
6. Harmony—A section: G major; B section: modulatory; significant chromaticism; varied harmonic rhythm.
7. Melody—right-hand, lyrical, scalar melody on top of chords split between the two hands.
8. Articulation—*legato*, with some *marcato* sections.
9. Dynamics—*pp-f*, with extensive *crescendo* and *diminuendo*.
10. Musical Expression/Character—sweet, pastorale.
11. Pedaling—overlapping pedaling of various depths ranging from shallow to full pedaling; some notated, intermittent pedaling could be interpreted as overlapping pedaling.

Op. 126, No. 5: <u>Ballade</u>
Level: MI

1. Keyboard Skills/Technique/Mobility—right-hand melody with frequent hand-position changes; descending, left-hand, parallel intervals with challenging fingering.

2. Notation—range is D2-G5.
3. Tempo/Meter/Rhythm—*Allegro moderato*; 12/8 ; rhythmic patterns through the division of the beat; notated tempo *rubato* and multiple tempo changes with *fermatas* followed by a return to tempo.
4. Texture—homophonic: primarily right-hand melody with inconsistent number of voices; some chordal passages.
5. Form—AA¹BA²; four-measure phrases, with one six-measure phrase.
6. Harmony—A section: G minor; B section: D minor, G minor.
7. Melody—fragmented, right-hand melody with many two-note slurs and rests.
8. Articulation—a significant variety of articulations: short slurs, *marcatos*, and accents; contrasts between *dolce* and *marcato* sections.
9. Dynamics—*pp-f*, with sudden dynamic changes.
10. Musical Expression/Character—jaunty, excited, dramatic.
11. Pedaling—additional overlapping and intermittent pedaling could be used in addition to the notated pedaling.

<u>Op. 126, No. 6: *Scherzo-Valse*</u>
Level: MI

1. Keyboard Skills/Technique/Mobility—the left-hand melody flows frequently to the right hand through passagework.
2. Notation—range is D2-D6.
3. Tempo/Meter/Rhythm—*Allegro*; 3/8 ; rhythmic patterns through the subdivision of the beat.
4. Texture—homophonic: A section: left-hand melody flows to the right hand through scalar passages; mixed-texture accompaniments, including a left-hand jump bass; B section: right-hand melody on top of chords, interspersed with chromatic passagework flowing from the left hand to the right hand, and with sections of right-hand, single-line melodies.
5. Form—A-BA¹-BA¹; eight-measure phrases.
6. Harmony—A section: D major; B section: A major.

7. Melody—A section: left-hand, single-line melody with occasional additional voices; right-hand, single-line melody with occasional additional voices; B section: right-hand melody with wide leaps on top of chords.
8. Articulation—a variety of articulations: short slurs, accents, *staccatos*.
9. Dynamics—*p-f*.
10. Musical Expression/Character—waltz.
11. Pedaling—intermittent and overlapping pedaling.

<u>Op. 126, No. 7: *Élégie*</u>
Level: MI

1. Keyboard Skills/Technique/Mobility—difficult texture due to the diversity between the two hands; there are many threats to the pulse, including the scalar passagework in the B section that changes hands frequently but inconsistently with the meter.
2. Notation—range is D2-B-flat5; B section: both hands are written on the same staff.
3. Tempo/Meter/Rhythm—*Andante sostenuto*; $^6_8$; rhythmic patterns through the subdivision of the beat.
4. Texture—homophonic: A section: right-hand, lyrical melody; B section: chordal, with the melody on top of the chords, followed by passagework split between the two hands.
5. Form—Introduction A (extended) BA¹; four-measure phrases.
6. Harmony—D minor; varied harmonic rhythm.
7. Melody—right-hand, scalar, lyrical melody with a few short ornaments.
8. Articulation—*legato*, with short slurs and some accents.
9. Dynamics—*p-f*, with *crescendo* and *diminuendo*.
10. Musical Expression/Character—sad, mournful.
11. Pedaling—overlapping pedaling.

<u>Op. 126, No. 8: *Novelette*</u>
Level: LI

1. Keyboard Skills/Technique/Mobility—rapid hand-position and range changes as well as shifts of musical material between the two hands.

2. Notation—range is C2-C6; some rolled intervals.
3. Tempo/Meter/Rhythm—*Allegretto*; $\frac{2}{4}$; rhythmic patterns through the subdivision of the beat; some notated tempo *rubato*.
4. Texture—homophonic, with much diversity between the two hands.
5. Form—A-BA¹-BA¹; four- and eight-measure phrases, with one five-measure phrase.
6. Harmony—A section: F major; B section: C major; fast harmonic rhythm.
7. Melody—A section: right-hand, disjunct melody with inconsistent number of voices; B section: various textures, including some polyphony with the musical material switching hands and a chordal section.
8. Articulation—a variety of articulations including short slurs, accents, and *tenutos*.
9. Dynamics—*p-f*.
10. Musical Expression/Character—quirky, fun, carefree.
11. Pedaling—intermittent and overlapping pedaling.

Op. 126, No. 9: *Patrouille*
Level: MI

1. Keyboard Skills/Technique/Mobility—challenging fingering due to quick hand-position changes and diverse patterns between the two hands.
2. Notation—range is G1-E-flat5; both hands on the same staff at the end.
3. Tempo/Meter/Rhythm—*Allegretto moderato*; **C**; rhythmic patterns through the division of the beat, with some dotted-eighth and sixteenth-note patterns.
4. Texture—homophonic: A section: mostly chordal, with the melody on top of the chords; B section: includes a left-hand melody with right-hand accompaniment; A¹ section: right-hand melody with additional voice and left-hand, broken-interval accompaniment (including some broken octaves).

5. Form—ABA¹B¹ + coda; four-measure phrases.
6. Harmony—A section: G minor; B section: D minor; B¹ section: G minor.
7. Melody—A section: scalar, limited-range, right-hand melody on top of chords; B section: disjunct melody on top of chords repeated in the left hand as a single-line melody.
8. Articulation— a variety of articulations including short slurs, accents, and *staccatos*; diverse articulations between the two hands.
9. Dynamics—*p-ff*, with sudden dynamic changes.
10. Musical Expression/Character—dark, tragic, scary, dramatic.
11. Pedaling—overlapping and limited, intermittent pedaling.

<u>Op. 126, No. 10: *Villanelle*</u>
Level: MI

1. Keyboard Skills/Technique/Mobility—quick range and hand-position changes in each hand.
2. Notation—range is E2–A5; both hands occasionally notated on the same staff.
3. Tempo/Meter/Rhythm—*Allegretto*; $\frac{3}{4}$; rhythmic patterns through the division of the beat; emphasis on the second beat of the measure.
4. Texture—homophonic: melody with mixed-texture accompaniment; some parallel interval passages between the two hands.
5. Form—A-BCA-BCA; eight-measure phrases.
6. Harmony—A major; varied harmonic rhythm.
7. Melody—right-hand melody with short slurs and inconsistent number of voices; some grace notes; the left hand sometimes has the melody or a countermelody.
8. Articulation— a variety of articulations, including short slurs, accents, and *portatos*.
9. Dynamics—*p-f*, with sudden dynamic changes.
10. Musical Expression/Character—rustic dance, folk music.
11. Pedaling—waltz pedaling by the measure; overlapping pedaling.

Op. 126, No. 11: *Conte de Fées*
Level: MI

1. Keyboard Skills/Technique/Mobility—wide-ranging melody in various settings; C section: the pulse is difficult to maintain when the left-hand ostinato does not fit the compound meter pattern well.
2. Notation—wide range: A1–E6; use of two treble clefs; both hands are sometimes notated on the same staff.
3. Tempo/Meter/Rhythm—*Allegretto*; 6/8; rhythmic patterns through the division of the beat.
4. Texture—varied: right-hand, single musical line; right-hand melody with a left-hand countermelody; right-hand melody accompanied by left-hand chords; right-hand melody with a left-hand ostinato accompaniment.
5. Form—ABCAB¹ + coda; variable phrase lengths.
6. Harmony—A minor, C major; varied harmonic rhythm.
7. Melody—right-hand, single musical line; right-hand melody with a countermelody; a few grace notes.
8. Articulation—mostly *legato*, with short slurs and accents.
9. Dynamics—*pp-f*, with sudden dynamic changes.
10. Musical Expression/Character—"fairy tale"
11. Pedaling—overlapping and intermittent pedaling.

Op. 126, No. 12: *Valse Mignonne*
Level: LI

1. Keyboard Skills/Technique/Mobility—rapid hand-position and range changes.
2. Notation—range is C2-F6; use of two treble clefs; both hands are occasionally notated on the same staff.
3. Tempo/Meter/Rhythm—*Allegro vivo*; 3/4; rhythmic patterns through the division of the beat.
4. Texture—homophonic: right-hand melody with occasional added voice and left-hand, mixed-texture accompaniment.

5. Form—AA¹-BB¹ + coda; four- and eight-measure phrases, with a seven-measure coda.
6. Harmony—B-flat major; varied harmonic rhythm.
7. Melody—right-hand, lyrical melody with wide leaps.
8. Articulation—*legato*, with short slurs and accents.
9. Dynamics—*p-f*
10. Musical Expression/Character—dainty, petite waltz.
11. Pedaling—waltz pedaling and overlapping pedaling.

William Gillock—*Lyric Preludes in Romantic Style*

Forest Murmurs
Level: EI

1. Keyboard Skills/Technique/Mobility—right-hand passagework with line-within-a-line melody on the top; rapid hand contraction and extension.
2. Notation—range is C2-G6.
3. Tempo/Meter/Rhythm—"Gently"; 3/4 ; rhythmic patterns through the subdivision of the beat; notated tempo *rubato*.
4. Texture—homophonic: right-hand passagework with line-within-a-line melody on the top and left-hand, jump-bass accompaniment.
5. Form—AA[1] + coda; eight-measure phrases.
6. Harmony—C major; varied harmonic rhythm.
7. Melody—right-hand, lyrical melody; long notes may cause fading sound challenges.
8. Articulation—*legato*, with *portatos*.
9. Dynamics—*pp-mp*, with *crescendo* and *diminuendo*.
10. Musical Expression/Character—murmuring, shimmering.
11. Pedaling—overlapping pedaling; *una corda* notated for the entire piece.

Seascape
Level: EI

1. Keyboard Skills/Technique/Mobility—left-hand crossings over the right hand with large leaps, then both hands cross over each other with rapid range changes; memorization will be helpful to play this piece well.

2. Notation—wide range: C1-C7; use of two treble clefs and two bass clefs, with frequently changing clefs; use of commas as musical "breath marks."
3. Tempo/Meter/Rhythm—"In a stormy mood"; $\frac{4}{4}$; rhythmic patterns through the division of the beat.
4. Texture—homophonic: right-hand chords alternating with left-hand single notes.
5. Form—AA¹ + coda; eight-measure phrases, with a six-measure coda.
6. Harmony—C minor; slow harmonic rhythm.
7. Melody—motivic melody, alternating hands between single notes and the top notes of the chords.
8. Articulation—*legato*.
9. Dynamics—wide dynamic range: *pp-ff*, with quick dynamic changes.
10. Musical Expression/Character—restless, surging.
11. Pedaling—consistent pedaling with the left-hand bass notes, but with sound breaks notated by the commas; pedaling depth can be varied to support the dynamic changes.

October Morning
Level: EI

1. Keyboard Skills/Technique/Mobility—right-hand, lyrical melody with intermittent, chordal accompaniment.
2. Notation—range is G1-G5; use of two bass clefs; clef changes, with rapid range changes in both hands.
3. Tempo/Meter/Rhythm—"Happily; with much freedom"; $\frac{4}{4}$; rhythmic patterns through the division of the beat; notated tempo *rubato*.
4. Texture—homophonic: right-hand, single-line melody with sparse chordal accompaniment in both hands.
5. Form—one four-measure and one six-measure phrase.
6. Harmony—G major; slow harmonic rhythm.
7. Melody—right-hand, lyrical melody with frequent direction changes.
8. Articulation—*legato*.
9. Dynamics—*pp-f*.

10. Musical Expression/Character—happy, content.
11. Pedaling—intermittent and overlapping pedaling as notated.

Deserted Ball Room
Level: EI

1. Keyboard Skills/Technique/Mobility—rapid hand crossings to play arpeggios across a wide range in the coda.
2. Notation—range is G2-G7.
3. Tempo/Meter/Rhythm—"In a sad and ghostly manner"; $\frac{3}{4}$; rhythmic patterns through the division of the beat.
4. Texture—homophonic: left-hand, single-line melody with intermittent, right-hand accompaniment.
5. Form—AA^1 + coda; eight-measure phrases.
6. Harmony—G minor; slow harmonic rhythm.
7. Melody—left-hand, single-line, lyrical melody; long notes may cause fading sound challenges.
8. Articulation—*legato*, with short slurs.
9. Dynamics—*p-mf*, with extensive *crescendo* and *diminuendo*.
10. Musical Expression/Character—sad, reflective.
11. Pedaling—intermittent and overlapping pedaling as notated.

Legend
Level: EI

1. Keyboard Skills/Technique/Mobility—chromatic chords split between the two hands; quick hand-position and range changes.
2. Notation—range is D1-B-flat5.
3. Tempo/Meter/Rhythm—"Pensively; weighing each thought carefully"; $\frac{2}{4}$; rhythmic patterns through the division of the beat.
4. Texture—homophonic: right-hand melody on top of chords with changing number of voices.

5. Form—through-composed, with a brief restatement of the opening chord progression at the climax of the piece.
6. Harmony—D major, with extensive chromaticism; fast harmonic rhythm.
7. Melody—limited-range, chromatic, right-hand melody on top of chords with changing number of voices.
8. Articulation—*legato*, with *tenutos* and two-note slurs.
9. Dynamics—*pp-f*, with extensive *crescendo* and *diminuendo*.
10. Musical Expression/Character—pensive, reflective.
11. Pedaling—notated, overlapping pedaling is challenging due to the rhythmic placement of the chromatic chords and the fast harmonic rhythm.

Interlude
Level: EI

1. Keyboard Skills/Technique/Mobility—polyphonic texture with overlapping phrases between the two hands.
2. Notation—range is C-sharp2-F5.
3. Tempo/Meter/Rhythm—"Moderately slowly"; $\frac{4}{4}$; rhythmic patterns through the division of the beat; notated tempo *rubato*.
4. Texture—polyphonic: two-voice texture with overlapping phrases between the two hands.
5. Form—AA¹ + coda; four-measure phrases.
6. Harmony—D minor, with chromaticism; fast harmonic rhythm.
7. Melody—broken-chord patterns in both hands.
8. Articulation—*legato*, with short slurs in both hands requiring careful control.
9. Dynamics—*pp-mf*, with extensive *crescendo* and *diminuendo*.
10. Musical Expression/Character—restless.
11. Pedaling—intermittent pedaling as notated.

Song of the Mermaid
Level: EI

1. Keyboard Skills/Technique/Mobility—some awkward fingerings needed for the *legato* melody.

2. Notation—range is A1-A5.
3. Tempo/Meter/Rhythm—"In a flowing manner"; $\frac{4}{4}$; rhythmic patterns through the subdivision of the beat.
4. Texture—homophonic: right-hand, lyrical melody with changing number of additional voices; left-hand, sweeping, scalar passagework accompaniment.
5. Form—through-composed; four-measure phrases.
6. Harmony—A major; varied harmonic rhythm.
7. Melody—right-hand, lyrical melody with changing number of additional voices.
8. Articulation—*legato*, with slurs and combination *staccato/tenuto* markings.
9. Dynamics—*p-f*, with extensive *crescendo* and *diminuendo*.
10. Musical Expression/Character—flowing, peaceful.
11. Pedaling—frequent, shallow pedaling.

Summer Storm
Level: MI

1. Keyboard Skills/Technique/Mobility—difficult left-hand passagework.
2. Notation—range is E1-A5; left-hand leger lines may be challenging.
3. Tempo/Meter/Rhythm—"Dramatically"; $\frac{2}{4}$; rhythmic patterns through the subdivision of the beat.
4. Texture—homophonic: left-hand melody with right-hand, chordal accompaniment; both parts share equal importance.
5. Form—through-composed; four- and six-measure phrases.
6. Harmony—A minor; varied harmonic rhythm.
7. Melody—left-hand, disjunct passagework interspersed with right-hand chords; right-hand chords become the melody at measure nine.
8. Articulation—*legato*, with *staccatos*, accents, *tenutos*, and combination markings.
9. Dynamics—*f-fff*, with *sfz*.
10. Musical Expression/Character—dramatic, stormy, passionate.
11. Pedaling—intermittent pedaling for sustaining chords and increasing volume.

A Faded Letter
Level: EI

1. Keyboard Skills/Technique/Mobility—finger independence required in the right hand; some awkward fingering.
2. Notation—range is B1-C-sharp5.
3. Tempo/Meter/Rhythm—"Tenderly; expressively"; $\frac{3}{4}$; rhythmic patterns through the division of the beat; notated tempo *rubato*.
4. Texture—homophonic: four-voice texture split between the two hands, with the melody in the upper voice.
5. Form—AA¹; four- and six-measure phrases.
6. Harmony—E Major; varied harmonic rhythm; tension/resolution through the two-note slur "sighing."
7. Melody—slow, lyrical, right-hand melody with some awkward fingering; long notes may cause fading sound challenges.
8. Articulation—*legato*, with two-note slurs.
9. Dynamics—*ppp-mp*, with *crescendo* and *diminuendo*.
10. Musical Expression/Character—tender, reflective.
11. Pedaling—consistent, overlapping pedaling with the chord changes.

Dragon Fly
Level: EI

1. Keyboard Skills/Technique/Mobility—fast, right-hand passagework requiring rotation and rapid hand extension and contraction.
2. Notation—range is B2-E7; use of two treble clefs.
3. Tempo/Meter/Rhythm—"Moving quickly; in strict time"; $\frac{2}{4}$; rhythmic patterns through the subdivision of the beat.
4. Texture—homophonic: right-hand passagework with left-hand chordal accompaniment.
5. Form—AA¹ + coda; two- and four-measure phrases.
6. Harmony—E minor; fast harmonic rhythm.

7. Melody—right-hand, instrumental passagework with broken intervals and scalar passages.
8. Articulation—implied non-*legato* passages with many accents interspersed with *legato* passages.
9. Dynamics—*pp-mp*, with fast *crescendo* and *diminuendo*.
10. Musical Expression/Character—urgent, determined.
11. Pedaling—none notated; direct pedaling at different depths can be used on the chords to enhance accents and support dynamics.

Moonlight Mood
Level: MI

1. Keyboard Skills/Technique/Mobility—melody on top of chords alternating rapidly between the two hands; detailed fingering; *legato* passagework flowing between the two hands, sometimes with both hands crossing; difficult improvisatory-like passage with numerous accidentals, including double sharps.
2. Notation—wide range: B1-B6; use of two treble clefs and two bass clefs, with multiple clef changes in both hands.
3. Tempo/Meter/Rhythm—"Mist-like; always lingering"; $\frac{4}{4}$; rhythmic patterns through the subdivision of the beat, plus some asymmetrical scalar passages; notated tempo *rubato*; syncopation.
4. Texture—homophonic: melody on top of chords alternating between the two hands.
5. Form—AA¹ + coda; variable phrase lengths; longer phrases may be difficult due to the many pauses of the rhythmic motion.
6. Harmony—B major, difficult key with significant chromaticism; varied harmonic rhythm.
7. Melody—disjunct melody that moves rapidly between the two hands; careful voicing is needed within each hand and between the two hands to maintain control of the melodic line.
8. Articulation—*legato*, requiring focused aural connections between the two hands.
9. Dynamics—*ppp-pp*; very soft dynamic levels with subtle tonal shading.

10. Musical Expression/Character—dreamy, transparent.
11. Pedaling—primarily overlapping pedaling, which is challenging due to chord changes on the offbeats; use of *una corda* throughout.

Autumn Sketch
Level: EI

1. Keyboard Skills/Technique/Mobility—playing a smooth melodic contour with upbeat to downbeat rhythmic patterns and changing note values may be challenging; frequent position shifts in both hands.
2. Notation—range is F-sharp2-D6; use of two treble clefs.
3. Tempo/Meter/Rhythm—"Moving subtly"; 3/4; rhythmic patterns through the division of the beat.
4. Texture—homophonic: A section: right-hand, lyrical melody of continuous short slurs; B section: more rhythmically varied right-hand melody; left-hand, broken-chord accompaniment throughout.
5. Form—AA^1-BB^1 + coda; eight-measure phrases.
6. Harmony—B minor; moderate harmonic rhythm.
7. Melody—right-hand, single-line, lyrical melody with occasional added voice.
8. Articulation—*legato*, with numerous short slurs, *tenutos*, and *portatos*.
9. Dynamics—*pp-mf*, with *crescendo* and *diminuendo*.
10. Musical Expression/Character—elegant waltz.
11. Pedaling—A section: challenging pedaling on the offbeats as notated; B section: consistent, overlapping pedaling on the downbeats as notated.

Procession of the Mandarin
Level: EI

1. Keyboard Skills/Technique/Mobility—primarily parallel intervals alternating between the two hands; interlocking hands and rapid hand-position changes.

2. Notation—wide range: G-flat1–G-flat6; use of two treble clefs; numerous clef changes in both hands; the notation makes it difficult to follow the melody visually.
3. Tempo/Meter/Rhythm—"With a slow, swaying motion"; $\frac{4}{4}$; rhythmic patterns through the division of the beat.
4. Texture—homophonic: primarily parallel intervals alternating between the two hands with the melody on top; A¹ section has primarily parallel intervals in both hands at the same time.
5. Form—ABA¹ + coda; four-, six-, and eight-measure phrases.
6. Harmony—G-flat major; slow harmonic rhythm determined by the bass notes.
7. Melody—repetitive, pentatonic melody alternating between the two hands.
8. Articulation—bell-tone effects of playing *staccato* on the pedal; accents, and accents combined with *staccatos*.
9. Dynamics—wide range: *mp-fff*, with *sfz*.
10. Musical Expression/Character—grand processional.
11. Pedaling—consistent pedaling as notated.

Winter Scene
Level: MI

1. Keyboard Skills/Technique/Mobility—instrumental passagework in both hands with awkward fingering; frequently changing textures; finger independence required for multiple voices within one hand, including the use of finger pedaling; both hands crossing in the coda; requires sophisticated voicing and balancing of textures.
2. Notation—range is F-sharp2–F-sharp6; use of two treble clefs.
3. Tempo/Meter/Rhythm—"With grace and delicacy"; $\frac{3}{4}$; rhythmic patterns through the division of the beat; several *fermatas* and notated tempo *rubato* that require careful pacing; the rhythmic pattern in the coda may cause metrical challenges due to the upbeat start and the hand crossing groupings.

4. Texture—homophonic: the melody switches between the two hands with various accompaniments.
5. Form—AA¹-BA² + coda; four-measure phrases.
6. Harmony—F-sharp minor, with significant chromaticism; slow harmonic rhythm.
7. Melody—scalar, lyrical passagework that flows between the two hands; some use of the melodic minor scale pitches.
8. Articulation—*legato*, with short slurs.
9. Dynamics—wide range: *ppp-mf*.
10. Musical Expression/Character—delicate waltz.
11. Pedaling—intermittent and overlapping pedaling.

Serenade
Level: MI

1. Keyboard Skills/Technique/Mobility—right-hand, lyrical melody that moves below the left-hand accompaniment, putting both hands in awkward positions and making voicing challenging; some finger substitutions on long notes with hand contraction and extension.
2. Notation—wide range: A-flat1-D-flat7; use of two treble clefs and two bass clefs.
3. Tempo/Meter/Rhythm—"Moderately"; $\frac{4}{4}$; rhythmic patterns through the division of the beat.
4. Texture—homophonic: right-hand, single-line, lyrical melody with mixed-texture accompaniment.
5. Form—AA¹ + coda; two long phrases of sixteen and eighteen measures.
6. Harmony—D-flat major; varied harmonic rhythm.
7. Melody—wide-ranging, right-hand, scalar melody that moves below the accompaniment; long note values in the melody may cause fading sound challenges; coda has wide vocal leaps.
8. Articulation—*legato*, with two-note slurs, *portatos*, and *tenutos*; "bell-tone" effect of playing *staccato* on the pedal.
9. Dynamics—*pp-mf*.

10. Musical Expression/Character—vocal aria, song without words.
11. Pedaling—overlapping pedaling as notated, but the pianist may choose to use more continuous overlapping pedaling.

Humming Bird
Level: MI

1. Keyboard Skills/Technique/Mobility—fast, light, right-hand passagework with rapid directional changes and hand crossings with both hands; rapid alternation of pitches between the two hands with *accelerando* just before the Tempo I.
2. Notation—wide range: C-sharp2-C-sharp7; use of two treble clefs.
3. Tempo/Meter/Rhythm—"Quickly and smoothly"; $\frac{2}{4}$; rhythmic patterns through the subdivision of the beat; tempo changes.
4. Texture—homophonic: right-hand, figurational melody with left-hand, intermittent, mixed-texture accompaniment.
5. Form—AA^1-B-AA^1 + coda; two- and four-measure phrases.
6. Harmony—C-sharp minor, with extensive chromaticism; slow harmonic rhythm.
7. Melody—fast, light, chromatic, right-hand passagework.
8. Articulation—*legato*, with *staccato* chords, *tenutos*, accents, and combination markings.
9. Dynamics—wide range: *ppp-mf*.
10. Musical Expression/Character—flittering bird.
11. Pedaling—limited, shallow pedaling as notated.

Fountain of Diana
Level: EI

1. Keyboard Skills/Technique/Mobility—fast sixteenth-note rolling passagework that moves between the two hands; rapid hand crossings with both hands.
2. Notation—wide range: B-flat1-A-flat6; use of two treble clefs.
3. Tempo/Meter/Rhythm—"Smoothly flowing"; $\frac{3}{4}$; rhythmic patterns through the subdivision of the beat; notated tempo *rubato*.

4. Texture—homophonic: left-hand, lyrical melody with occasional added voices, needing careful voicing; flowing, sixteenth-note accompaniment that moves between the two hands.
 5. Form—through-composed; four-measure phrases, with short interpolations in between the phrases.
 6. Harmony—A-flat major; slow harmonic rhythm.
 7. Melody—left-hand, singing *legato* melody; grace notes.
 8. Articulation—*legato*, with *tenutos*, *staccatos*, and combination markings.
 9. Dynamics—*pp-f*, with extensive *crescendo* and *diminuendo*.
 10. Musical Expression/Character—flowing water.
 11. Pedaling—continuous, shallow, overlapping pedaling.

Phantom Rider
Level: MI

 1. Keyboard Skills/Technique/Mobility—very fast hand-over-hand arpeggios alternating with chords in both hands.
 2. Notation—wide range: G-sharp2-G-sharp7; use of two treble clefs.
 3. Tempo/Meter/Rhythm—"Mysteriously; terrifying"; $\frac{4}{4}$; rhythmic patterns through the division of the beat; extensive use of triplets.
 4. Texture—homophonic: single musical line alternating hands interspersed with triads doubled between the two hands.
 5. Form—AA¹ + coda; four-measure phrases.
 6. Harmony—G-sharp minor, challenging key, including the use of double sharps and chromaticism; varied harmonic rhythm.
 7. Melody—hand-over-hand arpeggios split between the two hands, alternating with chords with the melody on top; *fortissimo* chords need strong voicing.
 8. Articulation—contrasts of *legato* and *marcato* sections, with accents and *tenutos*.
 9. Dynamics—*pp-ff*, with quick *crescendo* and sudden dynamic changes.
 10. Musical Expression/Character—frightening.
 11. Pedaling—consistent pedaling on the broken chords as notated; short direct pedals on the chords for more volume.

Soaring
Level: EI

1. Keyboard Skills/Technique/Mobility—right-hand, broken-chord passagework with line-within-a-line melody on the bottom, requiring finger independence within the right hand; rapid octave changes in both hands.
2. Notation—range is B-flat1-C7; use of two treble clefs and two bass clefs; both hands are occasionally notated on the same staff.
3. Tempo/Meter/Rhythm—"In a romantically intense manner"; $\frac{4}{4}$; rhythmic patterns through the division of the beat; extensive use of triplets; notated tempo *rubato*.
4. Texture—homophonic: right-hand, lyrical melody with left-hand, sustained, chordal accompaniment.
5. Form—through-composed; eight-measure phrases.
6. Harmony—E-flat major; varied harmonic rhythm.
7. Melody—right-hand, lyrical passagework with line-within-a-line melody on the bottom.
8. Articulation—*legato*, with *tenutos*.
9. Dynamics—*mp-f*.
10. Musical Expression/Character—soaring, passionate.
11. Pedaling—continuous, overlapping pedaling as notated.

The Silent Snow
Level: EI

1. Keyboard Skills/Technique/Mobility—limited position shifts and one left-hand crossing.
2. Notation—range is E-flat2-E-flat5.
3. Tempo/Meter/Rhythm—"Slowly; quietly"; $\frac{6}{8}$; rhythmic patterns through the division of the beat.
4. Texture—homophonic: melody with chordal accompaniment that switches between the two hands.
5. Form—through-composed; four-measure phrases.

6. Harmony—E-flat minor; moderate harmonic rhythm; tension/resolution.
7. Melody—lyrical melody that switches between the two hands.
8. Articulation—*legato*, with short slurs.
9. Dynamics—*pp-mp*, with *crescendo* and *diminuendo*.
10. Musical Expression/Character—tender, gentle.
11. Pedaling—limited, intermittent pedaling.

Night Song
Level: EI

1. Keyboard Skills/Technique/Mobility—right-hand, broken-chord passagework with line-within-a-line melody on both the top and the bottom; awkward fingering with hand extension and contraction.
2. Notation—range is F1-B-flat5; use of two bass clefs.
3. Tempo/Meter/Rhythm—"Moderately"; $^6_8$; rhythmic patterns through the division of the beat; hemiola; syncopation; multiple pauses requiring careful pacing.
4. Texture—homophonic: right-hand, line-within-a-line melody on both top and bottom, with very active left-hand accompaniment.
5. Form—through-composed; various phrase lengths.
6. Harmony—B-flat major; varied harmonic rhythm.
7. Melody—right-hand, line-within-a-line melody with the melody on both the top and bottom within angular passagework with many directional changes.
8. Articulation—*legato*.
9. Dynamics—*p-mf*, with *crescendo* and *diminuendo*.
10. Musical Expression/Character—sweet, reflective song without words.
11. Pedaling—"Pedal lightly if desired," as notated; challenging pedaling to prevent blurring of the texture.

Night Journey
Level: MI

1. Keyboard Skills/Technique/Mobility: fast broken octaves within each hand and doubled in both hands; slurs between the two hands.

2. Notation—range is F1-B-flat5; use of two bass clefs.
3. Tempo/Meter/Rhythm—"Boldly"; 4/4; rhythmic patterns through the division of the beat; triplet upbeats might cause metrical problems.
4. Texture—homophonic: dramatic melody in broken octaves with intermittent, chordal accompaniment, with the melody and accompaniment switching hands.
5. Form—AA-B-A¹B¹; four-measure phrases.
6. Harmony—B-flat minor, with a Picardy third at the end; fast harmonic rhythm.
7. Melody—broken octaves with intermittent chords.
8. Articulation—extensive articulations: two-note and other short slurs, *staccatos*, *marcatos*, *tenutos*, accents, and combination markings.
9. Dynamics—*p-ff*, with some *crescendo* and *diminuendo*.
10. Musical Expression/Character—dramatic, scary.
11. Pedaling—intermittent pedaling as notated.

An Old Valentine
Level: MI

1. Keyboard Skills/Technique/Mobility—multi-voice texture, with inconsistent number of voices in each hand; some awkward fingerings needed for *legato* playing; rolled chords.
2. Notation—range is F2-C6; use of two treble clefs.
3. Tempo/Meter/Rhythm—"Quietly reminiscing"; 3/4; rhythmic patterns through the division of the beat.
4. Texture—homophonic: right-hand melody with left-hand accompaniment, with an inconsistent number of voices within each hand.
5. Form—AA¹; eight-measure phrases.
6. Harmony—F major; fast harmonic rhythm.
7. Melody—right-hand, lyrical melody.
8. Articulation—*legato*, with short slurs.
9. Dynamics—*pp-mf*, with *crescendo* and *diminuendo*, and many dynamic level changes.

10. Musical Expression/Character—tender, reflective.
11. Pedaling—intermittent pedaling needing significant aural attention.

A Witch's Cat
Level: MI

1. Keyboard Skills/Technique/Mobility—numerous quick range changes in both hands; broken arpeggios with many finger crossings; rapid hand crossings in both hands.
2. Notation—wide range: C2-C7; use of two treble clefs and two bass clefs.
3. Tempo/Meter/Rhythm—"Fancifully caricatured"; $\frac{2}{4}$; rhythmic patterns through the subdivision of the beat.
4. Texture—homophonic: A section: right-hand melody with left-hand mixed-texture accompaniment; B section: passagework alternating between the two hands.
5. Form—AA^1-BB^1-AA^1 + coda; four-measure phrases.
6. Harmony—F minor; fast harmonic rhythm; tension/resolution.
7. Melody—*legato* melody of broken arpeggios, sometimes split between the two hands.
8. Articulation—extensive articulation: short slurs, accents, *staccatos*, *tenutos*, and combination markings.
9. Dynamics—*p-ff*, with both sudden and slower dynamic changes.
10. Musical Expression/Character—quirky, scary.
11. Pedaling—intermittent pedaling to enhance slurs or tone quality on long notes.

Edvard Grieg—*Lyric Pieces*, Opp. 12, 38, 43, 47, 54, 57, 62, 65, 68, 71 (Selections)

Op. 12, No. 1: *Arietta*
Level: MI, JM6

1. Keyboard Skills/Technique/Mobility—three-part texture requiring careful voicing and balance; finger independence required within each hand; awkward fingering needed for the *legato* melody.
2. Notation—range is E-flat2-G5.
3. Tempo/Meter/Rhythm—*Poco Andante e sostenuto*; $\frac{2}{4}$; rhythmic patterns through the subdivision of the beat; some syncopation.
4. Texture—homophonic: three-part texture consisting of a lyrical melody, inner voice split between the two hands, and bass line.
5. Form—AA¹; four-measure phrases.
6. Harmony—E-flat major; varied harmonic rhythm; tension/resolution.
7. Melody—right-hand, single-line, lyrical, narrow-range melody with many repeated notes.
8. Articulation—*legato*, with slurs in the inner voice.
9. Dynamics—*p-pp*, with some *crescendo* and *diminuendo*.
10. Musical Expression/Character—dreamy, floating.
11. Pedaling—frequently changing, overlapping pedaling.

Op. 12, No. 2: *Waltz*
Level: MI, JM6

1. Keyboard Skills/Technique/Mobility—finger independence needed between the two hands for different articulations; limited-range, waltz-bass accompaniment.

2. Notation—range is A2-E5; use of two treble clefs.
3. Tempo/Meter/Rhythm—*Allegro moderato*; ¾; rhythmic patterns through the division of the beat; some notated tempo *rubato* at the ends of phrases.
4. Texture—homophonic: A section: right-hand, articulated melody with left-hand, waltz-bass accompaniment; B section: chords split between the two hands with the melody on top of the chords; C section: left-hand melody with right-hand, intermittent, chordal accompaniment.
5. Form—Introduction AB-AB-CC¹ (interpolation) AB + coda; four- and eight-measure phrases, with shorter sub-phrases.
6. Harmony—A section: A minor; B section: C major, modulatory; C section, coda: A major, with a final A minor chord.
7. Melody—A section: single-line melody with melodic minor pitch content; B section: melody on top of chords; C section: left-hand, single-line, lyrical melody; grace notes.
8. Articulation—light *staccatos*; two-note and other short slurs.
9. Dynamics—*pp-f*, with *crescendo*.
10. Musical Expression/Character—waltz.
11. Pedaling—A section: waltz-bass pedaling on beats one and two; B section: intermittent, direct pedaling; C section: frequently changing, intermittent pedaling to enhance long notes, slurs, and accents.

Op. 12, No. 3: *Watchman's Song*
Level: MI, JM5

1. Keyboard Skills/Technique/Mobility—melody doubled in octaves between the two hands interspersed with chordal sections; finger independence required in the right hand to play inconsistent number of voices; successive chord inversions split between the two hands.
2. Notation—range is E2-F5: both hands occasionally notated on the same staff.
3. Tempo/Meter/Rhythm—*Molto Andante e semplice*; ₵; rhythmic patterns through the subdivision of the beat, plus fast septuplets.
4. Texture—homophonic: melody doubled in octaves between the two hands interspersed with chordal sections; two parts in the right hand, requiring finger independence.

5. Form—ABA¹B-CC-BA²; 4-measure phrases.
6. Harmony—A section: E major; B section: E minor.
7. Melody—single-line, scalar melody with limited range and many repeated notes; melody on top of chords.
8. Articulation—*legato*, with slurs and *portatos*.
9. Dynamics—*pp-f*, with sudden dynamic changes in the C section.
10. Musical Expression/Character—mysterious *Intermezzo* section depicts ghosts in the night and the watchman's shout (Grieg composed this piece after he saw a production of Macbeth).[1]
11. Pedaling—quick, shallow, overlapping pedaling as needed, primarily in the chordal sections.

Op. 12, No. 4: *Fairy-dance*
Level: MI, JM6

1. Keyboard Skills/Technique/Mobility—left hand written high in the range; chords alternating with passagework; passagework with broken intervals.
2. Notation—wide range: F-sharp2-E6; both hands frequently notated on the same staff.
3. Tempo/Meter/Rhythm—*Molto Allegro e sempre staccato*; $\frac{3}{4}$; rhythmic patterns through the division of the beat.
4. Texture—homophonic: right-hand melody on top of chords, or as passagework with mixed-texture settings.
5. Form—AAB-AB-AA¹ + coda; variety of phrase lengths.
6. Harmony—E minor; varied harmonic rhythm.
7. Melody—A section: repeated notes on top of chords alternating with single-line passagework; B section: broken-interval passagework.
8. Articulation—light, *staccato* chords with *legato* passagework.
9. Dynamics—wide dynamic range: *ppp-f*, with rapid dynamic changes.
10. Musical Expression/Character—light elfin dance.
11. Pedaling—very little notated pedaling; intermittent, direct pedaling to enhance the dynamics.

Op. 12, No. 5: *Popular Melody*
Level: LI

1. Keyboard Skills/Technique/Mobility—some awkward right-hand fingering; left-hand parallel thirds; left-hand waltz bass with wide leaps; finger independence required within each hand and between hands; some right-hand notes are redistributed to the left hand.
2. Notation—range is E2-F-sharp5; both hands are sometimes notated on the same staff.
3. Tempo/Meter/Rhythm—*Con moto*; 3/4 ; rhythmic patterns through the subdivision of the beat; the rhythm has much in common with a *mazurka*.
4. Texture—homophonic: A section: right-hand, single-line melody with chordal accompaniment; B section: right-hand melody over long notes that are sometimes redistributed to the left hand.
5. Form—AB-A¹B-A²; four-measure phrases.
6. Harmony—F-sharp minor; varied harmonic rhythm.
7. Melody—right-hand, single-line melody with many different rhythmic patterns; limited ornamentation.
8. Articulation—*marcato* style implied by the rhythmic patterns, with short slurs and accents.
9. Dynamics—*p-mf*, with very few notated dynamic changes, but the pianist will need to play with significant phrase shaping.
10. Musical Expression/Character—folk dance.
11. Pedaling—A section: waltz-bass pedaling as notated; B section: rapidly changing, overlapping pedaling.

Op. 12, No. 6: *Norwegian Melody*
Level: LI, JM7

1. Keyboard Skills/Technique/Mobility—finger independence required in both hands to play multiple voices simultaneously; C section: right-hand melody with rapid hand extension and contraction when shifting from single notes to octaves; left-hand, fast, repeated *staccato* chords.

2. Notation—range is G1-D6; use of two treble clefs.
3. Tempo/Meter/Rhythm—*Presto marcato*; $\frac{3}{4}$; rhythmic patterns through the division of the beat; frequent changes from duple to triple division of the beat.
4. Texture—homophonic: A section: three-part texture with long notes on the top in the right hand and fast melodic passagework on the bottom, accompanied by a left-hand pedal point; B section: melody on top of chords with multiple voices and difficult voicing; C section: right-hand, mostly scalar melody with quick octave interruptions over a left-hand, guitar-like, chordal accompaniment.
5. Form—ABA-CC-ABA; eight-measure phrases.
6. Harmony—A, B sections: D major; C section: D minor; varied harmonic rhythm.
7. Melody—A section: triadic, inner-voice melody; B section: scalar melody on top of chords; C section: scalar folk tune interrupted by *fz* octaves.
8. Articulation—limited articulation markings; B section: *staccato* accompaniment chords.
9. Dynamics—*pp-fz*, with sudden *fz* appearing on different beats in different sections.
10. Musical Expression/Character—Norwegian "springar" couple's dance.[2]
11. Pedaling—intermittent, direct pedaling as desired to enhance the *fz* chords.

Op. 12, No. 7: *Album-Leaf*
Level: LI, JM6

1. Keyboard Skills/Technique/Mobility—quick finger changes on repeated notes in the right-hand melody; quick, left-hand, jump-bass accompaniment with wide leaps; B section: awkward fingering for the left-hand melody and some quick, wide leaps in the right-hand accompaniment.
2. Notation—range is E2-E6.

3. Tempo/Meter/Rhythm—*Allegretto e dolce*; 2/4 ; rhythmic patterns through the subdivision of the beat.
4. Texture—homophonic: A section: right-hand, single-line melody with quick hand-position changes, including quick hand contraction and extension, accompanied by a left-hand jump bass; B section: left-hand melody with right-hand, offbeat, chordal accompaniment.
5. Form—ABB¹-ABB¹-A; eight-measure phrases.
6. Harmony—A section: E minor; B section: G major, modulatory; moderate harmonic rhythm.
7. Melody—A section: right-hand, single-line melody with many wide leaps and grace notes; B section: left-hand, scalar melody.
8. Articulation—short slurs, accents, and *staccato* notes; A section: awkward left-hand slurs.
9. Dynamics—*p*, with some *crescendo* to *fz*.
10. Musical Expression/Character—sweetly, dance-like.
11. Pedaling—quick, shallow pedaling, with careful listening required to avoid obscuring the articulation; A section: pedal with the left-hand slurs; B section: pedal mainly on the long notes to add resonance.

Op. 12, No. 8: *National Song*
Level: MI, JM5

1. Keyboard Skills/Technique/Mobility—quick hand crossings on single notes; chords played in close positions with both hands; some awkward fingerings and chord position changes.
2. Notation—range is E-flat2-E-flat5; both hands occasionally notated on the same staff.
3. Tempo/Meter/Rhythm—*Maestoso*; C ; rhythmic patterns through the subdivision of the beat.
4. Texture—homophonic: primarily homorhythmic chordal texture with the melody on top of the chords.
5. Form—ABB; 4-measure phrases; many inconclusive phrases.

6. Harmony—E-flat major, with chromatic chord progressions; fast harmonic rhythm.
7. Melody—right-hand, scalar melody on top of the chords, with many repeated notes.
8. Articulation—accents, two-note slurs, and *staccato* chords.
9. Dynamics—*p-ff*, with sudden dynamic changes.
10. Musical Expression/Character—grand, patriotic.
11. Pedaling—intermittent pedaling with the chords.

Op. 38, No. 2: *Popular Melody*
Level: MI

1. Keyboard Skills/Technique/Mobility—A section: awkward fingering required for the right-hand passagework of rapidly changing intervals in dotted rhythms; left-hand octave leaps; large right-hand chords; B section: finger independence required in the right hand to play multiple parts.
2. Notation—range is E1-F-sharp5.
3. Tempo/Meter/Rhythm—*Allegro con moto*; $\frac{2}{4}$; rhythmic patterns through the subdivision of the beat; B section: changes between the duple and triple division of the beat.
4. Texture—homophonic: right-hand melody in mixed textures.
5. Form—Introduction AB (interpolation) A; four- and eight-measure phrases, with a three-measure interpolation.
6. Harmony—A section: E minor; B section: G major; varied harmonic rhythm.
7. Melody—A section: right-hand, limited-range, folk melody with dotted rhythms; B section: right-hand, lyrical melody, followed by thematic material from the A section.
8. Articulation—short slurs, accents, and *staccato* chords.
9. Dynamics—*pp-f*
10. Musical Expression/Character—Norwegian "springar" couple's dance.[3]
11. Pedaling—frequently changing, shallow, overlapping pedaling, releasing on the *staccato* chords.

Op. 38, No. 6: *Elegie*
Level: A

1. Keyboard Skills/Technique/Mobility—complicated, chromatic, mixed textures requiring finger independence within each hand and between the two hands; complicated rhythmic patterns within each hand and between the two hands; technically and musically difficult textures requiring significant control of the various layers.
2. Notation—range is B1-F5.
3. Tempo/Meter/Rhythm—*Allegretto semplice*; 3/4 ; rhythmic patterns through the subdivision of the beat; frequent changes from duple to triple division of the beat; polyrhythms (two against three, including rests); tempo changes through *fermatas*.
4. Texture—homophonic: A section: right-hand melody with a countermelody in the tenor voice, alternating with chordal sections with the melody on top of the chords; B section: left-hand, lyrical, single-line melody with right-hand, repeated-chord accompaniment; right-hand melody with additional offbeats and left-hand, chromatic, changing-interval accompaniment.
5. Form—AB-A¹B-A¹; four-measure phrases, with some five-measure phrases due to phrase extensions.
6. Harmony—A section: A minor, obscured by significant chromaticism and inconclusive phrases; B section: C major, modulatory; fast harmonic rhythm; tension/resolution.
7. Melody—chromatic, winding melody within mixed textures; A section: right-hand melody; B section: left-hand then right-hand melody.
8. Articulation—*legato*.
9. Dynamics—*pp*, with *crescendo* to *mf* or *fp*; *fp* on *fermatas*.
10. Musical Expression/Character—emotional, passionate.
11. Pedaling—challenging, frequently changing, overlapping pedaling requiring very careful listening.

Op. 38, No. 7: *Waltz*
Level: LI

1. Keyboard Skills/Technique/Mobility—waltz-bass accompaniment split between the two hands, requiring finger independence in the right hand; some wide stretches in both hands; very fast passagework in the middle section.
2. Notation—range is E2-B5.
3. Tempo/Meter/Rhythm—*Poco Allegro, Presto*; 3/4 ; rhythmic patterns through the division of the beat; *Presto* middle section almost doubles the tempo; at Tempo I, a single-line, right-hand melody facilitates the transition back to the A section; notated long tempo *rubato* at the end of the A section; multiple tempo changes.
4. Texture—homophonic: A section: right-hand melody with waltz-bass accompaniment split between the two hands; B section: right-hand passagework with mixed-texture accompaniment.
5. Form—ABA; four- and eight-measure phrases; many inconclusive phrases.
6. Harmony—E minor; significant chromaticism; moderate harmonic rhythm.
7. Melody—A section: right-hand, primarily scalar, lyrical melody followed by a heavily articulated section; B section: instrumental passagework.
8. Articulation—primarily *legato*, with *staccatos* and *portatos*.
9. Dynamics—*pp-f*.
10. Musical Expression/Character—A section: waltz; B section: lively, agitated.
11. Pedaling—significant notated pedaling, with many breaks to avoid obscuring the articulation.

Op. 43, No. 1: *Butterfly*
Level: A, JM9

1. Keyboard Skills/Technique/Mobility—significant technical and musical demands; wide leaps in both hands; rapid hand contraction and

    extension; broken chords and broken intervals; coordination of the continuous, right-hand passagework with the intermittent, left-hand passagework; rapid alternation of single notes with chords; right-hand passagework with line-within-a-line melody on the bottom.
2. Notation—extremely wide range: A0-A6; use of two treble clefs and two bass clefs.
3. Tempo/Meter/Rhythm—*Allegro grazioso*; **C** ; rhythmic patterns through the subdivision of the beat; *stretto* and tempo *rubato*.
4. Texture—homophonic: right-hand, instrumental melody, with a section of line-within-a-line melody with additional voices; left-hand, intermittent, broken-chord accompaniment.
5. Form—AAB (interpolation) A^{1}BA^2; varying phrase lengths.
6. Harmony—A major, with the tonal center obscured by the various chord progressions and chromaticism; fast harmonic rhythm.
7. Melody—A section: right-hand, single-line, instrumental passagework; B section: right-hand passagework with additional voices and line-within-a-line melody on the bottom.
8. Articulation—*legato*, with accents to highlight melodic notes.
9. Dynamics—*pp-ffz*.
10. Musical Expression/Character—flittering, shimmering.
11. Pedaling—many notated pedal markings, including *una corda*; intermittent, light, shallow pedaling.

Op. 43, No. 2: *Solitary Traveller*
Level: LI, JM7-8

1. Keyboard Skills/Technique/Mobility—*legato* parallel sixths; finger independence required within both hands; awkward fingering, including finger substitutions for *legato* playing; the melody is frequently doubled in octaves between the soprano and bass or tenor lines.
2. Notation—range is B1-B5; use of two treble clefs.
3. Tempo/Meter/Rhythm—*Allegretto semplice*; $^6_8$; rhythmic patterns through the subdivision of the beat, plus thirty-second-note triplets;

some hemiola; very slow tempo makes some of the awkward passages easier.
4. Texture—homophonic: chordal texture with the melody on top and often doubled at the octave or in a duet with the tenor or bass lines.
5. Form—AB-A¹B-A¹; four- and seven-measure phrases.
6. Harmony—B minor, with significant chromaticism.
7. Melody—right-hand, scalar, descending melody in mixed textures.
8. Articulation—*legato*; unusual accents on the upbeats should be emphasized with timing rather than dynamics.
9. Dynamics—*p-f*.
10. Musical Expression/Character—introspective, reflective.
11. Pedaling—some notated pedal markings; additional frequently changing pedaling is needed to enhance the *legato* connection and the tone quality, but without obscuring the melodic lines.

Op. 43, No. 3: *In My Native Country*
Level: A

1. Keyboard Skills/Technique/Mobility—significant finger independence required within each hand and between the two hands to carefully balance all of the voices; difficult key of F-sharp major.
2. Notation—range is F-sharp1-C6; use of two treble clefs and two bass clefs.
3. Tempo/Meter/Rhythm—*Poco Andante*; **C**; rhythmic patterns through the division of the beat; some syncopation; several tempo changes.
4. Texture—homophonic: overall chordal texture, but with many moving voices and a *legato* melody on top of the right hand.
5. Form—AB-A¹B-A¹ + coda; four-measure phrases.
6. Harmony—F-sharp major; with many chord progressions away from the tonal center and many inconclusive phrases; fast harmonic rhythm.
7. Melody—right-hand, lyrical melody with many directional changes.
8. Articulation—*legato*, with some short slurs.
9. Dynamics—wide dynamic range: *ppp-f*.
10. Musical Expression/Character—sincere, gentle.

11. Pedaling—frequently changing, overlapping pedaling to enhance the *legato* and tone quality; shallow pedaling needed for the softest dynamic levels.

Op. 43, No. 6: *To the Spring*
Level: A

1. Keyboard Skills/Technique/Mobility—difficult key of F-sharp major; wide dynamic range; finger independence needed within the right hand; careful voicing and balance of textures needing significant musical control.
2. Notation—wide range: F-sharp1-A-sharp6; use of two treble clefs, two bass clefs, and three staves (two for the right hand).
3. Tempo/Meter/Rhythm—*Allegro appassionato*; $\frac{9}{4}$; rhythmic patterns through the division of the beat: notated tempo *rubato* and tempo changes; *fermata* over a barline; B section: some hemiola.
4. Texture—homophonic: A section: left-hand, primarily single-line, lyrical melody with right-hand, intermittent, repeated-chord accompaniment; B section: melody doubled in octaves between the two hands with right-hand, intermittent, repeated-chord accompaniment in between; A¹ section: right-hand melody in octaves with intermittent, repeated chords and left-hand, arpeggio accompaniment.
5. Form—AABA¹ + coda; four-measure phrases.
6. Harmony—F-sharp major, with some unexpected chord progressions; varied harmonic rhythm; tension/resolution.
7. Melody—A section: left-hand, primarily single-line, lyrical melody; B section: melody doubled between the two hands; A¹ section: right-hand melody in octaves.
8. Articulation—*legato*, with some accents and *portatos*.
9. Dynamics—wide dynamic range: *ppp-ff*; long *crescendo* and *diminuendo* requiring careful pacing of dynamics.
10. Musical Expression/Character—calm and serene, passionate and dramatic.
11. Pedaling—extensive notated pedaling, which may be interpreted as continuous, overlapping pedaling.

Op. 47, No. 6: *Norwegian Dance*
Level: A

1. Keyboard Skills/Technique/Mobility—parallel sixths with quickly changing hand positions; left-hand crossings over the right hand in large leaps; large chords within both hands; finger independence needed within the right hand.
2. Notation—range is A1-G6; use of two treble clefs; frequent, quick clef changes.
3. Tempo/Meter/Rhythm—*Allegro vivace*; $\frac{3}{4}$; rhythmic patterns through the division of the beat; frequent changes from duple to triple subdivision of the beat.
4. Texture—homophonic: A section: right-hand melody in parallel sixths, with left-hand drone-bass accompaniment; B section: right-hand, repetitive melody with mixed-texture accompaniment; C section: right-hand, independent melody on top of large chords.
5. Form—Introduction ABC-A^{1}BC-A^2 + coda; three- and four-measure phrases.
6. Harmony—A section: G major; B, C sections: modulatory; varied harmonic rhythm.
7. Melody—right-hand, disjunct, motivic, folk melody with significant repetition; grace notes.
8. Articulation—short and long slurs, accents, and *staccatos*.
9. Dynamics—wide dynamic range: *ppp-ff*, with *crescendo* and *diminuendo*.
10. Musical Expression/Character—folk dance.
11. Pedaling—both overlapping and intermittent, direct pedaling.

Op. 54, No. 2: *Norwegian March*
Level: A

1. Keyboard Skills/Technique/Mobility—finger independence required within each hand and between the two hands; large leaps in the left hand; left-hand melody in octaves with frequent directional changes; melody

frequently shifting between the two hands; both hands required to play *ppp* in a very high range; large chords consisting of octaves with filled-in thirds or fourths; numerous range changes; hand crossings; parallel thirds; fast passages shifting rapidly from single notes to chords while using fingers 3,4, and 5; long, multi-sectional, repetitive piece requiring musical maturity.
2. Notation—wide range: F1-C7; use of two treble clefs and two bass clefs.
3. Tempo/Meter/Rhythm—*Allegretto marcato*; $^6_8$; rhythmic patterns through the subdivision of the beat; extensive use of syncopation.
4. Texture—homophonic: A section: four voices with right-hand melody on top; B section: mixed-texture settings with the melody frequently switching hands with sudden dynamic changes; D2 section: left-hand melody in octaves with right-hand, chordal accompaniment; E section: right-hand melody on top of large chords with left-hand accompaniment of large chords.
5. Form—AABC (interpolation) DD^{1}D^{2}E (interpolation) BC (interpolation) DD^{1}D^{2}E + coda; all sections except section C have closely related thematic material, giving the effect of a theme with variations.
6. Harmony—A section: C major with pedal point; B section: modulatory; C section: "on" G, followed by sequential chord progressions back to C major; D sections: C major; E section: A-flat major, C major.
7. Melody—repetitive, motivic, folk melody with short trills.
8. Articulation—*legato*, with short slurs and accents on syncopated notes.
9. Dynamics—wide range: *ppp-fff*, with *ffp* and sudden dynamic changes, as well as long *crescendo* or *diminuendo*.
10. Musical Expression/Character—Norwegian "gangar" dance, with a feeling of leisurely walking from side to side, but maintaining a steady rhythm.[4]
11. Pedaling—extensive notated pedaling.

Op. 54, No. 4: *Notturno*
Level: A, JM8

1. Keyboard Skills/Technique/Mobility—substantial trills; awkward fingering required to play changing parallel intervals in the right hand; quick range changes and hand crossings; complicated rhythmic

patterns within each hand and between the two hands; extensive musical demands to control the wide dynamic range as well as the balance and voicing of the entire texture.
2. Notation—range is C1-A-flat6; use of two treble clefs and two bass clefs; frequent clef changes.
3. Tempo/Meter/Rhythm—*Andante*; $\frac{6}{8}$; rhythmic patterns through the subdivision of the beat; extensive use of ties obscures the beat and creates a feeling of suspension; difficult polyrhythms (two against three) including rests and ties within each hand and between the two hands; full-measure rests used for dramatic effects.
4. Texture—homophonic: right-hand melody with intermittent chordal or arpeggiated accompaniments.
5. Form—AB-C-A^{1}B^1 + coda; varying phrase lengths; many inconclusive phrases, often sequential.
6. Harmony—C major, with extensive chromaticism and unexpected harmonic progressions; varied harmonic rhythm; tension/resolution.
7. Melody—multiple types of thematic material: right-hand, lyrical melody with large vocal leaps: broken-interval "bird calls"; parallel interval passages similar to horn fifths; lyrical, scalar passages.
8. Articulation—*legato*, with some *tenutos*.
9. Dynamics—*pp-ff*, with extensive *crescendo* and *diminuendo*; sudden dynamic changes as well as both long *crescendo* and *diminuendo* passages requiring mature pacing.
10. Musical Expression/Character—colorful, pictorial "night piece" with many dramatic effects.
11. Pedaling—extensive notated pedaling; overlapping pedaling, with many adjustments needed in the pedal depth for the rapidly changing wide dynamic ranges.

Op. 54, No. 5: *Scherzo*
Level: A

1. Keyboard Skills/Technique/Mobility—very fast tempo; left-hand melody with rapid hand contraction and extension and quick fingering changes;

rapid range changes, some with hand crossings; large rolled chords; awkward *legato* fingering in the middle section.
2. Notation—wide range: E1-B6; use of two treble and two bass clefs; extensive, quick clef changes; both hands notated on the same staff.
3. Tempo/Meter/Rhythm—*Prestissimo leggiero*; $\frac{3}{4}$; rhythmic patterns through the subdivision of the beat; meter changes; polyrhythms (two against three); tempo changes; full-measure rests used for dramatic effect.
4. Texture—homophonic: A section: frequently changing textures: instrumental, left-hand melody with right-hand, broken-chord accompaniment; rapidly changing textures of scalar passages that switch hands, sometimes with chordal accompaniment, interspersed with chords in both hands; right-hand, single-line melody with ostinato accompaniment; B section: right-hand, lyrical melody accompanied by left-hand sustained chords.
5. Form—large ABA scherzo and trio; four- and eight-measure phrases.
6. Harmony—A section: E minor, with many unexpected harmonic progressions and modulations; B section: E major, with modulations; varied harmonic rhythm.
7. Melody—motivic melody with repeating scalar and rhythmic patterns.
8. Articulation—primarily *legato*.
9. Dynamics—*ppp-ff*, with many sudden dynamic changes.
10. Musical Expression/Character—A section: mischievous, dramatic; B section: tranquil, calm.
11. Pedaling—extensive notated pedaling, including *una corda*; B section: overlapping pedaling, with frequent pedal changes and different pedal depths needed to match the dynamic levels and tonal colors.

Op. 57, No. 2: *Gade*
Level: A

1. Keyboard Skills/Technique/Mobility—broken intervals with wide stretches in both hands; finger independence required in both hands; significant hand extension and contraction in both hands; rapid shifts between single notes and chords; rapid directional changes; wide-ranging arpeggios.

2. Notation—range is A1-A6; use of two treble clefs.
3. Tempo/Meter/Rhythm—*Allegro grazioso*; ¢ ; rhythmic patterns through the subdivision of the beat; many offbeat rhythmic patterns.
4. Texture—homophonic: mixed textures with the melody in either hand and multiple simultaneous voices.
5. Form—AB (interpolation) AB (interpolation) A¹ + coda; variable phrase lengths.
6. Harmony—A major, with extensive chromaticism and modulations.
7. Melody—vocal melody with many leaps and direction changes; extensive melodic imitation between the two hands; free, cadenza-like interpolation.
8. Articulation—*legato*.
9. Dynamics—*pp-ff*, with long *crescendo* and *diminuendo* sections.
10. Musical Expression/Character—This piece is a tribute to the Danish composer Niels W. Gade.[5]
11. Pedaling—extensive notated pedaling, although more pedal changes may be needed through the lengthy pedals; primarily continuous, overlapping pedaling.

Op. 57, No. 3: *Illusion*
Level: LI

1. Keyboard Skills/Technique/Mobility—extensive use of parallel sixths and descending seventh chords; slurred broken octaves; left-hand, single-line melody with additional voices requiring significant finger independence; awkward fingering and frequent hand-position changes.
2. Notation—range is D1-E6; use of two bass clefs.
3. Tempo/Meter/Rhythm—*Allegretto serioso*; 6/8 ; meter changes from 6/8 to 9/8 ; rhythmic patterns through the subdivision of the beat; *fermata* on the opening note; dramatic use of rests; notated tempo *rubato*.
4. Texture—homophonic: A section: right-hand melody doubled in sixths or with other voices and left-hand, broken-octave accompaniment, then reversing hands; B section: melody in parallel sixths between the two hands, alternating with melody on top of chords; C section: chordal,

with the melody on top of the chords over a pedal point accompaniment; interpolation: right-hand, rising, chromatic melody with left-hand, descending, chromatic chords.
5. Form—ABC (interpolation) ABC (interpolation) A¹; four- and five-measure phrases.
6. Harmony—A minor, with extensive chromaticism, unexpected harmonic progressions, and modulations; quartal harmonies; moderate harmonic rhythm; tension/resolution.
7. Melody—motivic, descending, scalar patterns in parallel sixths, alternating with melody on top of chords.
8. Articulation—*legato*, with short slurs.
9. Dynamics—*pp-f*, with *crescendo* and *diminuendo*; both quick and slower dynamic changes.
10. Musical Expression/Character—pastorale; the opening *fermata* may represent the sound of a *lur*, an indigenous instrument that resembles an alpenhorn.[6]
11. Pedaling—overlapping pedaling.

Op. 57, No. 6: *Homesickness*
Level: LI

1. Keyboard Skills/Technique/Mobility—finger independence needed in the right hand; B section: both hands high in the range; tricky passagework.
2. Notation—range is E2-B6; use of two treble clefs; high pitches, requiring many leger lines; double sharps.
3. Tempo/Meter/Rhythm—A section: *Andante*; B section: *Molto piu Vivo*; 3/4; rhythmic patterns through the subdivision of the beat; use of hemiola; multiple *fermatas* over both notes and bar lines (rests); multiple tempo changes and notated tempo *rubato*.
4. Texture—homophonic: A section: right-hand, lyrical melody with chordal accompaniment, repeated with a left-hand, imitative countermelody; B section: right-hand, dotted-rhythm, folk melody with

an additional voice, accompanied by left-hand, broken intervals and blocked chords.

5. Form—ABA; variable phrase lengths, primarily four- and eight-measure phrases.
6. Harmony—A section: E minor; B section: E major, with extensive chromaticism.
7. Melody—right-hand, scalar, lyrical melody; B section: disjunct folk melody with extensive use of the Lydian mode; grace notes.
8. Articulation—A section: *legato*, with *tenutos*; B section: short slurs and *staccatos*.
9. Dynamics—*pp*, *p*, with *fz* and *fp*; *crescendo* and *diminuendo*.
10. Musical Expression/Character—pensive, mournful; the B section is like a Norwegian springar couple's dance.[7]
11. Pedaling—frequent, overlapping pedaling needed—the pianist can use more than is notated.

Op. 62, No. 1: *Sylphide*
Level: A

1. Keyboard Skills/Technique/Mobility—wide stretches within each hand; rapid leaps, often with range changes; *leggiero* passages requiring light but precise finger action; wide dynamic range and sudden dynamic changes requiring significant technical and musical control.
2. Notation—wide range: F-sharp1-D7; use of two treble clefs.
3. Tempo/Meter/Rhythm—*Allegretto con moto*; 3/4 ; rhythmic patterns through the subdivision of the beat; extensive use of dotted rhythms; meter changes; many notated tempo changes.
4. Texture—homophonic: right-hand, disjunct melody with two-beat, jump-bass accompaniment.
5. Form—Introduction ABA¹ + coda; variable phrase lengths, primarily four and eight measures; B section: lengthy figurational transition.
6. Harmony—B minor, B major; extensive chromaticism and unexpected chord progressions obscure the tonality; varied harmonic rhythm.

7. Melody—right-hand, fragmented, disjunct melody of two-note slurs in dotted rhythms with many wide leaps; grace notes.
8. Articulation—extensive two-note slurs; left-hand *staccato* notes on the pedal for playing bell-tones.
9. Dynamics—wide dynamic range: *ppp-ff*, with sudden dynamic changes.
10. Musical Expression/Character—quirky, flittering waltz.
11. Pedaling—extensive notated pedaling, primarily with the two-beat jump-bass pattern.

Op. 62, No. 2: *Gratitude*
Level: LI

1. Keyboard Skills/Technique/Mobility—finger independence required within each hand and between the two hands; awkward fingering needed to play the *legato* lines; large rolled chords in both hands; B section: right-hand-position shifts with left-hand wide leaps at the same time.
2. Notation—range is D1-E6; use of two treble clefs; B section: rapid clef changes.
3. Tempo/Meter/Rhythm—*Allegretto semplice*; 𝐂 ; rhythmic patterns through the division of the beat; notated tempo *rubato*.
4. Texture—homophonic: right-hand, lyrical melody with multiple parts in each hand.
5. Form—AA-BA¹-BA¹ + coda; varied phrase lengths, primarily four and eight measures.
6. Harmony—G major, with modulations and unexpected chord progressions.
7. Melody—right-hand, lyrical melody with frequent directional changes.
8. Articulation—*legato*, with *tenutos* and both long and short slurs.
9. Dynamics—*pp-f*, with *fz*; both long and short *crescendo* and *diminuendo*.
10. Musical Expression/Character—A section: sincere, peaceful; B section: ethereal, emotional.
11. Pedaling—overlapping pedaling with a range of pedal depths needed.

Op. 62, No. 5: Phantom
Level: LI

1. Keyboard Skills/Technique/Mobility—widely spaced, frequently changing, left-hand, broken-chord ostinato; right-hand finger substitutions needed for the *legato* lines; *legato* melodic octaves; notated, left-hand finger pedaling to hold bass line notes.
2. Notation—range is A1-A6; use of two bass clefs.
3. Tempo/Meter/Rhythm—*Poco Andante ed espressivo*; 6/8 ; rhythmic patterns through the subdivision of the beat; polyrhythms (two against three).
4. Texture—homophonic: right-hand, lyrical melody with broken-chord, ostinato accompaniment; melody doubled in octaves.
5. Form—four-measure theme repeated in multiple tonalities; short interpolation in the middle of the piece.
6. Harmony—A major; many unexpected chord progressions and inconclusive phrases; slow harmonic rhythm.
7. Melody—right-hand, lyrical melody with many vocal leaps; extended trills and small ornaments; unusual repeated melodic "E" for thirteen measures at the end of the piece.
8. Articulation—*legato*.
9. Dynamics—*pp-p*, with *crescendo* and *diminuendo*.
10. Musical Expression/Character—dreamy.
11. Pedaling—continuous, shallow, overlapping pedaling; variable pedaling change speeds can be considered.

Op. 65, No. 2: The Peasant's Song
Level: LI

1. Keyboard Skills/Technique/Mobility—multi-voice texture requiring finger independence within each hand and between the hands; finger substitutions and other awkward fingerings; large rolled chords.
2. Notation—range is A1-A6; use of two treble clefs.
3. Tempo/Meter/Rhythm—*Andante semplice*; C ; rhythmic patterns through the division of the beat.

4. Texture—homophonic: right-hand, lyrical melody on top of chordal texture with multiple moving voices.
5. Form—AB-A¹B-A¹ + coda; four-measure phrases.
6. Harmony—A major, with extensive chromaticism; fast harmonic rhythm.
7. Melody—right-hand, lyrical melody with many directional changes and leaps; grace notes and other small ornaments.
8. Articulation—*legato*.
9. Dynamics—wide dynamic range: *ppp-f*, with extensive *crescendo* and *diminuendo*.
10. Musical Expression/Character—reflective song without words.
11. Pedaling—frequently changing, shallow, overlapping pedaling needed to maintain clarity of the voices.

Op. 65, No. 5: *Ballad*
Level: MI

1. Keyboard Skills/Technique/Mobility—melody doubled at the octave between hands, with the lower voice shifting between the two hands, requiring careful voicing; long phrases and long melodic notes may cause fading sound challenges; finger independence required within each hand and between hands; thick texture with large chords in each hand.
2. Notation—range is C1-B-flat4.
3. Tempo/Meter/Rhythm—*Lento lugubre*; ¢ ; rhythmic patterns through the subdivision of the beat; notated tempo *rubato* and tempo changes.
4. Texture—homophonic: right-hand melody within a multi-voice chordal texture; upon repetition the melody is doubled at the octave, with the lower voice shifting between the two hands.
5. Form—AA¹-BA²-B²A³; four- and eight-measure phrases.
6. Harmony—C minor, with extensive chromaticism; varied harmonic rhythm; tension/resolution.
7. Melody—right-hand, scalar, limited-range melody with frequent directional changes.
8. Articulation—*legato*.

9. Dynamics—*pp-ff*, with *crescendo* and *diminuendo* and quick dynamic changes.
10. Musical Expression/Character—sad, mournful.
11. Pedaling—frequently changing, overlapping pedaling with various pedaling depths.

Op. 68, No. 1: *Sailor's Song*
Level: MI, JM5

1. Keyboard Skills/Technique/Mobility—rapid chords, including open octaves and octaves with filled-in notes; rapid parallel thirds.
2. Notation—range is C1-D6.
3. Tempo/Meter/Rhythm—*Allegro Vivace e marcato*; ¢ ; rhythmic patterns through the subdivision of the beat; notated tempo *rubato*.
4. Texture—homophonic: primarily homorhythmic, with melody on top of chords.
5. Form—ABA¹-BA¹; four-measure phrases.
6. Harmony—C major; fast harmonic rhythm.
7. Melody—right-hand, scalar, articulated melody on top of chords.
8. Articulation—accented chords, *staccato* chords, and two-note slurs.
9. Dynamics—*p-ff*; with sudden dynamic changes.
10. Musical Expression/Character—jovial, boisterous.
11. Pedaling—direct pedaling on the chords to enhance accents and dynamics.

Op. 68, No. 2: *Grandmother's Minuet*
Level: MI

1. Keyboard Skills/Technique/Mobility—right-hand melody with rapid expansion from single notes to full chords; parallel motion between the two hands.
2. Notation—range is G1-F-sharp6; use of two treble clefs.
3. Tempo/Meter/Rhythm—*Allegretto grazioso e leggierissimo*; ¾ ; rhythmic patterns through the division of the beat; full-measure rests for dramatic effect.

4. Texture—homophonic: A section: right-hand, single-note melody that quickly expands to five-voice chords split between the two hands; B section: melody doubled in octaves between the two hands.
5. Form—AA¹-BA²-BA²; four-measure phrases.
6. Harmony—G major; fast harmonic rhythm.
7. Melody—*staccato* minuet melody with slurred, short ornaments.
8. Articulation—*staccatos* and short slurs.
9. Dynamics—*pp*, with *crescendo* to *fz*.
10. Musical Expression/Character—dainty minuet.
11. Pedaling—direct pedaling as notated.

<u>Op. 68, No. 3: *At Your Feet*</u>
Level: A

1. Keyboard Skills/Technique/Mobility—wide stretches in both hands; parallel thirds; large chords in the right hand; melody doubled in octaves; significant musical maturity needed to sustain long, inconclusive phrases and control a wide dynamic range.
2. Notation—range is G1-A6; use of two treble clefs.
3. Tempo/Meter/Rhythm—*Poco Andante e molto espressivo*; $\frac{2}{4}$; rhythmic patterns through the division of the beat; notated tempo *rubato*; many tempo changes.
4. Texture—homophonic: A section: right-hand, lyrical melody with many vocal leaps and numerous rests, with widely spaced, broken-chord accompaniment; B section: left-hand, continuous melody that leads to a right-hand, continuous melody in octaves; C section: right-hand, lyrical melody in open octaves and octaves with filled-in notes.
5. Form—Introduction A-BB¹-C-A¹ + coda; four- and eight-measure phrases; many inconclusive phrases.
6. Harmony—D major, but with key changes, extensive chromaticism and unexpected chord progressions; varied harmonic rhythm; tension/resolution.

7. Melody—melody in multiple textural settings: vocal melody in both hands, melody doubled in thirds or with additional voices, melody in open octaves, and melody in octaves with filled-in notes.
8. Articulation—*legato*, with short slurs.
9. Dynamics—wide dynamic range: *ppp-ff*, with extensive *crescendo* and *diminuendo*.
10. Musical Expression/Character—deeply personal, passionate work.
11. Pedaling—*legato*, with pedaling following the chord changes.

Op. 68, No. 4: *Evening in the Mountains*
Level: LI

1. Keyboard Skills/Technique/Mobility—wide leaps; large chords; finger independence within each hand and between the two hands.
2. Notation—range is E1-B5.
3. Tempo/Meter/Rhythm—*Allegretto*; ⅜; rhythmic patterns through the division of the beat; frequent changes between the duple and triple division of the beat; extensive notated tempo *rubato* and tempo changes.
4. Texture—long introduction consisting of a single note accompanied by broken octaves; A section: single-line folk melody; A¹ section: repeat of the same melody, accompanied by thick sustained chords in mixed textures.
5. Form—Introduction AA¹; four-, six-, and eight-measure phrases.
6. Harmony—E minor; fast harmonic rhythm.
7. Melody—right-hand, wide-range, folk melody with extensive articulation.
8. Articulation—*legato*, with short slurs, accents, and *tenutos*.
9. Dynamics—*pp-ff*, with sudden dynamic changes.
10. Musical Expression/Character—pastoral; Grieg initially called this piece "Cow Call" and felt that it is like an evening in Utladalen (Skogadalsbøen); the introduction is like a *lur*.[8]
11. Pedaling—A section: intermittent, direct pedaling on long notes to enhance the tone quality and dynamics; A¹ section: frequently changing, continuous, overlapping pedaling with different depths.

Op. 68, No. 5: *At the Cradle*
Level: LI

1. Keyboard Skills/Technique/Mobility—chordal texture with multiple moving voices; difficult fingering needed to play the *legato* lines, parallel thirds and parallel horn fifths; large chords in the right hand; wide stretches in both hands.
2. Notation—range is E2-G6; use of two treble clefs.
3. Tempo/Meter/Rhythm—*Allegretto tranquillamente*; 𝐂 ; rhythmic patterns through the division of the beat.
4. Texture—homophonic: right-hand melody on top of chordal texture with multiple moving voices.
5. Form—AABCA¹ + coda; four- and eight-measure phrases; many inconclusive phrases.
6. Harmony—E major, with chromaticism and "color chords."
7. Melody—vocal melody on top of chordal texture; short ornaments.
8. Articulation—*legato*.
9. Dynamics—*ppp*, with *crescendo* to *fz*.
10. Musical Expression/Character—pastorale, tranquil.
11. Pedaling—frequently changing, overlapping pedaling with various pedal depths.

Op. 71, No. 3: *Puck*
Level: LI, JM8

1. Keyboard Skills/Technique/Mobility—difficult *staccato* passagework switching rapidly between single notes and thirds; successive, chromatic, *staccato* chords; wide stretches and quick hand-position changes.
2. Notation—range is A-flat1-G-flat6; use of two treble clefs and two bass clefs.
3. Tempo/Meter/Rhythm—*Allegro molto*; ₵ : rhythmic patterns through the subdivision of the beat; full-measure rests used for dramatic effect.
4. Texture—homophonic: A section: right-hand passagework alternating with melody on top of *staccato* chords; melody doubled in parallel

octaves between the two hands; B section: left-hand, single-note passagework and melody on top of *staccato* chords; descending, *staccato* chromatic scale.
5. Form—Introduction ABA; four- and eight-measure phrases.
6. Harmony—E-flat minor, with temporary excursions to many other keys; varied harmonic rhythm.
7. Melody—rapid, figurational passagework alternating with the melody on top of chords.
8. Articulation—extensive *staccatos*; accents.
9. Dynamics—*pp-ff*, with *fz* and sudden dynamic contrasts.
10. Musical Expression/Character—mischievous.
11. Pedaling—limited to notated pedaling.

Op. 71, No. 7: *Remembrances*
Level: MI

1. Keyboard Skills/Technique/Mobility – finger independence required in the right hand to play the lyrical melody in addition to the added inner voices that are a part of the left-hand chordal accompaniment; finger independence also required in the left hand to sustain the low bass notes while playing the upper chords.
2. Notation – range is B-flat1-G5.
3. Tempo/Meter/Rhythm – *Tempo di Valse*; $\frac{3}{4}$; rhythmic patterns through the division of the beat; syncopation in the melodic line; *fermatas*.
4. Texture – homophonic: right-hand, single-line melody with additional voices that are part of the left-hand accompaniment chords; the left hand has some brief two-part texture sections that include a sustained bass line in addition to the chords.
5. Form – A A^1 (interpolation) A^2 + coda; four- and eight-measure phrases.
6. Harmony – E-flat major, with modulations to D major and B-flat major before returning to E-flat major; moderate harmonic rhythm.
7. Melody – right-hand, single-line, lyrical, narrow-range melody with many repeated notes.
8. Articulation – *legato*, with many short slurs.

9. Dynamics – *ppp-f*, with *crescendo* and *diminuendo*.
10. Musical Expression/Character – this piece uses the same melody as Grieg's Op. 12, No. 1 *Arietta*, now transformed into a gentle waltz.
11. Pedaling – overlapping pedaling with the chord changes, except during a few measures where the left hand drops out; notated use of the *una corda* in the D major section.

Notes

1 Einar Steen-Nøkleberg, *Onstage with Grieg: Interpreting His Piano Music* (Bloomington, IN: Indiana University Press, 1997), 237.
2 Steen-Nøkleberg, *Onstage with Grieg*, 239.
3 Steen-Nøkleberg, *Onstage with Grieg*, 245.
4 Steen-Nøkleberg, *Onstage with Grieg*, 274–5.
5 Steen-Nøkleberg, *Onstage with Grieg*, 286.
6 Steen-Nøkleberg, *Onstage with Grieg*, 289.
7 Steen-Nøkleberg, *Onstage with Grieg*, 293.
8 Steen-Nøkleberg, *Onstage with Grieg*, 329–30.

Cornelius Gurlitt—*Album for the Young*, Op. 140

Op. 140, No.1: *March*
Level: EI, JM3

1. Keyboard Skills/Technique/Mobility—finger changes on repeated notes; diverse articulation between the two hands.
2. Notation—range is G3-G5; use of two treble clefs.
3. Tempo/Meter/Rhythm—*Vivace, ma non troppo*; $\frac{2}{4}$; rhythmic patterns through the subdivision of the beat.
4. Texture—homophonic: chords split between the two hands with the melody on top of the chords; chords alternating with single notes in each hand; some imitation between the two hands.
5. Form—AA^1-BA^{1}BA^1; eight-measure phrases.
6. Harmony—A section: C major; B section: G major; varied harmonic rhythm.
7. Melody—right-hand, articulated melody on top of chords alternating with single-note passages.
8. Articulation—non-*legato* touch, two-note slurs, *staccatos*, accents; some differing articulations between the two hands.
9. Dynamics—*f-ff*.
10. Musical Expression/Character—march.
11. Pedaling—intermittent, direct pedaling to enhance the slurs and give resonance to the chords.

Op. 140, No. 2: *Morning Song*
Level: EI, JM3-4

1. Keyboard Skills/Technique/Mobility—chordal texture with an inconsistent number of voices in each hand.
2. Notation—range is C3-F5.
3. Tempo/Meter/Rhythm—*Andantino*; $\frac{2}{4}$; rhythmic patterns through the beat level.
4. Texture—homophonic, with chords split between the two hands.
5. Form—ABABA; four-measure phrases.
6. Harmony—F major; fast harmonic rhythm; tension/resolution.
7. Melody—mostly scalar melody on top of chords with an inconsistent number of voices in each hand.
8. Articulation—*portato*s and two-note slurs.
9. Dynamics—*p-mf*, with *crescendo* and *diminuendo*.
10. Musical Expression/Character—reverent, calm.
11. Pedaling—direct pedaling on the *portato* chords, and overlapping pedaling to enhance the two-note slurs and give resonance to the chords.

Op. 140, No. 3: *The Sky is Bright*
Level: EI, JM3

1. Keyboard Skills/Technique/Mobility—left-hand finger pedaling of Alberti-bass patterns; fast finger changes on repeated notes.
2. Notation—range is G3-D6; use of two treble clefs.
3. Tempo/Meter/Rhythm—*Allegretto grazioso*; $\frac{2}{4}$; rhythmic patterns through the division of the beat.
4. Texture—homophonic: right-hand, single-line melody with left-hand, Alberti-bass accompaniment.
5. Form—ABA; eight-measure phrases.
6. Harmony—A section: C major; B section: G major; varied harmonic rhythm.
7. Melody—A section: scalar; B section: wide leaps, requiring some hand extension.

8. Articulation—two-note slurs and *portatos*.
9. Dynamics—*p-f*, with some *crescendo* and *diminuendo*.
10. Musical Expression/Character—graceful, dance-like.
11. Pedaling—none for more clarity, or frequently changing, very shallow, overlapping pedaling for more blending.

Op. 140, No. 4: *In the Garden*
Level: MI, JM4

1. Keyboard Skills/Technique/Mobility—finger independence needed in the right hand when the melody is combined with intermittent additional voices.
2. Notation—range is E3-D5.
3. Tempo/Meter/Rhythm—*Allegretto*; 6/8; rhythmic patterns through the division of the beat.
4. Texture—homophonic: A, B sections: left-hand, single-line melody with right-hand, intermittent, chordal accompaniment; A¹ section: right-hand melody is doubled between the two hands, with additional voices.
5. Form—A-BA¹-BA¹ + coda; four-measure phrases.
6. Harmony—A section: C major; B section: modulatory; moderate harmonic rhythm.
7. Melody—left-hand, mostly scalar melody with few leaps.
8. Articulation—*legato*.
9. Dynamics—*pp-p*, with some *crescendo* and *diminuendo*.
10. Musical Expression/Character—happy.
11. Pedaling—frequent, shallow pedaling to enhance the *legato* line.

Op. 140, No. 5: *Murmuring Brook*
Level: EI, JM4

1. Keyboard Skills/Technique/Mobility—both hands have broken-chord passagework with line-within-a-line melody on the top requiring finger independence within each hand at different times; parallel thirds; broken intervals; inner-voice repeated notes must be played lightly.

2. Notation—range is G3-G5; use of two treble clefs.
3. Tempo/Meter/Rhythm—*con moto*; $\frac{2}{4}$; rhythmic patterns through the subdivision of the beat; phrases start on the upbeats, requiring careful metrical perception to lead to the downbeats.
4. Texture—homophonic: duet between the two hands; each hand alternates the line-within-a-line melody sections with single-note passages.
5. Form—AA-BA-BA + coda; four-measure phrases.
6. Harmony—A section: G major; B section: D major; fast harmonic rhythm.
7. Melody—line-within-a-line melody in each hand at different times requiring rotation on the broken intervals.
8. Articulation—*legato*.
9. Dynamics—*pp-mf*, with quick *crescendo* and *diminuendo*.
10. Musical Expression/Character—"murmuring"
11. Pedaling—frequent, shallow, overlapping pedaling.

Op. 140, No. 6: *Catch Me!*
Level: MI

1. Keyboard Skills/Technique/Mobility—rapid range changes within the right-hand melody.
2. Notation—range is G3-F6; use of two treble clefs.
3. Tempo/Meter/Rhythm—*Poco Vivace*; $\frac{2}{4}$; rhythmic patterns through the subdivision of the beat; extensive dotted rhythms and phrases beginning on weak beats.
4. Texture—homophonic: A section: wide-ranging, right-hand melody with sparse, left-hand accompaniment; B section: left-hand melody with right-hand, repeated-interval accompaniment.
5. Form—AA^1-BA^{1}BA^1; four-measure phrases.
6. Harmony—A section: C major; B section: revolves around the note A.
7. Melody—A section: right-hand, disjunct, fragmented melodic line; B section: chromatic, narrow-range, left-hand melody.
8. Articulation—multiple short slurs.

9. Dynamics—*mf-ff.*
10. Musical Expression/Character: light, flitting.
11. Pedaling: none.

Op. 140, No. 7: *The Festive Dance*
Level: EI

1. Keyboard Skills/Technique/Mobility—large leaps in the right-hand melodic passagework requiring hand extension and contraction, as well as fast position changes.
2. Notation—range is C3-C6.
3. Tempo/Meter/Rhythm—*Tempo di valse*; $\frac{3}{4}$; rhythmic patterns through the division of the beat; A section: phrases begin on weak beats; syncopation on beat three.
4. Texture—homophonic: right-hand melody with waltz-bass accompaniment within a limited range.
5. Form—ABA; eight-measure phrases.
6. Harmony—A section: F major; B section: C major; slow harmonic rhythm.
7. Melody—wide-range, disjunct melody.
8. Articulation—short slurs coinciding with the patterned, upbeat phrasing.
9. Dynamics—*p-f.*
10. Musical Expression/Character—graceful, elegant waltz.
11. Pedaling—waltz-bass pedaling from beats one through two.

Op. 140, No. 8: *The Music Box*
Level: EI, JM3

1. Keyboard Skills/Technique/Mobility—B section: single musical line split between the two hands may cause metrical challenges.
2. Notation—range is G3-B5; entire piece is notated in two treble clefs.
3. Tempo/Meter/Rhythm—*Allegretto*; $\frac{2}{8}$; rhythmic patterns through the subdivision of the beat.

4. Texture—A section: homophonic: right-hand, patterned melody with left-hand, chordal accompaniment; B section: monophonic: broken-chord patterns split between the two hands may present musical, metrical, and technical challenges.
5. Form—AA^1-BA^2; four-measure phrases.
6. Harmony—A section: C major; A^1 section: G major; B section: C major; A^2 section: C major; moderate harmonic rhythm.
7. Melody—A and A^1 sections: right-hand, scalar melody; B section: single musical line of broken-intervals in each hand.
8. Articulation—numerous short slurs.
9. Dynamics—*pp-mf*.
10. Musical Expression/Character—graceful, elegant.
11. Pedaling—A section: frequently changing shallow pedaling; A^1 and B sections: none.

Op. 140, No. 9: *Thoughtful Moments*
Level: EI

1. Keyboard Skills/Technique/Mobility—B section: fragmented melody must be perceived across rests.
2. Notation—range is E2-F-sharp5; use of two treble clefs.
3. Tempo/Meter/Rhythm—*Andante con moto*; $\frac{2}{4}$; rhythmic patterns through the division of the beat; many phrases begin on a weak beat; syncopation.
4. Texture—homophonic: A section: right-hand, single-line melody with *legato* parallel thirds or chordal accompaniment; B section: chordal, with melody on top of the chords.
5. Form—ABA; four-measure phrases with some phrase extensions; many inconclusive phrases.
6. Harmony—A section: A minor, modulatory; B section: C major; varied harmonic rhythm.
7. Melody—A section: right-hand, lyrical passagework with wide leaps that begins on a weak beat; B section: melody notes on top of *portato* chords suspended across rests may cause challenges with phrase continuity.

8. Articulation—A section: long *legato* slurs consistent with the phrasing; B section: *portato* chords slurred across rests.
9. Dynamics—*pp-f*, with long *crescendo* and *diminuendo*; sudden dynamic changes.
10. Musical Expression/Character—A section: passionate, restless; B section: calm within the storm.
11. Pedaling—challenging, overlapping pedaling due to phrases beginning on upbeats.

Op. 140, No. 10: *The Little Norwegian*
Level: EI, JM4

1. Keyboard Skills/Technique/Mobility—broken-interval passagework requiring rotation as well as hand contraction and extension.
2. Notation—range is A2-A5; use of two treble clefs.
3. Tempo/Meter/Rhythm—*Con moto*; $\frac{3}{4}$; rhythmic patterns through the division of the beat; some notated tempo *rubato* at ends of phrases.
4. Texture—homophonic: right-hand melody with sparse chordal accompaniment.
5. Form—ABA[1] + coda; varying phrase lengths.
6. Harmony—A section: A minor; B section: A major; slow harmonic rhythm.
7. Melody—A section: dotted-rhythm motive on top of chords alternating with passagework; B section: broken-interval passagework; all passagework includes some awkward fingering.
8. Articulation—*staccato* chords, *portatos*, and both shorter and longer slurs.
9. Dynamics—*pp-f*, with sudden dynamic changes.
10. Musical Expression/Character—spirited, lively.
11. Pedaling—B section: consistent, overlapping pedaling for each measure.

Op. 140, No. 11: *Longing*
Level: MI, JM4

1. Keyboard Skills/Technique/Mobility—right-hand, broken-interval passagework with line-within-a-line melody on top requiring finger independence and some awkward fingerings needed for the *legato*.

2. Notation—range is E2-E5.
3. Tempo/Meter/Rhythm: *Con moto*; 2/4 ; rhythmic patterns through the division of the beat.
4. Texture—homophonic: right-hand, line-within-a-line melody on top in duet with the left-hand bass line.
5. Form: AB-AB¹-A¹; eight-measure phrases.
6. Harmony: A section: F major; B section: modulatory; fast harmonic rhythm.
7. Melody—right-hand, lyrical, line-within-a-line melody.
8. Articulation—*legato*.
9. Dynamics—*p-f*.
10. Musical Expression/Character—yearning, restless.
11. Pedaling—quick, overlapping pedaling.

Op. 140: No. 12: *In the Church*
Level: MI, JM5
Praeludium and Chorale

1. Keyboard Skills/Technique/Mobility—Praeludium: right-hand, single-line passagework with many broken intervals requiring careful attention to fingering; Chorale: chordal texture with the melody on top.
2. Notation—range is G2-C6; Praeludium: use of two treble clefs.
3. Tempo/Meter/Rhythm—*Moderato*; 3/4 ; rhythmic patterns through the division of the beat.
4. Texture—Praeludium: polyphonic: two-voice texture of right-hand passagework with a left-hand melodic line; Chorale: homophonic: chordal.
5. Form—Praeludium: AA¹; eight-measure phrases; Chorale: through-composed; four-measure phrases.
6. Harmony—G major; fast harmonic rhythm.
7. Melody—Praeludium: right-hand passagework with broken intervals; left-hand, lyrical line; Chorale: mostly scalar melody on top of the chords.
8. Articulation—*legato*.
9. Dynamics—Praeludium: *p-mf*; Chorale: *f*.

10. Musical Expression/Character—Praeludium: flowing, peaceful; Chorale: grand, noble.
11. Pedaling—Praeludium: frequent, shallow pedaling with the fast harmonic rhythm; Chorale: overlapping pedaling with the chord changes.

Op. 140, No. 13: *The Little Wanderer*
Level: EI, JM4

1. Keyboard Skills/Technique/Mobility—occasional awkward fingering.
2. Notation—range is A2-D6.
3. Tempo/Meter/Rhythm—*Allegretto grazioso*; $\frac{2}{4}$; rhythmic patterns through the subdivision of the beat.
4. Texture—homophonic: A section: mostly chordal; B section: right-hand passagework with a left-hand, broken-chord accompaniment.
5. Form—AA^1-B-AA^2-B-AA^2; eight-measure phrases.
6. Harmony—A section: G major; B section: D major; moderate harmonic rhythm; tension/resolution.
7. Melody—A section: melody on top of chords; B section: flowing passagework with some leaps.
8. Articulation—two-note slurs.
9. Dynamics—*p-f*, with quick *crescendo* and *diminuendo*.
10. Musical Expression/Character—happy, jovial.
11. Pedaling—A section: overlapping pedaling with the chords, except for in the measures with the dotted rhythms; B section: no pedaling.

Op. 140, No. 14: *Hunting Song*
Level: MI, JM5

1. Keyboard Skills/Technique/Mobility—quick hand-position changes in the right hand to play repeated notes with finger changes; wide stretches in the left hand at a fast tempo; quick shifts from single notes to thirds in the right hand.
2. Notation—range is C3-F5; use of two treble clefs.

3. Tempo/Meter/Rhythm—*Vivace*; 6/8; rhythmic patterns through the division of the beat; tempo changes and *fermatas*; rhythmic patterns may be challenging to synchronize between the two hands due to articulations and syncopation; maintaining a larger metrical pulse grouping is important.
4. Texture—homophonic: right-hand, fragmented melody with various accompaniments.
5. Form—ABA; four-measure phrases.
6. Harmony—A section: F major; B section: B-flat major; fast harmonic rhythm.
7. Melody—A section: right-hand, fragmented melody with many two-note slurs; B section: lyrical, single-line melody; some parallel thirds.
8. Articulation—extensive use of two-note slurs and diverse articulations between the two hands.
9. Dynamics—*mf-f*.
10. Musical Expression/Character—lively hunting song.
11. Pedaling—on the *fortissimo* chords.

Op. 140, No. 15: *Will-o-the-Wisp*
Level: MI, JM5

1. Keyboard Skills/Technique/Mobility—melodic and rhythmic patterns require careful coordination between the two hands; B section: some finger independence within the right hand.
2. Notation—range is E2-C6; use of two treble clefs.
3. Tempo/Meter/Rhythm—*Vivace*; 6/8; rhythmic patterns through the subdivision of the beat.
4. Texture—homophonic: A section: right-hand, fragmented melody with sparse, chordal accompaniment; B section: right-hand, lyrical melody with some polyphony.
5. Form—ABA, with many sub-sections; eight-measure phrases.
6. Harmony—A section: C major; B section: A minor; fast harmonic rhythm.
7. Melody—A section: right-hand, fragmented melody with consistent rhythmic motives; B section: lyrical melody.

8. Articulation—extensive use of two-note slurs.
9. Dynamics—*pp-mf*.
10. Musical Expression/Character—skipping, hopping.
11. Pedaling—limited to the B section.

Op. 140, No. 16: *Loss*
Level: MI

1. Keyboard Skills/Technique/Mobility—left-hand wide stretches; right-hand parallel thirds; abstract phrasing.
2. Notation—wide range: F1-F5.
3. Tempo/Meter/Rhythm—*Adagio*; $\frac{2}{4}$; rhythmic patterns through the subdivision of the beat.
4. Texture—homophonic: A section: chordal; B section: right-hand passagework with left-hand, two-part texture requiring finger independence.
5. Form—ABA¹; eight-measure phrases with asymmetrical subphrases 5+3.
6. Harmony—A section: F major; B section: F minor; varied harmonic rhythm.
7. Melody—A section: right-hand melody with parallel thirds; B section: right-hand, mostly scalar, lyrical melody.
8. Articulation—extensive use of *portato* notes and chords, some connected across rests; numerous two-note slurs.
9. Dynamics—*pp*, with *crescendo* and *diminuendo*.
10. Musical Expression/Character—sad.
11. Pedaling—quick pedaling, mostly to enhance the chords and two-note slurs.

Op. 140, No. 17: *Scherzo*
Level: EI, JM3

1. Keyboard Skills/Technique/Mobility—quick range changes; extensive use of *sf* on beat three may cause problems with maintaining a one-measure metrical pulse.

2. Notation—range is F2-B5; use of two treble clefs.
3. Tempo/Meter/Rhythm—*Allegretto*; $\frac{3}{4}$; rhythmic patterns through the subdivision of the beat.
4. Texture—homophonic: right-hand melody with intermittent added voice interspersed with a chordal accompaniment.
5. Form—A (interpolation) A^1 + coda; four-measure phrases.
6. Harmony—F major, with a brief section in C major.
7. Melody—right-hand melody with intermittent added voice.
8. Articulation—extensive use of two-note and other short slurs.
9. Dynamics—*mf*, with *sf* on weak beats.
10. Musical Expression/Character—playful.
11. Pedaling—intermittent pedaling on the chords to enhance *sf*.

Op. 140, No. 18: *Serenade*
Level: MI, JM4

1. Keyboard Skills/Technique/Mobility—A section: *cantabile* melody with many leaps requiring rotation of arm weight; B section: quick hand-position shifts with finger changes on repeated notes.
2. Notation—range is E3-E-flat6; extensive use of two treble clefs.
3. Tempo/Meter/Rhythm—*Andantino con moto*; $\frac{6}{8}$; rhythmic patterns through the division of the beat.
4. Texture—homophonic: right-hand, single-line, lyrical melody with left-hand, broken-chord, scalar accompaniment.
5. Form—ABA^1 + coda; eight-measure phrases; many inconclusive phrases.
6. Harmony—A section: B-flat major; B section: G minor, modulatory; varied harmonic rhythm.
7. Melody—right-hand, lyrical melody with many leaps; some grace notes and a short trill.
8. Articulation—*legato*, with shorter slurs that might be connected as longer phrases.
9. Dynamics—*pp-f*, with some *crescendo* and *diminuendo*.
10. Musical Expression/Character—sweet, innocent.
11. Pedaling—frequently changing, shallow, overlapping pedaling.

Op. 140, No. 19: *Impromptu*
Level: MI

1. Keyboard Skills/Technique/Mobility—large leaps in the left-hand melody; parallel thirds; finger independence required in both hands.
2. Notation—range is B-flat1-B-flat5; use of two treble clefs.
3. Tempo/Meter/Rhythm—*Vivace*; $\frac{2}{4}$; rhythmic patterns through the division of the beat.
4. Texture—homophonic: A section: right-hand, single-line melody with mixed-texture accompaniment; B section: chordal, with an independent melody on top.
5. Form—ABA + coda; A section: four-measure phrases; B section: eight-measure phrases.
6. Harmony—A section: F major; B section: B-flat major; fast harmonic rhythm; tension/resolution.
7. Melody—A section: melody switches quickly between the two hands.
8. Articulation—*legato*, with *staccatos* and accents.
9. Dynamics—*p-f*, with sudden dynamic changes.
10. Musical Expression/Character—passionate.
11. Pedaling—little or none, due to the very fast tempo; B section: some quick, overlapping pedaling could enhance the tone quality and provide some extra blending.

Op. 140, No. 20: *Storm and Stress*
Level: MI, JM5

1. Keyboard Skills/Technique/Mobility—quick passagework with some difficult arpeggiated sections covering a wide range; parallel passagework between the two hands, including trill-like oscillations.
2. Notation—range is C-sharp2-B-flat5; use of two bass clefs.
3. Tempo/Meter/Rhythm—*Molto vivace*; $\frac{3}{8}$; rhythmic patterns through the subdivision of the beat.
4. Texture—homophonic: parallel passages doubled at the octave between the two hands, alternating with right-hand passagework with single-note or broken-chord accompaniment.

5. Form—AA-BA¹-C-AA-BA¹-C¹; four-measure phrases.
6. Harmony—D minor (often using melodic minor pitch content).
7. Melody—passagework in one or both hands with many directional changes.
8. Articulation—*legato*.
9. Dynamics—*pp-ff*.
10. Musical Expression/Character—stormy, mysterious, dramatic.
11. Pedaling—none.

Robert Schumann—*Album for the Young*, Op. 68

Op. 68, No. 1: *Melodie* (Melody)
Level: EI, JM3

1. Keyboard Skills/Technique/Mobility—some notated right-hand finger substitutions to play the *legato* lines; voicing needed to balance the duet between the right-hand melody and left-hand countermelody.
2. Notation—range is G3-A5; entire piece uses two treble clefs.
3. Tempo/Meter/Rhythm—(none); **C** ; rhythmic patterns through the division of the beat.
4. Texture—polyphonic: right-hand, single-line, lyrical melody accompanied by a left-hand, single-line, eighth-note countermelody.
5. Form—AA-BA¹-BA¹; four-measure phrases.
6. Harmony—C major; fast harmonic rhythm.
7. Melody—right-hand, single-line, lyrical melody.
8. Articulation—*legato*, with short slurs.
9. Dynamics—*p*, with notated *diminuendo*.
10. Musical Expression/Character—flowing, peaceful.
11. Pedaling—light, shallow, overlapping pedaling on each quarter-note beat.

Op. 68, No. 2: *Soldatenmarsch* (Soldier's March)
Level: EI, JM3

1. Keyboard Skills/Technique/Mobility—chordal texture with an inconsistent number of voices in each hand; perceived phrase continuity across the rests may be challenging.

2. Notation—range is C3-G5; brief use of two treble clefs.
3. Tempo/Meter/Rhythm—*Munter und straff* (cheerfully and strictly); 12/8 ; rhythmic patterns through the subdivision of the beat.
4. Texture—homophonic and homorhythmic, with chords split between the two hands and an inconsistent number of voices in each hand.
5. Form—AA-BA¹BA¹; four-measure phrases.
6. Harmony—G major; fast harmonic rhythm.
7. Melody—fragmented, right-hand melody on top of chords.
8. Articulation—none notated; a crisp, detached touch is implied by the character.
9. Dynamics—*f*.
10. Musical Expression/Character—cheerful march.
11. Pedaling—limited, direct pedaling on the longer notes.

Op. 68, No. 3: *Trällerliedchen* (Humming Song)
Level: EI, JM3

1. Keyboard Skills/Technique/Mobility—left-hand passagework with a line-within-a-line melody on the bottom alternating with right-hand passagework with a line-within-a-line melody on the top; balance and voicing needed for the duet between the melody and countermelody.
2. Notation—range is D3-A5; use of two treble clefs.
3. Tempo/Meter/Rhythm—*Nicht schnell* (not fast); C ; rhythmic patterns through the division of the beat.
4. Texture—polyphonic: A section: right-hand, single-line, lyrical melody with left-hand, line-within-a-line countermelody on the bottom; A¹ section: right-hand, line-within-a-line melody on the top with left-hand, single-line countermelody.
5. Form—AA¹A; eight-measure phrases.
6. Harmony—C major; fast harmonic rhythm.
7. Melody—right-hand, single-line melody, alternating with line-within-a-line melody on the top.
8. Articulation—*legato*.

9. Dynamics—*p*, with phrase shaping needed, even though there is no notated *crescendo* or *diminuendo*.
10. Musical Expression/Character—flowing, peaceful.
11. Pedaling—light, shallow, overlapping pedaling on the quarter-note beats.

Op. 68, No. 4: *Ein Choral* (Chorale)
Level: EI, JM5

1. Keyboard Skills/Technique/Mobility—chorale texture; some notated finger substitutions to play the *legato* melody on top of the chords; shaping of the chord progression and voicing of the melodic line is needed.
2. Notation—range is G2-C5.
3. Tempo/Meter/Rhythm—(none); ¢; almost exclusively half notes.
4. Texture—homophonic and homorhythmic: chords split between the two hands with the melody on the top.
5. Form—AA¹-AA¹; four-measure phrases defined by *fermatas* at the ends of the phrases.
6. Harmony—G major; fast harmonic rhythm.
7. Melody—right-hand, scalar melody on top of chords in consistent half notes.
8. Articulation—*legato*.
9. Dynamics—*p*, with phrase shaping needed.
10. Musical Expression/Character—serene, reverent.
11. Pedaling—consistent, overlapping pedaling on each chord.

Op. 68, No. 5: *Stückchen* (Little Piece)
Level: EI, JM3

1. Keyboard Skills/Technique/Mobility—left-hand passagework with line-within-a-line melody on the bottom; voicing and balance needed for the duet between the melody and line-within-a-line accompaniment.
2. Notation—range is F3-A5; entire piece uses two treble clefs.
3. Tempo/Meter/Rhythm—*Nicht schnell* (not fast); C; rhythmic patterns through the division of the beat; careful perception is needed for the

metrical grouping, since the piece starts in the middle of the measure and should lead to the next downbeat (continuing through the piece).
4. Texture—polyphonic: consistent, right-hand, single-line, lyrical melody with left-hand, line-within-a-line countermelody.
5. Form—theme with multiple subtle variations; four-measure phrases.
6. Harmony—C major; fast harmonic rhythm.
7. Melody—right-hand, single-line, lyrical melody within a limited range.
8. Articulation—*legato*.
9. Dynamics—*p*, with phrase shaping needed, even though there is no notated *crescendo* or *diminuendo*.
10. Musical Expression/Character—peaceful, flowing.
11. Pedaling—light, shallow pedaling needed on the quarter notes.

Op. 68, No. 6: *Armes Waisenkind* (Poor Orphan)
Level: MI

1. Keyboard Skills/Technique/Mobility—chordal texture with inconsistent number of voices; extensive parallel thirds.
2. Notation—range is E3-G5; use of two treble clefs.
3. Tempo/Meter/Rhythm—*Langsam* (slowly); $\frac{2}{4}$; rhythmic patterns through the subdivision of the beat; several tempo changes, requiring careful pacing.
4. Texture—homophonic: right-hand melody on top of chords.
5. Form—ABABA; four-measure phrases.
6. Harmony—A minor; fast harmonic rhythm.
7. Melody—right-hand melody with additional voice.
8. Articulation—*portatos* and short slurs.
9. Dynamics—*p*, with quick *crescendo* and *diminuendo*.
10. Musical Expression/Character—uncertain, halting, insecure.
11. Pedaling—careful, intermittent pedaling as needed to assist slurs, enhance long notes, and assist *portatos*, without obscuring the many articulations.

Op. 68, No. 7: *Jägerliedchen* (Hunting Song)
Level: MI, JM5

1. Keyboard Skills/Technique/Mobility—melody doubled in parallel octaves between the two hands; quick shifts from intervals to single notes; wide stretches in both hands; quick, repeated, *staccato* chords; some difficult notated fingering.
2. Notation—range is A2-A5; use of two treble clefs.
3. Tempo/Meter/Rhythm—*Frisch und fröhlich* (fresh and cheerful); 6/8; rhythmic patterns through the division of the beat.
4. Texture—homophonic: some doubling of the melody in both hands; chords split between the two hands.
5. Form—through-composed, with some repetition of similar material; two repeated sections; four-measure phrases.
6. Harmony—F major; varied harmonic rhythm.
7. Melody—disjunct, *staccato* melody alternating between single notes and intervals; a few grace notes.
8. Articulation—*staccatos, marcatos*, accents, and combination markings.
9. Dynamics—*p-ff*, with sudden dynamic changes.
10. Musical Expression/Character—cheerful, lively hunting song.
11. Pedaling—limited pedaling as notated.

Op. 68, No. 8: *Wilder Reiter* (Wild Rider or Wild Horseman)
Level: MI, JM3

1. Keyboard Skills/Technique/Mobility—rapid hand contraction and extension required for the passagework in both hands.
2. Notation—range is C3-F5; use of two treble clefs with quick clef changes.
3. Tempo/Meter/Rhythm—(none); 6/8; rhythmic patterns through the division of the beat; there is no tempo marking, but a fast, lively tempo is implied by the character.
4. Texture—homophonic: detached melody with intermittent, chordal accompaniment; A section: melody in the right hand; B section: melody in the left hand.

5. Form—AABA; four-measure phrases.
6. Harmony—A section: A minor; B section: F major; harmonic rhythm varies.
7. Melody—triadic, disjunct melody.
8. Articulation—*staccato*s and short slurs.
9. Dynamics—*mf*, with some *sf*.
10. Musical Expression/Character—wild, dramatic.
11. Pedaling—direct pedaling on the *sf* chords.

Op. 68, No. 9: *Volksliedchen* (Folk Song)
Level: MI

1. Keyboard Skills/Technique/Mobility—difficult independence of articulation needed between the two hands; A¹ section: careful voicing needed for the left-hand melody on top of the chords.
2. Notation—range is G3-D6; use of two treble clefs for the entire piece.
3. Tempo/Meter/Rhythm—*Im klagenden Ton* (in a plaintive tone); **C**; rhythmic patterns through the subdivision of the beat, with additional thirty-second notes and rests; several tempo changes.
4. Texture—homophonic: A section: right-hand, lyrical melody with occasional added voices over a chordal accompaniment with inconsistent number of voices; B section: articulated melody with chordal accompaniment; A¹ section: left-hand, lyrical melody on top of chords.
5. Form—ABA¹; four-measure phrases.
6. Harmony—A section: D minor; B section: D major; fast harmonic rhythm.
7. Melody—A section: right-hand, single-line, plaintive melody with occasional added voices; B section: disjunct, uneven-rhythm melody with a variety of articulations.
8. Articulation—A section: *legato*, with *portatos*; B section: quick changes between slurs and *staccatos*.
9. Dynamics—*p*, with *fp* and quick *crescendo* and *diminuendo*.
10. Musical Expression/Character—A section: plaintive; B section: humorous.

11. Pedaling—A section: varies for each measure; pianists should not pedal through the rests; B section: no pedaling; A¹ section: overlapping pedaling.

Op. 68, No. 10: *Fröhlicher Landmann, von der Arbeit zurückkehrend* (The Happy Farmer Returning from His Work)
Level: MI, JM3-4

1. Keyboard Skills/Technique/Mobility—wide stretches in the melody; finger independence required for multiple voices in the right hand.
2. Notation—range is B-flat2-F5.
3. Tempo/Meter/Rhythm—*Frisch und munter* (fresh and cheerful); 𝄴; rhythmic patterns through the division of the beat.
4. Texture—homophonic: A section: left-hand, single-line melody with intermittent, right-hand, chordal accompaniment; B section: right-hand melody in thirds with the left hand and doubled at the octave with the left hand, with additional right-hand inner voices.
5. Form—AA-BA¹-BA¹; two- and four-measure phrases.
6. Harmony—F major; moderate harmonic rhythm.
7. Melody—triadic, disjunct melody.
8. Articulation—mostly *legato*, with accents and *staccatos*.
9. Dynamics—*f*.
10. Musical Expression/Character—cheerful, happy.
11. Pedaling—intermittent, shallow pedaling.

Op. 68, No. 11: *Sizilianisch* (Sicilienne)
Level: MI, JM4-5

1. Keyboard Skills/Technique/Mobility—rapid finger changes notated on repeated notes; right-hand, broken-interval passagework with left-hand, quickly changing, chordal accompaniment.
2. Notation—range is B2-G5; use of two treble clefs.

3. Tempo/Meter/Rhythm—*Schalkhaft* (mischievous); $\frac{6}{8}$; rhythmic patterns through the division of the beat; $\frac{2}{4}$; rhythmic patterns through the subdivision of the beat.
4. Texture—homophonic: right-hand, single-line melody with left-hand, chordal accompaniment.
5. Form—AABBA-CDC-ABA; four-measure phrases.
6. Harmony—A minor; varied harmonic rhythm.
7. Melody—A section: right-hand, single-line melody with many repeated notes and leaps; B section: passagework with broken intervals.
8. Articulation—short slurs, *portatos*, and accents.
9. Dynamics—*p-f*, with quick dynamic changes.
10. Musical Expression/Character—folk dance.
11. Pedaling—A section: short pedals on the longer chords and slurs; B section: short, direct pedaling on the accented chords.

Op. 68, No. 12: *Knecht Ruprecht* (Knight Rupert)
Level: LI, JM7

1. Keyboard Skills/Technique/Mobility—A section: passagework in unison octaves between the two hands, with two-note slurs and slurred parallel thirds; B section: difficult, broken-interval passagework with line-within-a-line melodies.
2. Notation—range is A1-A5; use of two bass clefs, with many clef changes.
3. Tempo/Meter/Rhythm—(none); $\frac{2}{4}$; rhythmic patterns through the subdivision of the beat.
4. Texture—A section: homophonic: passagework doubled at the octave between the two hands, with some parallel thirds and additional chords; B section: polyphonic: difficult broken-interval passagework in each hand; one sub-section has a difficult three-part texture requiring right-hand finger independence.
5. Form—large ABA form with many repeated sub-sections; four-measure phrases.

6. Harmony—A section: A minor; B section: F major; both sections have modulatory, sequential passages in other keys.
7. Melody—A section: patterned, instrumental passagework; B section: diverse, instrumental passagework between the two hands.
8. Articulation—A section: *marcatos* and short slurs; B section: *legato*.
9. Dynamics—*p-ff*, with *fp* and fast *crescendo* and *diminuendo*.
10. Musical Expression/Character—dramatic.
11. Pedaling—intermittent, direct pedaling on the accented notes and chords; careful, limited, quick pedaling is needed during the polyphonic section to assist with the *legato* melody.

Op. 68, No. 13: *Mai, lieber Mai—Bald bist Du wieder da!* (May, Sweet May— You'll be back soon!)
Level: A

1. Keyboard Skills/Technique/Mobility—difficult complex texture, with much diversity in multiple musical elements between the two hands; challenging musical and technical demands.
2. Notation—range is C-sharp3-C-sharp6; use of two treble clefs, with frequently changing clefs in the left hand; extensive chromaticism, including the use of double sharps.
3. Tempo/Meter/Rhythm—*Nicht schnell* (not fast); ⅜; rhythmic patterns through the subdivision of the beat; the tempo must not be rushed, due to the significant chromaticism and complicated harmonic progressions; extensive tempo *rubato* is needed.
4. Texture—homophonic, with a clear instrumental melody, but with extensive counterpoint between the two hands.
5. Form—AABB, with variations of A recurring in B; inconclusive phrases with a variety of phrase lengths.
6. Harmony—E major, with extensive chromaticism and complicated harmonic progressions; fast harmonic rhythm; tension/resolution needs careful aural attention.
7. Melody—disjunct, instrumental melody with many quick directional changes.

8. Articulation—great variety of articulations within each hand and between the two hands.
9. Dynamics—*p-f*, with *fp* and *crescendo* and *diminuendo*.
10. Musical Expression/Character—sincere, wistful, romantic.
11. Pedaling—sophisticated, constantly changing, shallow, short pedals to enhance tone, volume, accents, articulations, and tension/resolution.

Op. 68, No. 14: *Kleine Studie* (Little Study)
Level: EI, JM4

1. Keyboard Skills/Technique/Mobility—single musical line of broken arpeggios alternating hands on every beat.
2. Notation—range is G2-G5.
3. Tempo/Meter/Rhythm—*Leise und sehr egal zu spielen* (play quietly with all of the notes even); $\frac{6}{8}$; consistent eighth notes.
4. Texture—monophonic: one musical line alternating between the two hands.
5. Form—AA-BA¹BA¹; sixteen-measure phrases.
6. Harmony—G major; moderate harmonic rhythm.
7. Melody—implied line-within-a-line melody on the top notes of the right hand, although it is not notated.
8. Articulation—*legato*.
9. Dynamics—limited *crescendo* and *diminuendo*.
10. Musical Expression/Character—gentle, flowing.
11. Pedaling—overlapping pedaling with the chord changes.

Op. 68, No. 15: *Frühlingsgesang* (Spring Song)
Level: LI

1. Keyboard Skills/Technique/Mobility—difficult chordal texture with polyphonic sections, each requiring great finger independence within each hand and between the two hands.

2. Notation—range is F-sharp2-A5; use of two treble clefs.
3. Tempo/Meter/Rhythm—*Innig zu spielen* (tenderly); $^6_8$; rhythmic patterns through the subdivision of the beat; dotted rhythms; syncopation.
4. Texture—homophonic, with some polyphonic sections; homophonic: melody on top of right-hand chords, with inconsistent number of voices; polyphonic: melody with inner-voice countermelody.
5. Form—AA-BA^{1}BA^2 + coda; four-measure phrases; multiple inconclusive phrases.
6. Harmony—E major, with significant chromaticism and modulations; fast harmonic rhythm; tension/resolution.
7. Melody—vocal melody on top of right-hand chords, with many vocal leaps.
8. Articulation—*legato*, with *portatos*.
9. Dynamics—*pp-f*, with *fp* and quick *crescendo* and *diminuendo*.
10. Musical Expression/Character—tender, innocent.
11. Pedaling—*una corda* indicated by *Verschiebung*; sophisticated, constantly changing, shallow, short pedals to enhance tone, volume, articulations, and tension/resolution.

Op. 68, No. 16: *Erster Verlust* (First Loss)
Level: MI, JM3-4

1. Keyboard Skills/Technique/Mobility—awkward notated fingering and finger independence needed within one hand and between the two hands.
2. Notation—range is E2-G5; use of two treble clefs, with many clef changes.
3. Tempo/Meter/Rhythm—*Nicht schnell* (not fast); $^2_4$; rhythmic patterns through the division of the beat; some notated tempo *rubato*.
4. Texture—A section: homophonic: right-hand, single-line, lyrical melody with intermittent, mixed-texture, left-hand accompaniment; B section: polyphonic: melody alternating hands, with additional left-hand voice.
5. Form—AA^1-BA^2-BA^2; four- and eight-measure phrases.

6. Harmony—E minor, with extensive chromaticism.
7. Melody—right-hand, single-line, lyrical melody.
8. Articulation—*legato*, with short slurs and accents.
9. Dynamics—*p-f*, with *fp* and *crescendo* and *diminuendo*.
10. Musical Expression/Character—sad, sorrowful.
11. Pedaling—sophisticated, intermittent, shallow pedaling.

Op. 68, No. 17: *Kleiner Morgenwanderer* (The Little Morning Wanderer)
Level: LI

1. Keyboard Skills/Technique/Mobility—fast, dotted-rhythm chords; finger independence needed within each hand and between the two hands; thick chords; some voice crossings, requiring interlocking hands or potential redistribution of parts.
2. Notation—range is D2-A5; use of two bass clefs.
3. Tempo/Meter/Rhythm—*Frisch und kräftig* (fresh and strong); $\frac{2}{4}$; rhythmic patterns through the subdivision of the beat, plus double-dotted eighth notes, dotted-sixteenth notes, sixteenth-note triplets and thirty-second notes.
4. Texture—homophonic: chordal texture with the melody on top, with finger independence needed in both hands and between the two hands.
5. Form—AA¹-BA²-BA² + coda; four-measure phrases.
6. Harmony—A major, with extensive chromaticism; fast harmonic rhythm.
7. Melody—right-hand, primarily scalar melody on top of the chords.
8. Articulation—few articulation markings are provided, leaving the pianist to decide between a crisp, non-*legato* touch or a more *legato* approach.
9. Dynamics—wide dynamic range: *pp-ff*.
10. Musical Expression/Character—confident, exuberant, jaunty.
11. Pedaling—open to interpretation, depending upon the chosen character: direct pedaling to give sonority to the chords while maintaining an articulated touch or more overlapping pedaling for a more *legato* approach.

Op. 68, No. 18: *Schnitterliedchen* (The Reaper's Song)
Level: MI, JM4

1. Keyboard Skills/Technique/Mobility—finger independence needed in the right hand; awkward notated fingering to play the *legato* melody; passagework in parallel motion doubled at the octave between the two hands; parallel thirds and horn fifths.
2. Notation—range is C3-C6.
3. Tempo/Meter/Rhythm—*Nicht sehr schnell* (not very fast); 6/8; rhythmic patterns through the division of the beat.
4. Texture—A section: homophonic: melody on top of chordal texture; B section: polyphonic: three-voice texture with the melody in the middle; C section: homophonic: melody in parallel octaves between the two hands.
5. Form—AA-BB-A-CC-A^{1}B^1 + coda; four-measure phrases.
6. Harmony—A section: C major; B section: G major; C section: F major; A^1 section: F major; B^1 section: C major; coda: C major; moderate harmonic rhythm.
7. Melody—lyrical melody within various textures.
8. Articulation—primarily *legato*, with *staccato* passages in the coda.
9. Dynamics—*p* and *f*, with sudden dynamic contrasts.
10. Musical Expression/Character—flowing.
11. Pedaling—limited, to keep the texture clear.

Op. 68, No. 19: *Kleine Romanze* (Little Romance)
Level: LI, JM6

1. Keyboard Skills/Technique/Mobility—disjunct melody doubled in parallel octaves between the two hands with offbeat accompaniment chords in each hand; challenging notated fingering for playing the *legato* melody.
2. Notation—range is A2-A5.
3. Tempo/Meter/Rhythm—*Nicht schnell* (not fast); ¢; rhythmic patterns through the division of the beat.

4. Texture—A section: homophonic: melody doubled in parallel octaves between the two hands, with each hand also having offbeat accompaniment chords; B section: includes some homorhythmic chordal sections with the melody on top of the chords.
5. Form—AABB, with the B section including some musical material similar to the A section; four- and six-measure phrases.
6. Harmony—A minor; varied harmonic rhythm.
7. Melody—disjunct, *legato* melody.
8. Articulation—primarily *legato*.
9. Dynamics—*pp-f*, with *sfz* and sudden dynamic changes.
10. Musical Expression/Character—passionate, yearning.
11. Pedaling—quick, overlapping pedaling, being careful not to obscure various voices of the texture.

Op. 68, No. 20: *Ländliches Lied* (Rustic Song)
Level: LI

1. Keyboard Skills/Technique/Mobility—chordal texture with awkward notated fingering and quick hand-position changes; difficult left-hand, broken-chord accompaniment.
2. Notation—range is A2-A5; use of two treble clefs.
3. Tempo/Meter/Rhythm—*Im maßigen* Tempo (in moderate time); $\frac{2}{4}$; rhythmic patterns through the division of the beat.
4. Texture—homophonic: A section: chordal texture with melody on top of chords; B section: right-hand, single-line melody over left-hand, broken-chord accompaniment.
5. Form—AA^1-BA^2A^1-BA^2A^1; eight-measure phrases.
6. Harmony—A major; fast harmonic rhythm.
7. Melody—A section: right-hand, disjunct melody on top of chords; B section: right-hand, lyrical, primarily scalar melody; chord rolls; short trills.
8. Articulation—short slurs and *staccatos*.
9. Dynamics—*p-mf*.

10. Musical Expression/Character—folk dance.
11. Pedaling—intermittent, direct pedaling on longer notes and short slurs.

Op. 68, No. 21: ***
Level: LI, JM7

1. Keyboard Skills/Technique/Mobility—finger independence needed within each hand for multiple voices; awkward notated fingering to play the *legato* melody.
2. Notation—range is A2-C6; use of two treble clefs.
3. Tempo/Meter/Rhythm—*Langsam und mit Ausdruck zu spielen* (to play slowly and with expression); 𝐂 ; rhythmic patterns through the division of the beat; several tempo changes.
4. Texture—homophonic: right-hand, lyrical melody with mixed-texture accompaniment.
5. Form—ABA¹; four-measure phrases; multiple inconclusive phrases.
6. Harmony—C major; fast harmonic rhythm; extensive chromaticism; unexpected harmonic progressions; tension/resolution.
7. Melody—lyrical melody with a number of vocal leaps; notated ornamental turn.
8. Articulation—primarily *legato*, with *portatos* and short slurs.
9. Dynamics—*p*, with some *crescendo* and *diminuendo*.
10. Musical Expression/Character—intimate, gently passionate.
11. Pedaling—intermittent, shallow pedaling needed for clarity.

Op. 68, No. 22: *Rundgesang* (Roundelay)
Level: A

1. Keyboard Skills/Technique/Mobility—complex texture with frequently changing hand positions and number of voices; awkward notated fingering to play the *legato* parts; significant musical and technical challenges requiring great control.
2. Notation—range is A2-A5; use of two treble clefs.

3. Tempo/Meter/Rhythm—*Mäßig. Sehr geunden zu spielen* (Moderate. Play very *legato*); $\frac{6}{8}$; rhythmic patterns through the division of the beat.
4. Texture—homophonic: right-hand, lyrical melody within mixed textures with frequently changing number of voices; B section: includes polyphonic sections with multiple voices.
5. Form—AA-BA¹- BA¹; eight-measure phrases; inconclusive phrases.
6. Harmony—A major, with extensive chromaticism; fast harmonic rhythm; tension/resolution.
7. Melody—A section: lyrical, disjunct melody on top of the chordal texture with many leaps; B section: lyrical, melodic passages in both hands.
8. Articulation—*legato*.
9. Dynamics—*p-fp*, with *crescendo*.
10. Musical Expression/Character—flowing, joyful.
11. Pedaling—frequently changing, shallow, short pedals to enhance tone, volume, articulations, and tension/resolution.

Op. 68, No. 23: *Reiterstück* (Horseman's Song)
Level: MI, JM7

1. Keyboard Skills/Technique/Mobility—rapid broken octaves and other broken intervals; parallel thirds; large chords in both hands; wide stretches for both hands; both hands playing in the low range may cause balance problems, especially in the coda.
2. Notation—range is D1-A5; use of two treble clefs; both hands frequently notated on the same staff.
3. Tempo/Meter/Rhythm—*Kurz und bestimmt* (short and decisive); $\frac{6}{8}$; rhythmic patterns through the subdivision of the beat.
4. Texture—homophonic: primarily chordal, with occasional single notes.
5. Form—AA-BB-AB¹C + coda; four-measure phrases.
6. Harmony—D minor, with the coda in D major; varied harmonic rhythm.

7. Melody—detached melody with extensive parallel thirds.
8. Articulation—*marcatos* and *staccatos*; implied non-*legato* touch for most of the piece.
9. Dynamics—*pp-ff*, with *sf* and sudden dynamic contrasts.
10. Musical Expression/Character—determined, intense, passionate.
11. Pedaling—limited, direct pedaling on the chords and slurs; shallow, overlapping pedaling on the chords in the coda.

Op. 68, No. 24: <u>Ernteliedchen (Harvest Song)</u>
Level: MI

1. Keyboard Skills/Technique/Mobility—wide stretches; chords with awkward notated fingering needed for playing *legato*; finger independence needed within each hand.
2. Notation—range is E3-B5; use of two treble clefs, with frequent clef changes.
3. Tempo/Meter/Rhythm—*Mit frölichem Ausdruck* (with a happy expression); $\frac{6}{8}$; rhythmic patterns through the division of the beat.
4. Texture—homophonic: A section: right-hand melody on top of chords, with some doubling of the melody in the left hand; B section: right-hand melody with an inconsistent number of voices in mixed textures.
5. Form—AA-BA^1-BA^1; four-measure phrases.
6. Harmony—A major; varied harmonic rhythm.
7. Melody—A section: primarily triadic melody on top of chords; B section: primarily scalar, articulated melody.
8. Articulation—variety of articulations, including *legato*, *portatos*, accents, and *staccatos*.
9. Dynamics—*p-mf*, with *fp* and some *crescendo* and *diminuendo*.
10. Musical Expression/Character—happy, celebratory.
11. Pedaling—intermittent, direct pedaling and quick, shallow, overlapping pedaling on the lyrical, chordal sections.

Op. 68, No. 25: <u>Nachklänge aus dem Theater</u> (Echoes from the Theater)
Level: LI, JM6

1. Keyboard Skills/Technique/Mobility—rapid, repeated chords and octaves, sometimes in dotted rhythms; quick notated finger changes on repeated notes; difficult fingering in passagework; large right-hand chords; quick chord changes.
2. Notation—range is E2-C6; extensive use of two treble clefs.
3. Tempo/Meter/Rhythm—*Etwas agitiert* (a little agitated); $\frac{2}{4}$; rhythmic patterns through the subdivision of the beat, plus thirty-second notes.
4. Texture—homophonic: A section: right-hand, single-line passagework with left-hand, chordal accompaniment; B section: right-hand melody in various settings: doubled with left-hand octaves, on top of thick chords, and as part of a brief three-part texture.
5. Form—AA-BA¹-BA¹; many inconclusive phrases.
6. Harmony—A section: A minor; B section: C major, modulatory; varied harmonic rhythm.
7. Melody—disjunct passagework with awkward notated fingering.
8. Articulation—a variety of articulations: *legato*, with short slurs, accents, and *marcatos*.
9. Dynamics—wide dynamic range: *p-ff*, with *crescendo* and *diminuendo*.
10. Musical Expression/Character—dramatic, passionate, intense.
11. Pedaling—intermittent pedaling, primarily for the long notes, two-note slurs, *forte* octaves, and *forte* chords.

Op. 68, No. 26: ***
Level: LI

1. Keyboard Skills/Technique/Mobility—frequently changing musical texture with awkward notated fingering for playing the *legato* melody; finger independence required within the same hand and between the two hands; the texture needs careful balance and voicing.
2. Notation—range is F2-F5.

3. Tempo/Meter/Rhythm—*Nicht schnell, hübsch vorzutragen* (not fast, perform in a pretty way); **C**; rhythmic patterns through the division of the beat.
4. Texture—homophonic: lyrical melody that switches hands in a mixed-texture setting with intermittent, chordal accompaniment.
5. Form—AA-BA¹C-BA¹C; four-measure phrases.
6. Harmony—A section: F major; B section: C major; C section: modulatory; extensive chromaticism; fast harmonic rhythm.
7. Melody—lyrical melody that switches hands within a mixed-texture setting; long notes have the potential for fading sound challenges.
8. Articulation—primarily *legato*.
9. Dynamics—*p-mf*, with *fp*.
10. Musical Expression/Character—gentle, peaceful, serene.
11. Pedaling—intermittent, shallow, short pedals to enhance tone, volume, articulations, and tension/resolution.

Op. 68, No. 27: *Kanonisches Liedchen* (Little Song in Canon Form)
Level: A

1. Keyboard Skills/Technique/Mobility—complex polyphonic texture with difficult fingering and finger independence required within both hands; frequently changing number of voices in both hands; careful balance and voicing of the texture is needed.
2. Notation—range is A1-A5.
3. Tempo/Meter/Rhythm—*Nicht schnell und mit innigem Ausdruck* (not fast, and with heartfelt expression); $\frac{2}{4}$; rhythmic patterns through the division of the beat; syncopation in the B section; several notated tempo changes.
4. Texture—polyphonic, with multiple independent voices; canon at a one-measure interval between the soprano and the tenor voices.
5. Form—AABA¹; four- and eight-measure phrases; many inconclusive phrases.
6. Harmony—A section: A minor; B section: A major; fast harmonic rhythm.

7. Melody—A section: lyrical, scalar, ascending and descending melodic line with inconsistent number of additional voices; B section: disjunct melody with a variety of articulations.
8. Articulation—*legato*, with *staccatos, portatos*, and short slurs.
9. Dynamics—*pp-p*, with *fp* and *crescendo* and *diminuendo*.
10. Musical Expression/Character—A section: sad, sorrowful; B section: hopeful.
11. Pedaling—intermittent, shallow, short pedals to enhance tone, volume, and articulations.

Op. 68, No. 28: *Erinnerung* (In Memoriam or Remembrance)
Level: LI

1. Keyboard Skills/Technique/Mobility—awkward fingering needed to play the *legato* melodic line; frequently changing number of voices, especially in the right hand; left-hand arpeggios with wide stretches.
2. Notation—range is A1-F-sharp5.
3. Tempo/Meter/Rhythm—*Nicht schnell und sehr gesangvoll zu spielen* (not fast, and play very vocally); $\frac{2}{4}$; rhythmic patterns through the subdivision of the beat; several tempo changes and *fermatas*.
4. Texture—homophonic: right-hand, lyrical melody with chords within the same hand and left-hand, broken-chord accompaniment, with an inconsistent number of additional voices in both hands.
5. Form—ABA[1]; four- and six-measure phrases.
6. Harmony—A major; varied harmonic rhythm; tension/resolution.
7. Melody—lyrical melody within a mixed, inconsistent texture of various additional voices; ornamental turns.
8. Articulation—*legato*, with short slurs and *portatos*.
9. Dynamics—*p*, with some *crescendo* and *diminuendo*.
10. Musical Expression/Character—song without words; Felix Mendelssohn died on the date in the musical score (November 4, 1847).
11. Pedaling—intermittent pedaling as notated.

Op. 68, No. 29: _Fremder Mann_ (Strange Man)
Level: LI, JM8

1. Keyboard Skills/Technique/Mobility—octave passages in dotted rhythms; large dotted-rhythm chords with awkward notated fingering; tremolo-like, broken-chord patterns in both hands.
2. Notation—range is G1-D6; use of two treble clefs.
3. Tempo/Meter/Rhythm—_Stark und kräftig zu spielen_ (to play strong and powerful); $\frac{2}{4}$; rhythmic patterns through the subdivision of the beat; extensive use of dotted rhythms.
4. Texture—homophonic: right-hand melody as single notes and on top of chords, with a left-hand, octave-passage accompaniment.
5. Form—large ABA¹ + coda; four- and eight-measure phrases.
6. Harmony—D minor, with many unusual chord progressions through various keys; fast harmonic rhythm.
7. Melody—A section: detached melody on top of chords; B section: lyrical, with the melody on top of sustained chords alternating with the strong octaves and dotted rhythms.
8. Articulation—_marcato_, with some short slurs.
9. Dynamics—_pp-ff_, with _sf_ and sudden dynamic changes.
10. Musical Expression/Character—powerful and strong, with strange trembling interludes.
11. Pedaling—direct pedaling on the chords; some overlapping pedaling in the soft, lyrical sections.

Op. 68, No. 30: ***
Level: A

1. Keyboard Skills/Technique/Mobility—awkward notated fingering needed for playing the _legato_ melody within a complicated texture of multiple voices in each hand; finger independence needed within both hands for careful balancing of textures.
2. Notation—range is B-flat1-F5.

3. Tempo/Meter/Rhythm—*Sehr langsam* (very slow); **C**; rhythmic patterns through the subdivision of the beat; several notated tempo changes.
4. Texture—homophonic: A section: right-hand melody on top of chords with mixed-texture accompaniment; B section: right-hand melody with mixed-texture accompaniment, including a flowing, eighth-note inner voice.
5. Form—AA-BA^1-BA^2; four-measure phrases.
6. Harmony—F major; varied harmonic rhythm; tension/resolution; B section: extensive chromaticism.
7. Melody—right-hand, lyrical melody with many vocal leaps; long notes may cause fading sound challenges; ornamental turns.
8. Articulation—*legato*.
9. Dynamics—*pp-p*, with *sf* and *fp*.
10. Musical Expression/Character—dreamy, transparent.
11. Pedaling—overlapping, shallow pedaling with frequent changes.

Op. 68, No. 31: *Kriegslied* (Song of War)
Level: A, JM8

1. Keyboard Skills/Technique/Mobility—right-hand melody doubled with octaves in the left hand; octaves with inner voices; rapidly shifting chords and rapid shifts from single notes to chords.
2. Notation—range is D2-D6; use of two treble clefs.
3. Tempo/Meter/Rhythm—*Sehr kräftig* (very strong); ⁶⁄₈; dotted rhythms.
4. Texture—homophonic and homorhythmic: the melody appears in unison octave doublings between the two hands and on top of the chords in chordal passages.
5. Form—through-composed, with the theme presented differently in various keys and with various accompaniments; asymmetrical and inconclusive phrases make the form ambiguous.
6. Harmony—D major, with unusual and unexpected modulations to F-sharp major and G major.

7. Melody—disjunct melody in octaves alternating with passages with the melody on top of chords.
8. Articulation—implied non-*legato* touch, with accents and *marcatos*.
9. Dynamics—*f-ff*, with *sf* and *crescendo*.
10. Musical Expression/Character—strong, powerful.
11. Pedaling—intermittent pedaling for volume and sonority with clarity.

Op. 68, No. 32: *Sheherazade* (fictional character)
Level: A

1. Keyboard Skills/Technique/Mobility—awkward notated fingering to play the *legato* right-hand melody while also playing the eighth-note inner voice with rolled chords, requiring significant finger independence; extremely challenging to control balance, voicing, and articulation.
2. Notation—range is A2-A5.
3. Tempo/Meter/Rhythm—*Ziemlich langsam, leise* (rather slow, gentle); **C**; rhythmic patterns through the division of the beat; several notated tempo changes.
4. Texture—homophonic: right-hand, lyrical melody with rolled chords on top of continuous eighth-note passagework.
5. Form—AA-BC (interpolation) BC + coda; varying phrase lengths.
6. Harmony—A section: A minor, C major; B section: A minor, F major; C section: D minor, A minor; varied harmonic rhythm; extensive use of non-diatonic harmonies and unusual chord progressions for expressive purposes.
7. Melody—right-hand, primarily scalar, vocal melody, with frequent long note values that may cause fading sound challenges.
8. Articulation—*legato*.
9. Dynamics—*pp-p*, with extensive use of *fp* and *sfp*.
10. Musical Expression/Character—gentle, harp-like.
11. Pedaling—shallow pedaling, following the melodic line and harmonic rhythm.

Op. 68, No. 33: *Weinlesezeit—Fröhliche Zeit!* (Grape Harvest, Happy Time)
Level: LI

1. Keyboard Skills/Technique/Mobility—chords with rapid inversion changes.
2. Notation—range is F-sharp2-G-sharp6; use of two treble clefs with frequent clef changes.
3. Tempo/Meter/Rhythm—*Munter* (lively); $\frac{2}{4}$; rhythmic patterns through the subdivision of the beat.
4. Texture—homophonic: right-hand melody on top of chords alternating with single-note passagework.
5. Form—AA¹-AA¹-BA²-BA²-CC + coda; four-, six-, and eight-measure phrases.
6. Harmony—E major, with extensive chromaticism.
7. Melody—right-hand, detached melody on top of chords, alternating with continuous, scalar passagework; trills.
8. Articulation—a variety of articulation, requiring independence between the two hands; accents, short slurs, and *staccatos*.
9. Dynamics—*p-f*, with *sf* and *fp*; some dynamic changes implied by character changes are not notated in the score.
10. Musical Expression/Character—happy, celebratory, exciting.
11. Pedaling—intermittent pedaling, including some additional pedaling possibilities not notated in the score.

Op. 68, No. 34: *Thema* (Theme)
Level: A

1. Keyboard Skills/Technique/Mobility—complicated, polyphonic texture requiring independence of voices in both hands; the number of actual sounding voices varies from three to four, due to note doublings; extensive dotted-rhythm motivic pattern throughout the entire piece.
2. Notation—range is B2-A5.
3. Tempo/Meter/Rhythm—*Langsam. Mit inniger Empfindung* (slow, with deep feeling); $\frac{2}{4}$; rhythmic patterns through the subdivision of the beat,

plus extensive use of the dotted-sixteenth and thirty-second note motive; several notated tempo changes.
4. Texture—polyphonic: significant finger independence required within each hand and between the hands.
5. Form—ABB, with extensive repetition and imitation using the main motive; ambiguous phrasing with many inconclusive phrases.
6. Harmony—C major; fast harmonic rhythm; extensive tension/resolution.
7. Melody—right-hand, fragmented, motivic melody.
8. Articulation—primarily *legato*, with short slurs.
9. Dynamics—*p*, with quick *crescendo* and *diminuendo*.
10. Musical Expression/Character—uncertain, restless, unfulfilled.
11. Pedaling—frequent, shallow pedaling needed to assist the *legato* while not obscuring the individual voices.

Op. 68, No. 35: *Mignon* (delicate, dainty)
Level: LI, JM8

1. Keyboard Skills/Technique/Mobility—right-hand, broken-chord passagework with fragmented line-within-a-line melody on the top; awkward notated fingering to play the *legato* melody; long accompaniment notes requiring control of fading sound; wide stretches in the left hand; challenging control of balance and voicing combined with dynamic shading.
2. Notation—range is D2-A5.
3. Tempo/Meter/Rhythm—*Langsam, zart* (slowly, tenderly); **C**; rhythmic patterns through the division of the beat.
4. Texture—homophonic: right-hand, fragmented, line-within-a-line melody within arpeggiated passagework; rhythmically consistent left-hand accompaniment pattern.
5. Form—AABB; four-, six-, and eight-measure phrases.
6. Harmony—E-flat major; slow harmonic rhythm.

7. Melody—right-hand, lyrical, fragmented, line-within-a-line melody within broken-chord passagework; continuity of the melodic line will likely be challenging.
8. Articulation—*legato*, with numerous two-note slurs and other short slurs.
9. Dynamics—*pp-p*, with *sf*, *fp*, and quick dynamic swells; unusual notation of *fp* within the accompaniment needs careful consideration.
10. Musical Expression/Character—delicate, tender.
11. Pedaling—the notation should be interpreted as continuous, overlapping pedaling, except for in the short cadenza-like passage.

Op. 68, No. 36: *Lied italienischer Marinari* (Italian Sailor's Song)
Level: MI

1. Keyboard Skills/Technique/Mobility—extensive right-hand, *staccato*, parallel thirds; broken-intervals and broken octaves in the left-hand accompaniment.
2. Notation—range is D2-B-flat5; use of two bass clefs and two treble clefs.
3. Tempo/Meter/Rhythm—*Langsam* (slow), *Schnell* (fast); $^6_8$; rhythmic patterns through the division of the beat, plus some dotted-sixteenth and thirty-second notes.
4. Texture—homophonic: right-hand, scalar melody with parallel thirds with left-hand accompaniment of broken intervals and broken octaves.
5. Form—Introduction AA-BA¹-BA¹ + coda; four-measure phrases.
6. Harmony—G minor, with various modulations; fast harmonic rhythm.
7. Melody—right-hand, *staccato* melody in parallel thirds with frequent directional changes.
8. Articulation—primarily *staccato* in both hands.
9. Dynamics—*pp-p*, with *fp*, *sfz*, *crescendo*, and sudden dynamic changes.
10. Musical Expression/Character—joyful, exuberant.
11. Pedaling—quick, intermittent pedaling to emphasize accents and slurs; some notated *legato* pedaling in the introduction and coda.

Op. 68, No. 37: *Matrosenlied* (Sailor's Song)
Level: LI, JM8

1. Keyboard Skills/Technique/Mobility—mixed texture with frequently changing number of voices; multiple voices in each hand requiring finger independence; rapid position shifts.
2. Notation—range is G1-G6; use of two bass clefs.
3. Tempo/Meter/Rhythm—*Nicht schnell* (not fast); ¢; rhythmic patterns through the division of the beat.
4. Texture—homophonic: A section: melody doubled in three octaves split between the two hands; B section: primarily homorhythmic chords with the melody on the top; C section: polyphonic: multiple voices in each hand requiring finger independence within each hand and between the two hands.
5. Form—ABBA^1-C-A^{2}B + coda; four-measure phrases.
6. Harmony—G minor; fast harmonic rhythm.
7. Melody—right-hand, *legato* melody within various textures; short trills; grace notes.
8. Articulation—*legato*, with *staccatos* and short slurs.
9. Dynamics—*p-f*, with *sf*, *crescendo*, and quick dynamic changes.
10. Musical Expression/Character—dramatic, strong.
11. Pedaling—frequently changing overlapping pedaling.

Op. 68, No. 38: *Winterzeit* (Wintertime I)
Level: LI

1. Keyboard Skills/Technique/Mobility—chordal, mixed texture with multiple voices, requiring finger independence within each hand and between the two hands; awkward notated fingering to play the multiple *legato* lines.
2. Notation—range is F3-C6; entire piece is written in two treble clefs.
3. Tempo/Meter/Rhythm—*Ziemlich langsam* (rather slow); ¢; rhythmic patterns through the subdivision of the beat; B section includes syncopation.

4. Texture—homophonic: chordal, mixed texture with multiple voices, requiring finger independence within each hand and between the two hands.
5. Form—AA^1-BA^{2}BA^2; thematic motives permeate both sections; four-measure phrases.
6. Harmony—A section: C minor; B section: E-flat major, modulating back to C minor; varied harmonic rhythm; tension/resolution.
7. Melody—right-hand, lyrical, fragmented melody within various textures.
8. Articulation—*legato*, with short slurs.
9. Dynamics—*pp-f*, with *crescendo* and *diminuendo*.
10. Musical Expression/Character—A section: sad, contemplative; B section: hopeful.
11. Pedaling—intermittent, shallow pedaling with frequent changes to avoid obscuring the texture.

Op. 68, No. 39: *Winterszeit* (Wintertime II)
Level: A

1. Keyboard Skills/Technique/Mobility—multi-sectional work with different textures and tempos for each section, requiring sophisticated musical and technical control; finger independence needed within each hand and between the two hands.
2. Notation—range is G1-B-flat5; use of two treble clefs and two bass clefs.
3. Tempo/Meter/Rhythm—*Langsam* (slow); *Nach und nach belebter* (more and more with an increasing passion); $\frac{2}{4}$; rhythmic patterns through the subdivision of the beat; changes between the duple and triple division of the beat; multiple tempo changes.
4. Texture—A section: homophonic: the melody is doubled in octaves between the hands, with continually increasing number of additional voices; B section: polyphonic: right-hand passagework with active left-hand, with frequent changes in the number of voices and texture types; C section: homophonic: complicated chordal texture; coda: polyphonic.
5. Form—ABAC + coda; four- and eight-measure phrases.

6. Harmony—A section: C minor; B section: G minor, C minor; C section: C major; coda: C minor, C major; fast harmonic rhythm.
7. Melody—A section: lyrical, instrumental melody with many leaps; B section: wide-ranging passagework; C section: chordal, with the melody on top of the chords; coda: single-line melody followed by a chordal section with the melody on the top.
8. Articulation—A, C sections and coda: *legato*; B section: a variety of articulations.
9. Dynamics—*pp-f*, with *sf* and *fp*; B section: sudden dynamic contrasts.
10. Musical Expression/Character—A section: mysterious; B section; excited, passionate: C section; calm, peaceful.
11. Pedaling—frequent, shallow, intermittent pedaling needed in the various sections; *Verschiebung* marking for the *una corda* pedal in the coda.

Op. 68, No. 40: *Kleine Fuge* (Little Fugue)
Level: A

1. Keyboard Skills/Technique/Mobility—Prelude: rapid passagework in both hands with difficult fingering and inconsistent number of voices; Fugue: three-voice polyphonic texture; difficult textures with many musical and technical elements to control at one time.
2. Notation—range is C-sharp2-C-sharp6; use of two treble clefs.
3. Tempo/Meter/Rhythm—Prelude: (none); $\frac{2}{4}$; rhythmic patterns through the subdivision of the beat; Fugue: *Lebhaft, doch nicht zu schnell* (lively, but not too fast); $\frac{6}{8}$; rhythmic patterns through the subdivision of the beat; includes some syncopation.
4. Texture—polyphonic: significant finger independence needed within each hand and between the two hands.
5. Form—Prelude: binary form; Fugue: fugue form.
6. Harmony—A major, with extensive chromaticism and modulations in the fugue; fast harmonic rhythm.
7. Melody—Prelude: *legato* sixteenth-note passagework; Fugue: dance-like, articulated passagework.
8. Articulation—Prelude: *legato*; Fugue: the fugue subject is marked *staccato*, while other voices have no articulation markings; accents and *sf*.

9. Dynamics—*p-f*, with *crescendo* and *diminuendo* and sudden dynamic contrasts.
10. Musical Expression/Character—Prelude: energetic; Fugue: dance-like.
11. Pedaling—none.

Op. 68, No. 41: *Nordisches Lied* (Nordic Song)
Level: MI, JM7

1. Keyboard Skills/Technique/Mobility—chordal texture with melody on top of chords.
2. Notation—range is F1-F5.
3. Tempo/Meter/Rhythm—*Im Volkston* (in the folk tone); ₵; rhythmic patterns through the division of the beat.
4. Texture—homophonic and homorhythmic, with the melody on top of the chords.
5. Form—AA^1-BA^2A^3-BA^2A^3; four-measure phrases; the A melody repeats with different harmonizations.
6. Harmony—D minor to F major, with extensive modulations; fast harmonic rhythm.
7. Melody—right-hand melody on top of the chords.
8. Articulation—none notated; the pianist has the option of playing the piece *legato* with overlapping pedaling or non-*legato* with direct pedaling on each of the chords.
9. Dynamics—*pp-f*, with *crescendo* and *diminuendo*.
10. Musical Expression/Character—strong, powerful.
11. Pedaling—consistent, overlapping pedaling on each chord change or direct pedaling on detached chords.

Op. 68, No. 42: *Figurierter Choral* (Figurative Chorale)
Level: LI

1. Keyboard Skills/Technique/Mobility—finger independence required in each hand; melody in half notes may cause challenges with fading sound;

long phrases require mature musicianship; difficult fingering with wide stretches.
2. Notation—range is C2-F6.
3. Tempo/Meter/Rhythm—(none); 𝐂 ; rhythmic patterns through the division of the beat.
4. Texture—homophonic: chorale with flowing inner voice.
5. Form—through-composed; four-measure phrases.
6. Harmony—F major, with some secondary harmonies and chromaticism.
7. Melody—chorale tune *Freu dich sehr, o meine Seele* (Rejoice greatly, o my soul) by Johann Sebastian Bach; right-hand, primarily scalar melody in half notes on top of chords.
8. Articulation—*legato*.
9. Dynamics—virtually none notated, but phrase shaping is needed.
10. Musical Expression/Character—calm, serene, reverent.
11. Pedaling—continuous, shallow pedaling is needed to connect the half notes to maintain the melodic line through the long phrases.

Op. 68, No. 43: *Silvesterlied* (New Year's Eve Song)
Level: LI

1. Keyboard Skills/Technique/Mobility—large chords in each hand, with frequent changes in hand positions and number of voices; awkward notated fingering needed to play the *legato* lines; some left-hand octave passagework.
2. Notation—range is A1-C6.
3. Tempo/Meter/Rhythm—*Im maßigen Tempo* (at a moderate pace); 𝐂 ; rhythmic patterns through the subdivision of the beat.
4. Texture—polyphonic: right-hand melody on top of chords, with an active bass line and multiple moving lines; inconsistent number of voices in both hands.
5. Form—AA-BA^1-BA^1; varying phrase lengths.
6. Harmony—A major, with extensive chromaticism; fast harmonic rhythm; tension/resolution.
7. Melody—right-hand, vocal melody on top of chords; ornamental turn.

8. Articulation—*legato*, with some short slurs.
9. Dynamics—*mf*, with *fp* and *crescendo*.
10. Musical Expression/Character—happy, content.
11. Pedaling—frequently changing overlapping pedaling.

Peter Ilyich Tchaikovsky—*Album for the Young*, Op. 39

Op. 39, No. 1: <u>Morning Prayer</u>
Level: MI, JM4

1. Keyboard Skills/Technique/Mobility—four-voice texture, requiring finger independence within each hand.
2. Notation—range is F-sharp2-G5; use of two bass clefs.
3. Tempo/Meter/Rhythm—*Lento*; 3/4 ; rhythmic patterns through the subdivision of the beat.
4. Texture—homophonic: consistent, four-voice chordal texture with the melody on top of the chords; some sections are homorhythmic and other sections have individual active parts.
5. Form—through-composed; eight-measure phrases.
6. Harmony—G major; fast harmonic rhythm.
7. Melody—right-hand, lyrical melody in the top voice.
8. Articulation—*legato*, with some short slurs.
9. Dynamics—*pp-f*, with many notated dynamic changes.
10. Musical Expression/Character—sincere, hopeful.
11. Pedaling—frequent, overlapping pedaling with the chord changes.

Op. 39, No. 2: <u>A Winter Morning</u>
Level: MI

1. Keyboard Skills/Technique/Mobility—frequent shifts of hand positions and ranges.

2. Notation—range is A2-B-flat5; use of two treble clefs.
3. Tempo/Meter/Rhythm—*Andante*; $\frac{2}{4}$; rhythmic patterns through the subdivision of the beat; extensive use of a dotted-rhythm motive.
4. Texture—homophonic: chordal texture with the melody on top of the chords.
5. Form—ABA + coda; A section: eight-measure phrases; B section: four-measure phrases.
6. Harmony—A section: D major; B section: B minor; fast harmonic rhythm; tension/resolution.
7. Melody—right-hand, fragmented, motivic melody on top of the chordal texture.
8. Articulation—numerous two-note slurs and accents.
9. Dynamics—*pp-mf*, with extensive *crescendo* and *diminuendo*.
10. Musical Expression/Character—restless.
11. Pedaling—frequent pedaling: A section: direct pedaling on each downbeat to enhance the two-note slurs; B section: frequently changing, overlapping pedaling.

Op. 39, No. 3: *The Hobby-Horse*
Level: LI, JM8

1. Keyboard Skills/Technique/Mobility—mixture of *staccato* repeated chords and changing chords in both hands at a very fast tempo.
2. Notation—range is D2-D6.
3. Tempo/Meter/Rhythm—*Vivo*; $\frac{3}{8}$; continuous eighth notes.
4. Texture—homophonic: consistent four-voice chords.
5. Form—ABA[1] + coda; eight-measure phrases.
6. Harmony—D major, with a D pedal point through much of the A section; fast harmonic rhythm.
7. Melody—right-hand, mostly scalar, limited-range melody on top of the chords.
8. Articulation—*staccato* (wrist combined with finger).
9. Dynamics—*pp-mf*, with long *crescendo* and *diminuendo*.
10. Musical Expression/Character—playful.
11. Pedaling—none.

Op. 39, No. 4: *Mamma*
Level: MI, JM6

1. Keyboard Skills/Technique/Mobility—left-hand, line-within-a-line melody on the bottom of the broken-interval accompaniment forms a countermelody with the right-hand melody.
2. Notation—range is G2-G5.
3. Tempo/Meter/Rhythm—*Andante espressivo*; 3/4 ; rhythmic patterns through the division of the beat; some use of hemiola.
4. Texture—homophonic: right-hand melody with intermittent additional voices and left-hand, broken-interval accompaniment.
5. Form—ABAC + coda; eight-measure phrases.
6. Harmony—A section: G major; B section: B minor, modulatory; C section: modulatory, sequential chromatic passage; fast harmonic rhythm; tension/resolution.
7. Melody—right-hand, *legato* melody with many leaps.
8. Articulation—*legatissimo*, with some short slurs.
9. Dynamics—*pp-mf*, with some *crescendo* and *diminuendo*.
10. Musical Expression/Character—gentle.
11. Pedaling—frequently changing, overlapping pedaling.

Op. 39, No. 5: *March of the Tin Soldiers*
Level: MI, JM6

1. Keyboard Skills/Technique/Mobility—right-hand melody with intermittent additional voice.
2. Notation—range is A3-G5; entire piece uses two treble clefs.
3. Tempo/Meter/Rhythm—*Tempo di Marcia*; 2/4 ; rhythmic patterns through the subdivision of the beat; extensive use of dotted rhythms.
4. Texture—homophonic: right-hand melody with left-hand, mixed-texture accompaniment of single notes, intervals, and chords.
5. Form—AA^1-BB^1-AA^2; eight-measure phrases.
6. Harmony—A section: D major; B section: A major; fast harmonic rhythm.

7. Melody—fragmented, motivic melody with phrasing across rests.
8. Articulation—short slurs and accents.
9. Dynamics—*pp-mf*, with some *crescendo* and *diminuendo*.
10. Musical Expression/Character—quirky march.
11. Pedaling—none, or intermittently on the slurs.

Op. 39, No. 6: *The Sick Doll*
Level: MI, JM3

1. Keyboard Skills/Technique/Mobility—long phrases at a slow tempo, with broken chords between the two hands, requiring careful control of tone quality, balance, and pacing of phrasing.
2. Notation—range is G2-B-flat5; use of two treble clefs.
3. Tempo/Meter/Rhythm—*Lento*; $\frac{2}{4}$; consistent rhythmic pattern through the division of the beat for the entire piece.
4. Texture—homophonic: right-hand melody in various textures split inconsistently between the two hands.
5. Form—AB-AB-A¹ + long coda; four-, six-, and eight-measure phrases; many inconclusive phrases.
6. Harmony—G minor; slow harmonic rhythm.
7. Melody—right-hand, descending, limited-range, fragmented melody consisting primarily of quarter notes interspersed with rests; B section: right-hand, continuous melody.
8. Articulation—*legato*, with the melody notes marked *tenuto*.
9. Dynamics—*pp-mf*, with long *crescendo* and *diminuendo*.
10. Musical Expression/Character—sad, distressed.
11. Pedaling—consistent, overlapping pedaling.

Op. 39, No. 7: *The Doll's Burial*
Level: MI, JM4

1. Keyboard Skills/Technique/Mobility—repeated-note "funeral march" motive; inconsistent number of voices in each hand; long phrases, requiring mature pacing and control of tone quality, dynamics, and balance.

2. Notation—range is G2-C5.
3. Tempo/Meter/Rhythm—*Grave*; 2/4 ; rhythmic patterns through the subdivision of the beat, with extensive dotted rhythms.
4. Texture—homophonic: chordal texture with an inconsistent number of voices in both hands from single notes to full chords, with the melody on top of the texture.
5. Form—ABA; eight-measure phrases.
6. Harmony—C minor; varied harmonic rhythm.
7. Melody—right-hand, limited-range melody with many repeated notes.
8. Articulation—short slurs, with some *portato* chords.
9. Dynamics—*pp-sf*, with some long *crescendo* and *diminuendo*.
10. Musical Expression/Character—funeral march.
11. Pedaling—overlapping, changing with the chords.

Op. 39, No. 8: <u>*Waltz*</u>
Level: MI

1. Keyboard Skills/Technique/Mobility—finger independence is needed within each hand to play sustained and moving voices.
2. Notation—range is A-flat2-A-flat5.
3. Tempo/Meter/Rhythm—*Vivace*; 3/4 ; rhythmic patterns through the division of the beat; some hemiola; emphasis on the weak second beat of the measure may cause metrical challenges.
4. Texture—homophonic: right-hand, fragmented melody with various accompaniments: easy waltz bass, sustained bass notes requiring finger pedaling, and drone fifths.
5. Form—ABC (interpolation) AB; four- and eight-measure phrases.
6. Harmony—A, B sections: E-flat major; C section: C minor; moderate harmonic rhythm.
7. Melody—right-hand, single-line, fragmented melody; C section has an additional voice.
8. Articulation—extensive use of frequently changing, detailed articulations: short slurs, *staccatos*, and accents.

9. Dynamics—*p-f*, with some *crescendo* and *diminuendo*.
10. Musical Expression/Character—elegant waltz.
11. Pedaling—none notated, but some intermittent, direct pedaling could be used on single notes to enhance the tone quality and the slurs, and to bring out the accents in the hemiola sections. Pianists should avoid continuous, overlapping pedaling that would obscure the extensive articulation.

Op. 39, No. 9: *The New Doll*
Level: MI

1. Keyboard Skills/Technique/Mobility—quick hand-position shifts; quick left-hand, repeated, *staccato* chords; diversity of articulation between the two hands.
2. Notation—range is B-flat2-C5; extensive use of two treble clefs.
3. Tempo/Meter/Rhythm—*Andantino*; $\frac{3}{8}$; rhythmic patterns through the division of the beat; two-note slurs starting on weak beats.
4. Texture—homophonic: right-hand, single-line melody with consistent, fragmented accompaniment of different intervals.
5. Form—AABAA¹ + coda; eight-measure phrases.
6. Harmony—A section: B-flat major; B section; modulatory.
7. Melody—A section: right-hand, long, *legato* melody with occasional added voice; B section: right-hand, fragmented melody consisting of two-note slurs.
8. Articulation—*legato*, with short slurs and left-hand, *staccato* chords.
9. Dynamics—*pp-f*, with *sf*; long *crescendo* and *diminuendo* phrase shaping.
10. Musical Expression/Character—gently playful.
11. Pedaling—none.

Op. 39, No. 10: *Mazurka*
Level: MI, JM5

1. Keyboard Skills/Technique/Mobility—right-hand melody with occasional additional voice and left-hand, modified, waltz-bass accompaniment on beats one and three requiring quick position shifts.

2. Notation—range is G2–G6; use of two treble clefs.
3. Tempo/Meter/Rhythm—*Tempo di Mazurka*; 3/4; rhythmic patterns through the subdivision of the beat; accents on weak beats.
4. Texture—homophonic: right-hand, single-line, fragmented melody with modified waltz-bass accompaniment.
5. Form—ABA + coda; four-measure phrases.
6. Harmony—A section: D minor; B section: C major; moderate harmonic rhythm.
7. Melody—right-hand, single-line, fragmented melody.
8. Articulation—extensive articulation of *staccatos*, two-note slurs, and accents.
9. Dynamics—*p-mf*, with *sf*; sudden dynamic changes and long *crescendo* and *diminuendo*.
10. Musical Expression/Character—rustic folk dance.
11. Pedaling—none.

Op. 39, No. 11: *Russian Song*
Level: MI

1. Keyboard Skills/Technique/Mobility—finger independence needed within each hand; rapid hand-position changes in both hands.
2. Notation—range is B-flat2–C5.
3. Tempo/Meter/Rhythm—*Comodo*; 2/4; rhythmic patterns through the division of the beat.
4. Texture—homophonic: right-hand, lyrical melody with inconsistent number of voices and left-hand, chordal accompaniment with inconsistent number of voices.
5. Form—theme with three variations + coda; six-measure phrases.
6. Harmony—F major; fast harmonic rhythm.
7. Melody—right-hand, folk melody with varying accompaniments.
8. Articulation—*legato*, with short slurs and a few *staccatos*.
9. Dynamics—*f*.
10. Musical Expression/Character—folk song.

11. Pedaling—none notated; intermittent pedaling to enhance single notes, chords, and slurs.

Op. 39, No. 12: *The Peasant Plays the Accordion*
Level: MI

1. Keyboard Skills/Technique/Mobility—chordal texture with quick changes in the number of pitches in each chord; thick chords with awkward fingering required to play subsequent quick sixteenth notes; phrasing and interpretation is challenging due to repetition of musical ideas.
2. Notation—range is F3-E-flat5.
3. Tempo/Meter/Rhythm—(none); 2/4; rhythmic patterns through the subdivision of the beat.
4. Texture—homophonic: thick chordal texture with the melody on top of the chords.
5. Form—theme with repetitions and variations + coda; six-measure phrases + four-measure coda.
6. Harmony—B-flat major, with a strong emphasis on the dominant; fast harmonic rhythm.
7. Melody—repetitive folk melody.
8. Articulation—short slurs.
9. Dynamics—*mf-f*, with a *diminuendo* to the end.
10. Musical Expression/Character—lively folk music.
11. Pedaling—intermittent, shallow pedaling to enhance the two-note slurs and add resonance to long notes.

Op. 39, No. 13: *Folk-Song*
Level: MI

1. Keyboard Skills/Technique/Mobility—difficult, right-hand, *staccato* passagework with wide leaps and quick hand-position changes; finger independence required in the left hand.
2. Notation—range is A2-D6; use of two treble clefs.

3. Tempo/Meter/Rhythm—*Comodo*; 2/4; rhythmic patterns through the division of the beat.
4. Texture—A section: polyphonic: three-part texture of right-hand, articulated, disjunct passagework, lyrical inner voice, and bass pedal point; B section: homophonic: disjunct, articulated passagework over detached chords; C section: homophonic and homorhythmic detached chords with melody on top; D section: homophonic: articulated, disjunct passagework over intermittent motivic accompaniment.
5. Form—ABCD, with each section repeated; six-measure phrases.
6. Harmony—D major; fast harmonic rhythm.
7. Melody—disjunct, articulated passagework.
8. Articulation—consistent *staccato* passagework with slurs and accents; independence of articulation required between the two hands.
9. Dynamics—*pp-f*, with limited dynamic changes.
10. Musical Expression/Character—rustic folk song.
11. Pedaling—none, due to significant articulation.

<u>Op. 39, No. 14: *Polka*</u>
Level: MI

1. Keyboard Skills/Technique/Mobility—challenging texture of complicated passagework in one hand with broken-chord accompaniment in the opposite hand; finger changes on fast repeated notes.
2. Notation—range is E2-B-flat6; use of two treble clefs.
3. Tempo/Meter/Rhythm—*Allegretto*; 2/4; rhythmic patterns through the subdivision of the beat.
4. Texture—homophonic: A section: right-hand, articulated, disjunct melody with left-hand, broken-chord accompaniment; B section: left-hand, articulated melody with rapid hand-position shifts and right-hand, chordal accompaniment; the melody shifts back to the right hand for the final A^1 section.
5. Form—AABA^1; four- and six-measure phrases.
6. Harmony—B-flat major; fast harmonic rhythm.

7. Melody—A section: right-hand, disjunct folk melody with numerous grace notes; B section: left-hand, articulated melody with rapid hand-position changes.
8. Articulation—significant articulation challenges, with numerous *staccato*s and short slurs.
9. Dynamics—*p-f*, with long *crescendo* and *diminuendo*.
10. Musical Expression/Character—quirky polka.
11. Pedaling—none.

Op. 39, No. 15: *Italian Song*
Level: MI, JM5

1. Keyboard Skills/Technique/Mobility—left-hand, waltz-bass accompaniment limited to one octave.
2. Notation—range is D2-E5.
3. Tempo/Meter/Rhythm—*Vivo*; 3/8; rhythmic patterns through the subdivision of the beat.
4. Texture—homophonic: right-hand, lyrical melody with waltz-bass accompaniment.
5. Form—AA¹-BC-BC¹; four- and eight-measure phrases.
6. Harmony—D major; moderate harmonic rhythm.
7. Melody—right-hand, single-line, lyrical melody.
8. Articulation—consistent *staccato* accompaniment; *legato* melody with occasional accents and *staccato*s.
9. Dynamics—*p-f*, with some *crescendo* and *diminuendo*.
10. Musical Expression/Character: joyful waltz.
11. Pedaling—none, due to consistent *staccato* accompaniment.

Op. 39, No. 16: *Old French Song*
Level: MI, JM5

1. Keyboard Skills/Technique/Mobility—finger independence required in the left hand.
2. Notation—range is G2-F5.

3. Tempo/Meter/Rhythm—*Moderato assai*; 2/4 ; rhythmic patterns through the division of the beat.
4. Texture—polyphonic: three-part texture consisting of right-hand, single-line, lyrical melody with left-hand, inner-voice countermelody and bass line.
5. Form—AABA; eight-measure phrases.
6. Harmony—G minor; slow harmonic rhythm.
7. Melody—right-hand, single-line, lyrical, scalar melody with a limited range.
8. Articulation—*legato*, with some short slurs.
9. Dynamics—*pp-p*, with some *crescendo* to *mf*.
10. Musical Expression/Character—pleading, yearning.
11. Pedaling—intermittent, shallow pedaling, primarily on long notes in the lyrical sections.

Op. 39, No. 17: <u>German Song</u>
Level: MI, JM6

1. Keyboard Skills/Technique/Mobility: finger changes on repeated notes; melody with parallel thirds; some awkward fingering; challenging accompaniment of waltz bass in a wider range, with chord changes on beats two and three requiring position shifts; wide, broken intervals requiring fast hand extensions following repeated notes; right-hand arpeggios.
2. Notation—range is B-flat2–B-flat5.
3. Tempo/Meter/Rhythm—*Tranquillo*; 3/4 ; rhythmic patterns through the subdivision of the beat.
4. Texture—homophonic: right-hand melody sometimes doubled in thirds, with left-hand, waltz-bass accompaniment.
5. Form—ABBA; four-measure phrases.
6. Harmony—E-flat major; slow harmonic rhythm.
7. Melody—right-hand, lyrical melody with many repeated notes and large leaps.

8. Articulation—short slurs, accents, and combination markings.
9. Dynamics—*mf-f*.
10. Musical Expression/Character: German waltz.
11. Pedaling—A section: waltz-bass pedaling; B section: intermittent pedaling on the dotted-eighth notes.

Op. 39, No. 18: *Neopolitan Dance-Song*
Level: MI, JM6

1. Keyboard Skills/Technique/Mobility—left-hand, rapid, repeated *staccato* chords with leaps; rapid repeated notes requiring quick finger changes; highly-articulated passagework with rapidly changing articulations; right-hand, full-octave scale passages.
2. Notation—range is B-flat2-F5.
3. Tempo/Meter/Rhythm—*Comodo*; $\frac{2}{4}$; rhythmic patterns through the subdivision of the beat; *piu mosso* tempo change for the last section.
4. Texture—homophonic: right-hand, single-line melody with consistent *staccato* chordal accompaniment.
5. Form—Introduction AABBCC + coda; eight-measure phrases.
6. Harmony—E-flat major; slow harmonic rhythm.
7. Melody—right-hand, single-line melody with many repeated notes and articulations.
8. Articulation—numerous *staccatos* and two-note slurs.
9. Dynamics—sections A, B: *piano*; section C: *forte*, with some *decrescendo*.
10. Musical Expression/Character—lively.
11. Pedaling—none, or limited, quick, direct pedaling on accented notes for emphasis.

Op. 39, No. 19: *The Nurse's Tale*
Level: MI

1. Keyboard Skills/Technique/Mobility—quick hand-position changes on successive chords with changing intervals, accidentals, articulations, and/or leaps; chromatic parallel thirds; rapid octave changes.

2. Notation—range is A2-E-flat6; use of two treble clefs.
3. Tempo/Meter/Rhythm—*Moderato*; $\frac{2}{4}$; syncopation.
4. Texture—homophonic: A section: chordal; B section: right-hand, single tonic pitch with left-hand, chromatic parallel thirds accompaniment.
5. Form—ABA; four-measure phrases.
6. Harmony—C major; fast harmonic rhythm.
7. Melody—A section: chromatic, articulated melody on top of chords; B section: single tonic pitch in syncopated rhythmic pattern.
8. Articulation—numerous articulations including *staccatos*, two-note slurs, and accents.
9. Dynamics—*p-f*, with long *crescendo* and *diminuendo*.
10. Musical Expression/Character—quirky.
11. Pedaling—intermittent, direct pedaling on slurred chords.

Op. 39, No. 20: *The Witch*
Level: A

1. Keyboard Skills/Technique/Mobility—difficult texture with rapidly changing, awkward hand positions, including fast hand extension and contraction; notated finger changes on fast repeated notes; rapidly changing articulations.
2. Notation—range is E2-G6; multiple voices with different rhythms resulting in a visually complicated notation.
3. Tempo/Meter/Rhythm—*Vivace*; $\frac{6}{8}$; rhythmic patterns through the division of the beat; the piece begins on the weak beat two, requiring careful metrical perception.
4. Texture—rapidly changing homophonic and polyphonic textures.
5. Form—through-composed, with many sections; the opening A section returns once; four- measure phrases, with a six-measure coda.
6. Harmony—E minor, with extensive chromaticism; varied harmonic rhythm.
7. Melody—*staccato* instrumental melody.
8. Articulation—*staccato*, with *sf* and short slurs.
9. Dynamics—*pp-f*, with some long *crescendo* and *diminuendo*.
10. Musical Expression/Character—mysterious, scary.
11. Pedaling—intermittent, direct pedaling on *sf* notes and chords.

Op. 39, No. 21: *Sweet Dreams*
Level: MI, JM6

1. Keyboard Skills/Technique/Mobility—requires holding melodic notes while playing chordal offbeats within the same hand; careful voicing and balancing of texture is difficult.
2. Notation—range is D3-A5; use of two treble clefs.
3. Tempo/Meter/Rhythm—*Andante*; $\frac{3}{4}$; rhythmic patterns through the subdivision of the beat; notated tempo *rubato* at the ends of phrases.
4. Texture—A section: polyphonic: three-part texture consisting of a right-hand, primarily single-line melody with a left-hand countermelody and offbeat, chordal accompaniment; B section: homophonic: left-hand, single-line melody with right-hand, offbeat, chordal accompaniment.
5. Form—AA¹-BB¹-AA¹: eight-measure phrases; many inconclusive phrases.
6. Harmony—A section: C major; B section: G major; fast harmonic rhythm; tension/resolution.
7. Melody—*legato*, vocal melody that alternates between the two hands.
8. Articulation—*legato*, with some use of accents on phrase peaks.
9. Dynamics—*p-f*, with quick *crescendo* and *diminuendo*.
10. Musical Expression/Character—sweet.
11. Pedaling—frequently changing, overlapping pedaling.

Op. 39, No. 22: *Song of the Lark*
Level: MI, JM6

1. Keyboard Skills/Technique/Mobility—finger independence needed within the left hand and between the two hands; diverse articulations between the two hands; quick right-hand range changes.
2. Notation—range is F-sharp3-E7; use of two treble clefs; extensive use of leger lines.
3. Tempo/Meter/Rhythm—*Lentamente*; $\frac{3}{4}$; rhythmic patterns through the subdivision of the beat, including sixteenth-note triplets; A section: hemiola, potentially causing metrical pulse challenges.

4. Texture—homophonic: A section: right-hand melody with left-hand, mixed-texture accompaniment; B section: right-hand, fragmented melody with left-hand, mostly sustained chordal accompaniment.
5. Form—AA^1-BB^1 (extension) A^2 + coda; four-measure phrases.
6. Harmony—A section: G major; B section: E minor.
7. Melody—right-hand, repetitive "bird-call" patterns; numerous grace notes.
8. Articulation—short slurs and *staccatos*.
9. Dynamics—*pp-p*, with limited *crescendo* and *diminuendo*.
10. Musical Expression/Character—birdsong.
11. Pedaling—intermittent, shallow pedaling.

Op. 39, No. 23: *The Handorgan Man*
Level: MI, JM5

1. Keyboard Skills/Technique/Mobility—finger independence needed within each hand and between the two hands; multiple parts, requiring careful balance and control, both melodically and harmonically; long phrases.
2. Notation—range is G2-F-sharp5; B section: multiple voices with different rhythms in a visually complicated notation.
3. Tempo/Meter/Rhythm—*Moderato*; 3/4; rhythmic patterns through the division of the beat.
4. Texture—A section: homophonic; B section: polyphonic: four-part texture consisting of a right-hand melody with offbeat, chordal accompaniment and a left-hand, bass pedal point with lyrical inner voice.
5. Form—ABB; eight-measure phrases.
6. Harmony—G major; varied harmonic rhythm.
7. Melody—A section: right-hand, primarily single-line, lyrical melody; B section: wide-range, right-hand melody with offbeat chords in the same hand.
8. Articulation—long *legato* slurs, with accents and *portatos*.
9. Dynamics—*pp-mf*, with *crescendo* and *diminuendo*.
10. Musical Expression/Character—peaceful, calm.

11. Pedaling—A section: overlapping pedaling; B section: quick, shallow, overlapping pedaling.

Op. 39, No. 24: *In Church*
Level: MI, JM5

1. Keyboard Skills/Technique/Mobility—*legato* repeated chords; finger independence required in the left hand; asymmetrical phrasing may be musically challenging.
2. Notation—range is E2-E6; treble clef leger lines.
3. Tempo/Meter/Rhythm—*Largo*; $\frac{2}{4}$; rhythmic patterns through the division of the beat.
4. Texture—homophonic: A section: chords split between the two hands; B section: right-hand chords with left-hand countermelody over a tonic pedal point.
5. Form—AA (interpolation) BB[1] + coda; A section: asymmetrical phrasing 2+3+3+4; B section: eight-measure phrases.
6. Harmony—E minor; varied harmonic rhythm.
7. Melody—right-hand, narrow-range, *legato* melody on top of chords.
8. Articulation—*legato*, with short slurs and some accents.
9. Dynamics—*ppp-mf*, with some *crescendo* and *diminuendo*.
10. Musical Expression/Character—calm, reverent.
11. Pedaling—overlapping pedaling with the chord changes.

21

Miscellaneous

Liszt: *Romance Oubliée (Forgotten Romance)*, S. 527
Level: LI

1. Keyboard Skills/Technique/Mobility—single-line, cadenza-like melody that moves between the two hands, requiring fluidity and mature rhythmic pacing; melodic octaves; multiple textures requiring careful voicing.
2. Notation—range is E2-G-sharp6; use of two treble clefs.
3. Tempo/Meter/Rhythm—*Andante malinconico*; 6/8 (3/4); rhythmic patterns through the subdivision of the beat; meter changes.
4. Texture—monophonic, cadenza-like sections; homophonic: right-hand, single-line melody with occasional added voices, with intermittent left-hand, chordal accompaniment.
5. Form—through-composed; various phrase lengths.
6. Harmony—E minor, E major; modulatory; varied harmonic rhythm.
7. Melody—single-line, cadenza-like, lyrical melody that moves between the two hands; right-hand, single-line, vocal melody with occasional additional voices; melody on top of chords; melody doubled in octaves; grace notes; arpeggios.
8. Articulation—*legato*, with light *staccatos*.
9. Dynamics—*pp-f*, with extensive *crescendo* and *diminuendo*; long *crescendo*.
10. Musical Expression/Character—expressive narrative with multiple emotions/characters such as uncertain, questioning, passionate, and tranquil.
11. Pedaling—direct pedaling on the long notes in the cadenza-like sections to enhance tone quality; limited notated pedaling should be applied to similar sections; overlapping pedaling.

References

Albergo, C., and R. Alexander (2011), *Piano Repertoire Guide: Intermediate and Advanced Literature*, 5th ed. Champaign, IL: Stipes.

Beach, A. (1897), *Children's Album*, Op. 36. Boston, MA: Arthur P. Schmidt. Available online https://imslp.org/wiki/Children's_Album,_Op.36_(Beach,_Amy_Marcy) (accessed December 10 2024).

Banowetz, J. (1992), *The Pianist's Guide to Pedaling*. Bloomington, IN: Indiana University Press.

Bastien, J. W. (1988), *How to Teach Piano Successfully*, 3rd ed. San Diego, CA: Neil A. Kjos Music.

Berman, B. (2000), *Notes from the Pianist's Bench*. New Haven, CT: Yale University Press.

Bluestine, E. (2000), *The Ways Children Learn Music: An Introduction and Practical Guide to Music Learning Theory*, rev. ed. Chicago, IL: GIA Publications.

Burgmüller, J. (1994), *18 Characteristic Studies*, Op. 109, ed. M. Hinson. Van Nuys, CA: Alfred Music.

Burgmüller, J. (1992), *25 Progressive Pieces*, Op. 100, ed. W. A. Palmer. Van Nuys, CA: Alfred Music.

Camp, M. (1992), *Teaching Piano: The Synthesis of Mind, Ear and Body*. Van Nuys, CA: Alfred Music.

Chaminade, C. (1989), *Album for the Young*, Book 1, Op. 123. Boca Raton, FL: Masters Music. Available online https://imslp.org/wiki/Album_des_enfants_-_1%C3%A8re_s%C3%A9rie%2C_Op.123_(Chaminade%2C_C%C3%A9cile) (accessed December 10, 2024).

Chaminade, C. (1989), *Album for the Young*, Book 2, Op. 126. Boca Raton, FL: Masters Music. Available online https://imslp.org/wiki/Album_des_enfants_-_2%C3%A8me_s%C3%A9rie%2C_Op.126_(Chaminade%2C_C%C3%A9cile) (accessed December 10, 2024).

Crappell, C. (2019), *Teaching Piano Pedagogy: A Guidebook for Training Effective Teachers*. New York, NY: Oxford University Press.

Czerny, C. (1893), *The School of Velocity, Op. 299*. New York, NY: G. Schirmer.

Donelson, J. (2006), "The Development of Expressive Playing and Interpretive Skills in Elementary and Early-Intermediate Piano Students." D.M.A. thesis, University of Nebraska–Lincoln.

Ester, D. (2021), *Sound Connections—A Comprehensive Approach to Teaching Music Literacy*. Muncie, IN: (self-published).

Faricy, K. (2004), *Artistic Pedal Technique: Lessons for Intermediate and Advanced Pianists*. Mississauga, ON: Frederick Harris Music.

Fink, S. (1992), *Mastering Piano Technique: A Guide for Students, Teachers, and Performers*. Pompton Plains, NJ: Amadeus Press.

Gillock, W. L. (1958), *Lyric Preludes in Romantic Style*. Secaucus, NJ: Summy-Birchard.

Grieg, E. (1985), *The Complete Lyric Pieces*. Miami, FL: Kalmus.

Gurlitt, C. (1971), *Album for the Young*, Op. 140. Van Nuys, CA: Alfred Music.

Hanon, C.-L. (1992), *The Virtuoso Pianist in 60 Exercises*, ed. A. Small, 2nd ed. Van Nuys, CA: Alfred Music.

Hinson, M. (2000), *Guide to the Pianist's Repertoire*, 3d.ed. Bloomington, IN: Indiana University Press.

Hoffman, R., W. Pelto, and J. W. White (1996), "Takadimi: A Beat-Oriented System of Rhythm Pedagogy." *Journal of Music Theory Pedagogy*, 10: 7–30.

Hoffman, R. (2025), "Takadimi Short Guide." Available online https://www.takadimi.net/shortGuide.html (accessed March 3, 2025).

Jacobson, J. M. (2015), *Professional Piano Teaching: A Comprehensive Piano Pedagogy Textbook, Vol. 2: Intermediate-Advanced Levels*, ed. E. L. Lancaster and A. Mendoza. Van Nuys, CA: Alfred Music.

Johnston, P. (2002), *The Practice Revolution*. Pearce: PracticeSpot Press.

Liszt, F. (1986), *At the Piano with Liszt*, ed. M. Hinson. Van Nuys, CA: Alfred Music.

Lyke, J., and Y. Enoch (1987), *Creative Piano Teaching*, 2nd ed. Champaign, IL: Stipes.

Lyke, J., G. Haydon, and C. Rollin (2011), *Creative Piano Teaching*, 4th ed. Champaign, IL: Stipes.

Magrath, J. (2021), *Piano Literature for Teaching and Performance: A Graded Guide and Annotated Bibliography*, ed. E. L. Lancaster and A. Mendoza. Kingston, NJ: The Frances Clark Center Piano Education Press.

Manno, M. A. (1993), "An Investigation into the Nature of Musical Expression and It's Application in Elementary Piano Teaching." D.M.A. diss., University of Texas at Austin.

Neuhaus, H. (1973), *The Art of Piano Playing*. New York, NY: Praeger.

O'Neill Breth, N. (2004), *The Piano Student's Guide to Effective Practicing*. Milwaukee, WI: Hal Leonard.

Sándor, G. (1995), *On Piano Playing: Motion, Sound, and Expression*. New York, NY: Simon & Schuster Macmillan.

Schmitt, A. (1922), *Preparatory Exercises for the Piano*, Op. 16. Milwaukee, WI: G. Schirmer.

Schumann, R. (1977), *Klavierwerke*. Band I. München: G. Henle Verlag.

Steen-Nøkleberg, E. (1997), *Onstage with Grieg: Interpreting His Piano Music*. Bloomington, IN: Indiana University Press.

Tchaikovsky, P. I. (n.d.), *Album for the Young*. Miami, FL: Kalmus/CPP Belwin.

Tiernan, S. (2011), *Contemporary Piano Technique: Coordinating Breath, Movement, and Sound*, ed. J. Feist. Boston, MA: Berklee Press.

Uszler, M., S. Gordon, and S. Smith (2000), *The Well-Tempered Keyboard Teacher*, 2nd ed. New York, NY: Schirmer.

Woody, R. H. (June 2000), "Learning Expressivity in Music Performance: An Exploratory Study," *Research Studies in Music Education*, 14 (1): 14–23.

Woody, R. H. (Summer 2006), "Musicians' Cognitive Processing of Imagery-Based Instructions for Expressive Performance," *Journal of Research in Music Education*, 54 (2): 125–37.

Index of Terms

articulation
    accent markings   100–1
    articulations that conflict with the meter   102–3
    combination of articulation markings   101
    legato
        creating the illusion of *legato*   98
        finger slides   98–9
        legato fingering   96–7
        pedal-assisted *legato*   99
        variety of *legato* overlap   97
    marcato or *martellato*   101
    staccato   99–100
    tenuto   101
    two-note slurs   97–8
    variety of articulation   102–4

fingering
    alternate fingerings for very loud dynamics   110
    awkward fingering   87–8, 96–7, 108
    fingering, repeated notes   83
    fingerings, performance tempo   109
    finger substitutions, repeated notes   108–9
    finger substitutions, sustained notes   108
    five-finger pattern positions   107
    hand extension and contraction   72, 82–3, 89, 108
    individual finger sizes and proportions   106
    legato fingering   118
    multiple notes played by one finger   110
    notation practices   107
    playing with the hand   110
    redistribution   107
    suggested/edited fingerings   106
    temporary fingering changes   109–10
    thumbs on black keys   109

harmony
    analysis   25
    color chords for expressive effects   28–9
    consonant   23
    dissonant   23
    functional harmony   23–4
    harmonic rhythm   26
    individual chords   23–4
    keys with more than four sharps or flats   27–8
    non-diatonic harmonies and modulations   26
    non-typical chord progressions   26, 142
    obscure tonalities and harmonic progressions   29
    progressions and cadences   24–6
    tension/resolution   142–3

melody
    analysis   10–11
    character   14
    fading sound challenges   16–17
    fragmented or interrupted melodies   20–21
    instrumental melodies   10
    large vocal leaps   19
    left-hand, single-line melodies   18
    musical gestures   13
    pitch content   11
    range   11–2
    rapid changes of direction   19–20
    right-hand, single-line melodies   17–18
    scale degrees   11
    vocal melodies   9

musical expression
    compositional elements   150–1
    dynamics
        alternate fingerings for very loud dynamics   110

dynamic levels   138
long *crescendo* or *diminuendo*   140
markings   136–7
mixture of dynamics   140
speed of attack   15
sudden dynamic changes   139–140
wide dynamic ranges   140
early musical experiences   148
form
   analysis   127–130
   harmony   142
   imagery and emotion   147–8
   listening   146
   musical character   144–5
   musical expression strategies   148–150
   performance elements   151–2
   phrasing
      asymmetrical phrasing   133–4
      cadential patterns   131
      chord progressions   131
      interpolations   134
      long musical phrases   136
      personal emotional connection   132
      phrase climaxes, arrival points   12
      phrase groupings   12
      phrase groups with multiple inconclusive phrases   133
      phrase hierarchy   132–3
      phrases consisting of continuous short motives   134–5
      phrase shaping   12
      phrasing that moves across rests   135–6
      structurally significant notes   131
   structures
      binary   128
      ternary   128–9
      theme and variations   129
      through-composed   129
   tension/resolution   143
teacher modeling   146–7
tempo changes   141–2
tempo *rubato* and pacing   141
tone color   143–4

pedaling
   aural pedaling   117
   damper pedal   113
   finger pedaling   125–6
   flutter pedaling   126
   frequent but patterned pedal changes   121–2
   frequent pedal changes in inconsistent or unpatterned settings   122–3
   historical style period considerations   119–20
   influences and variables   120
   intermittent and/or direct pedaling   124–5
   one-finger pedal exercise   117
   overlapping (syncopated) pedaling   117, 121
   partial or shallow pedaling   123–4
   pedaling with *legato* fingering   118
   pedal markings   115–16
   sostenuto pedal   114–15
   speed of pedaling   117–8
   una corda pedal   114
   when to pedal   118–9

rhythm
   changes from duple to triple division of the beat   63–4
   metrical pulse groupings   58–9
   metronome   59–60
   polyrhythms between hands   64–6
   precision within passagework   60–1
   syncopation   62–3
   takadimi syllable system   63–5
   tempo stability   59–60
   time signatures   58–9
   unmeasured, improvisatory lines   66–7
   upbeats/weak beats   61

technique
   arms, shoulders   71
   arpeggios   76

awkward positions
    chords with awkward fingering 87–8
    hands crossed for extended positions 86
    hands positioned in high or low ranges for an extended period 86–7
    interlocking hands 85–6
blocked and broken chords/intervals 89–91
fast scalar passagework 88–9
fingering 83–4
foundational principles 69
hands/wrists, hand motion
    contraction and extension 72, 82–3, 89, 108
    lateral motion 72
    pronation 72
    rotation 19–20, 72
    supination 72
octaves and large stretches 91–4
position shifts
    chords 80–2
    finger positions on the key 73
    fluid physical movements 71
    hand crossings 84–5
    injury prevention 73
    passagework 82–4
    proper use of the body
    sitting posture 70–1
scales 75–6
tone production 74
waltz bass 40–1, 77–80
texture
    accompaniments
        Alberti bass, broken chords, broken intervals 39–40
        chordal textures, detached or legato 49–51
        continuous blocked chords 37–8
        continuous or detached repeated chords 38–9
        intermittent blocked chords 38
    melodies
        alternating hands 50–1
        below or within the accompaniment 42
        doubled at the octave 35–7
        line-within-a-line texture 42–7
        parallel intervals 47–8
        multi-voice 41–2
        waltz-bass 40–1, 77–80
    homophonic
    monophonic
        single musical lines
            between hands 33
            between hands, with hand crossings 33
            between hands, with rapid alternation 34
            left hand 32
            right hand 32
    polyphonic
        four voices 52
        mixed textures
            chords or intervals alternating with single notes 53
            melodies in parallel octaves between hands, with accompaniment 55–6
            melodies with chords in the same hand, with accompaniment 54–5
            more than one independent voice in one or both hands 54
        three voices 52
        two voices 51

Index of Compositions

Beach, Amy
  Children's Album, Op. 36
    No. 1: Minuet   155
    No. 2: Gavotte   21, 155–6
    No. 3: Waltz   9, 17, 19, 41, 62, 121, 156–7
    No. 4: March   157
    No. 5: Polka   102, 103, 134, 158
Burgmüller, Johann
  25 Progressive Pieces, Op. 100
    No. 1: Sincerity   38, 159
    No. 2: Arabesque   82, 102, 159–60
    No. 3: Pastorale   9, 17, 19, 20, 38–9, 124, 160–1
    No. 4: The Little Party   48, 161
    No. 5: Innocence   103, 161–2
    No. 6: Progress   51, 91, 103, 162–3
    No. 7: The Clear Stream   18, 20, 40, 45, 46, 91, 122, 163
    No. 8: Gracefulness   39, 89, 163–4
    No. 9: The Chase   89, 164–5
    No. 10: Tender Flower   98, 109, 165
    No. 11: The Young Shepherdess   76, 91, 102, 109, 165–6
    No. 12: The Farewell   20, 90, 143, 166–7
    No. 13: Consolation   14, 47, 91, 167
    No. 14: Austrian Dance   41, 103, 167–8
    No. 15: Ballade   18, 19, 102, 168–9
    No. 16: Sorrow   17, 18, 90, 169
    No. 17: The Chatterbox   38, 89, 109, 169–70
    No. 18: Inquiétude   82, 135, 170
    No. 19: Ave Maria   49, 171
    No. 20: Tarantelle   38, 83, 109, 140, 171–2
    No. 21: Angels' Voices   33, 124, 172
    No. 22: Barcarolle   17, 19, 39, 172–3
    No. 23: The Return   39, 48, 50, 100, 173–4
    No. 24: The Swallow   33, 84, 98, 124, 174
    No. 25: The Knight Errant   53, 63, 81, 135, 139, 174–5
Burgmüller, Johann
  18 Characteristic Studies, Op. 109
    No. 1: Confidence   45, 122, 177
    No. 2: The Pearls   21, 89, 124, 178
    No. 3: The Shepherd's Return   10, 20, 79, 103, 124, 134, 178–9
    No. 4: The Gypsies   50, 102, 103, 124, 139, 140, 179–80
    No. 5: The Spring   21, 46, 89, 91, 92, 124, 140, 180
    No. 6: The Merry Maiden   100, 124, 181
    No. 7: Lullaby   21, 45, 91, 92, 98, 121, 140, 181–2
    No. 8: Agitato   21, 33, 122, 135, 140, 182
    No. 9: Morning Bell   17, 19, 79, 84, 103, 140, 143, 182–3
    No. 10: Velocity   10, 42, 89, 140, 183–4
    No. 11: Serenade   21, 45, 91, 100, 121, 135, 140, 184
    No. 12: Awakening in the Woods   93, 100, 140, 185
    No. 13: The Storm   40, 94, 124, 133, 140, 143, 185–6
    No. 14: Song of the Gondolier   9, 91, 92, 125, 139, 186–7
    No. 15: Sylphs   21, 35, 55, 89, 92, 93, 103, 124, 126, 135, 139, 187
    No. 16: Parting   36, 92, 139, 188
    No. 17: March   10, 21, 50, 76, 93, 104, 124, 140, 188–9
    No. 18: Spinning Song   10, 189–90

Chaminade, Cécile
  Album for the Young, Book 1,
    Op. 123
    No. 1: (untitled) 48, 134, 191
    No. 2: Intermezzo 191–2
    No. 3: Canzonetta 192–3
    No. 4: Rondeau 10, 193
    No. 5: Gavotte 10, 51, 102, 134, 193–4
    No. 6: Gigue 51, 194
    No. 7: Romance 195
    No. 8: Barcarolle 195–6
    No. 9: Orientale 196
    No. 10: Tarentelle 21, 196–7
    No. 11: Air de Ballet 9, 197–8
    No. 12: Marche Russe 50, 198
Chaminade, Cécile
  Album for the Young, Book 2,
    Op. 126
    No. 1: Idylle 9, 19, 40, 199
    No. 2: Aubade 18, 121, 199–200
    No. 3: Rigaudon 200–1
    No. 4: Eglogue 201
    No. 5: Ballade 201–2
    No. 6: Scherzo-Valse 104, 202–3
    No.7: Élégie 28, 40, 121, 203
    No.8: Novelette 203–4
    No.9: Patrouille 49, 81, 94, 204–5
    No.10: Villanelle 205
    No.11: Conte de Fées 142, 206
    No.12: Valse Mignonne 142, 206–7

Gillock, William
  Lyric Preludes in Romantic Style
    A Faded Letter 17, 52, 122, 214
    A Witch's Cat 85, 224
    An Old Valentine 9, 54, 223–4
    Autumn Sketch 17, 40, 82, 122, 135, 216
    Deserted Ball Room 18, 38, 211
    Dragon Fly 20, 214–15
    Forest Murmurs 45, 89, 124, 133, 209
    Fountain of Diana 85, 134, 219–20
    Humming Bird 84, 219
    Interlude 51, 212
    Legend 211–12
    Moonlight Mood 28, 51, 62, 85, 215–16
    Night Journey 28, 222–3
    Night Song 47, 222
    October Morning 134, 210–11
    Phantom Rider 28, 85, 139–40, 220
    Procession of the Mandarin 28, 51, 85, 86, 216–17
    Seascape 85, 209–10
    Serenade 17, 42, 86, 218–19
    Soaring 20, 45, 221
    Song of the Mermaid 212–213
    Summer Storm 213
    The Silent Snow 28, 221–2
    Winter Scene 217–18
Grieg, Edvard
  Lyric Pieces, Op. 12, 38, 43, 48, 54, 57, 62, 65, 68, 71
    Op. 12, No. 1: Arietta 28, 52, 96, 143, 225
    Op. 12, No. 2: Waltz 18, 39, 79, 104, 225–6
    Op. 12, No. 3: Watchman's Song 53, 81, 140, 226–7
    Op. 12, No. 4: Fairy-dance 53, 139, 227
    Op. 12, No. 5: Popular Melody 41, 62, 228
    Op. 12, No. 6: Norwegian Melody 63, 228–9
    Op. 12, No. 7: Album-Leaf 53, 90, 229–30
    Op. 12, No. 8: National Song 50, 140, 230–1
    Op. 38, No. 2: Popular Melody 48, 231
    Op. 38, No. 6: Elegie 17, 63, 66, 80, 89, 92, 96, 133, 232
    Op. 38, No. 7: Waltz 41, 142, 233
    Op. 43, No. 1: Butterfly 29, 40, 89, 91–2, 233–4
    Op. 43, No. 2: Solitary Traveller 28, 49, 55, 96, 234–5

Index of Compositions

Op. 43, No. 3: In My Native
  Country   28–9, 96, 235–6
Op. 43, No. 6: To the Spring   9, 17,
  18, 28, 54, 56, 63, 66, 76, 87, 92,
  133, 140, 236
Op. 47, No. 6: Norwegian
  Dance   20, 48, 64, 84, 134, 237
Op. 54, No. 2: Norwegian
  March   54, 62, 103, 140, 237–8
Op. 54, No. 4: Notturno   17, 28–9,
  48, 62, 64, 66, 133, 140, 143,
  238–9
Op. 54, No. 5: Scherzo   18, 66, 82,
  89, 140, 239–40
Op. 57, No. 2: Gade   28, 42, 91–2,
  140, 240–1
Op. 57, No. 3: Illusion   241–2
Op. 57, No. 6: Homesickness   20,
  52, 87, 142, 242–3
Op. 62, No. 1: Sylphide   78, 135,
  243–4
Op. 62, No. 2: Gratitude   54, 96,
  244
Op. 62, No. 5: Phantom   9, 19,
  28–9, 36, 66, 93, 245
Op. 65, No. 2: The Peasant's
  Song   54, 93, 97, 245–6
Op. 65, No. 5: Ballad   17, 56, 92,
  143, 246–7
Op. 68, No. 1: Sailor's Song   50,
  92, 247
Op. 68, No. 2: Grandmother's
  Minuet   35, 100, 247–8
Op. 68, No. 3: At Your Feet   28–9,
  64, 91, 93, 248–9
Op. 68, No. 4: Evening in the
  Mountains   17, 32, 142, 249
Op. 68, No. 5: At the Cradle   92,
  97, 250
Op. 71, No. 3: Puck   10, 28, 53,
  100, 133, 140, 250–1
Op. 71, No. 7: Remembrances   79,
  251
Gurlitt, Cornelius
  Album for the Young, Op.   140
    No. 1: March   253
    No. 2: Morning Song   49, 254
    No. 3: The Sky is Bright   17, 40,
      109, 126, 254–5
    No. 4: In the Garden   18, 56, 255
    No. 5: Murmuring Brook   47, 91,
      255–6
    No. 6: Catch Me!   135, 256–7
    No. 7: The Festive Dance   19, 41,
      63, 136, 257
    No. 8: The Music Box   38, 257–8
    No. 9: Thoughtful Moments   38,
      63, 258–9
    No. 10: The Little Norwegian   20,
      89, 90, 259
    No. 11: Longing   45, 91, 122,
      259–60
    No. 12: In the Church   49, 51, 90,
      260–1
    No. 13: The Little Wanderer   98,
      143, 261
    No. 14: Hunting Song   90, 261–2
    No. 15: Will-o-the-Wisp   82, 136,
      262–3
    No. 16: Loss   263
    No. 17: Scherzo   263–4
    No. 18: Serenade   17, 19, 40, 90,
      264
    No. 19: Impromptu   265
    No. 20: Storm and Stress   265–6
Liszt, Franz
  Romance Oubliée (Forgotten Romance),
    S. 527   32–3, 67, 315
Schumann, Robert
  Album for the Young, Op.   68
    No. 1: Melodie (Melody)   267
    No. 2: Soldatenmarsch (Soldier's
      March)   267–8
    No. 3: Trällerliedchen (Humming
      Song)   91, 268–9
    No. 4: Ein Choral (Chorale)   269
    No. 5: Stückchen (Little Piece)   18,
      40, 46, 91, 269–70
    No. 6: Armes Waisenkind (Poor
      Orphan)   53, 270
    No. 7: Jägerliedchen (Hunting
      Song)   53, 100, 139, 271

No. 8: Wilder Reiter (Wild Rider or Wild Horseman)   38, 83, 100, 271–2
No. 9: Volksliedchen (Folk Song)   142, 272–3
No. 10: Fröhlicher Landmann, von der Arbeit zurückkehrend (The Happy Farmer Returning from His Work)   10, 18, 39, 56, 102, 273
No. 11: Sizilianisch (Sicilienne)   39, 273–4
No. 12: Knecht Ruprecht (Knight Rupert)   10, 20, 36, 83, 91, 98, 135, 274–5
No. 13: Mai, lieber Mai—Bald bist Du wieder da! (May, Sweet May—You'll be back soon!)   10, 275–6
No. 14: Kleine Studie (Little Study)   33, 91, 121, 276
No. 15: Frühlingsgesang (Spring Song)   49, 63, 122, 133, 143, 276–7
No. 16: Erster Verlust (First Loss)   122, 277–8
No. 17: Kleiner Morgenwanderer (The Little Morning Wanderer)   86–7, 278
No. 18: Schnitterliedchen (The Reaper's Song)   279
No. 19: Kleine Romanze (Little Romance)   56, 87, 97, 123, 140, 279–80
No. 20: Ländliches Lied (Rustic Song)   124, 280–1
No. 21: ***   29, 133, 281
No. 22: Rundgesang (Roundelay)   84, 87, 97, 123, 281–2
No. 23: Reiterstück (Horseman's Song)   87, 124, 135, 282–3
No. 24: Ernteliedchen (Harvest Song)   283
No. 25: Nachklänge aus dem Theater (Echoes from the Theater)   92, 284

No. 26: ***   29, 54, 97, 102, 123, 284–5
No. 27: Kanonisches Liedchen (Little Song in Canon Form)   285–6
No. 28: Erinnerung (In Memoriam or Remembrance)   21, 53, 125, 286
No. 29: Fremder Mann (Strange Man)   50, 92–3, 287
No. 30: ***   87, 123–4, 287–8
No. 31: Kriegslied (Song of War)   36, 92–3, 288–9
No. 32: Sheherazade (fictional character)   29, 55, 87, 124, 289
No. 33: Weinlesezeit–Fröhliche Zeit! (Grape Harvest, Happy Time)   21, 64, 88, 125, 290
No. 34: Thema (Theme)   29, 123, 290–1
No. 35: Mignon (delicate, dainty)   52, 92, 121, 133, 291–2
No. 36: Lied italienischer Marinari (Italian Sailor's Song)   48, 94, 100, 292
No. 37: Matrosenlied (Sailor's Song)   36, 293
No. 38: Winterzeit (Wintertime I)   123, 293–4
No. 39: Winterszeit (Wintertime II)   103, 123, 142, 294–5
No. 40: Kleine Fuge (Little Fugue)   42, 295–6
No. 41: Nordisches Lied (Nordic Song)   50, 88, 92, 122, 296
No. 42: Figurierter Choral (Figurative Chorale)   296–7
No. 43: Silvesterlied (New Year's Eve Song)   88, 123, 134, 297–8

Tchaikovsky, Peter Ilyich
Album for the Young, Op. 39
   No. 1: Morning Prayer   17, 49, 54, 133, 299
   No. 2: A Winter Morning   81, 98, 136, 299–300

Index of Compositions

No. 3: The Hobby-Horse   50, 81, 100, 140, 300
No. 4: Mamma   103, 126, 301
No. 5: March of the Tin Soldiers   53, 136, 301–2
No. 6: The Sick Doll   302
No. 7: The Doll's Burial   49, 302–3
No. 8: Waltz   41, 63, 103, 136, 303–4
No. 9: The New Doll   304
No. 10: Mazurka   78, 304–5
No. 11: Russian Song   134, 305–6
No. 12: The Peasant Plays the Accordion   50, 306
No. 13: Folk-Song   83, 102, 134, 306–7
No. 14: Polka   40, 83, 91, 102, 135, 307–8
No. 15: Italian Song   18, 41, 90, 308
No. 16: Old French Song   9, 18, 42, 308–9
No. 17: German Song   48, 80, 109, 309–10
No. 18: Neopolitan Dance-Song   39, 79, 109, 310
No. 19: The Nurse's Tale   50, 81, 140, 310–11
No. 20: The Witch   53, 109, 311–12
No. 21: Sweet Dreams   18, 38, 42, 52, 143, 312
No. 22: Song of the Lark   103, 312–13
No. 23: The Handorgan Man   19, 52, 90, 134, 313–14
No. 24: In Church   50, 314